For Chrissie and the boys

Fat Freddie

The award-winning journalist Stephen Breen – most recently NewsBrands Ireland's Crime Journalist of the Year 2018 – is crime editor of the *Irish Sun* and has been writing about the Irish criminal world for nearly two decades. He is the co-author of the number-one-bestseller *The Cartel*, the definitive account of the rise of the Kinahan gang.

PENGUIN BOOKS

STEPHEN BREEN

Fat Freddie

*A Gangster's Life – the Bloody Career
of Freddie Thompson*

PENGUIN BOOKS

UK | USA | Canada | Ireland | Australia
India | New Zealand | South Africa

Penguin Books is part of the Penguin Random House group of companies
whose addresses can be found at global.penguinrandomhouse.com.

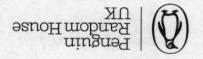

Penguin Random House
UK

First published by Penguin Ireland 2019
This updated edition published in Penguin Books 2020
001

Copyright © Stephen Breen, 2019, 2020

The moral right of the author has been asserted

Set in 12.01/14.33 pt Garamond MT Std
Typeset by Jouve (UK), Milton Keynes
Printed and bound in Great Britain by Clays Ltd, Elcograf S.p.A.

A CIP catalogue record for this book is available from the British Library

ISBN: 978–0–241–98666–0

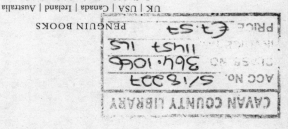

Contents

CONTENTS

Prologue

Daithi Douglas was enjoying being back at work.

Eight months earlier, the former IRA man and convicted drug dealer had cheated death when he had been shot three times by a gunman as he walked his dog close to his home in Cabra, north Dublin.

At the time of the attack, gardaí examined a number of theories to establish a motive for the shooting of a man who was no stranger to organized crime. Among the theories was that it might have been an assault orchestrated by the enemies of a veteran criminal, Gerry 'The Monk' Hutch, because of Douglas's close connections to the infamous criminal. However, gardaí soon had their main line of inquiry, after receiving intelligence Douglas was targeted because he had been involved in a row at a pub weeks earlier, with a north Dublin man who was involved in organized crime.

By the summer of 2016, Douglas was on the mend and was spending his days working at his wife Yumei's children's toy and shoe shop, Shoestown, located in Bridgefoot Street, south inner-city Dublin. Though lucky to be alive following the attempt on his life, Daithi followed a regular routine which was not that of a man under any type of threat. As far as Douglas was concerned, the dispute which had led to him being targeted by an assassin on 8 November 2015 had been resolved.

Unbeknownst to him, however, he was in the sights of one of Ireland's most dangerous gangland criminals – 'Fat

Freddie' Thompson – and his associates in the Kinahan cartel, the international crime syndicate led by Christy 'Dapper Don' Kinahan and his two sons, Daniel and Christopher. Worth an estimated billion euros, the gang had originated in south inner-city Dublin before moving their operations to southern Spain. Once there, the cartel established contacts with drugs gangs across the world, including in Colombia, Holland and Morocco. Through their drugs shipments and connections to international criminals, the cartel made a fortune, snapping up properties in Brazil and Dubai as a way of laundering cash. Other business ventures included expanding into the food industry in China.

By June 2016, Thompson and his associates were in the middle of a brutal gangland feud with Gerry Hutch's gang, which resulted in eight lives being lost. Among those murdered was Thompson's first cousin and cartel lieutenant, the 34-year-old David Byrne. He was mown down in a hail of bullets as gunmen, posing as members of the gardaí's Emergency Response Unit, stormed into the Regency Hotel, north Dublin, on 5 February 2016.

Within days of the incident, widely regarded as the most audacious attack in Irish gangland history, 'Fat Freddie' Thompson had been summoned to a council of war with his boss and friend, Daniel Kinahan. Apart from his role in sourcing guns and drugs, Thompson also acted as an enforcer for the cartel, regularly collecting debts from gangs who owed money and from desperate drug users. His remit was to instil fear and to use vicious intimidation against those who refused to pay up. It wasn't long before he had a fierce reputation for violence. By the end of the meeting Thompson, who had led the war against gangster Brian 'King

Ratt' Rattigan's gang in the Crumlin–Drimnagh feud, was promoted to Dublin leader of the cartel's feud.

As the body count continued to rise in the months following the attack at the Regency Hotel, Thompson was busy identifying targets – and Daithi Douglas's name was near the top of his hit list.

1. Young Guns

> There's no doubt there was a steely determination
> there for him to become one of the main players in
> organized crime. There were times when he tried to
> be the joker, when he would hug gardaí or talk
> about incidents that had been reported in the
> media, but deep down the only thing that
> mattered to him was crime.
> Former Detective Superintendent Gabriel O'Gara

The two detectives listened intently as their eighteen-year-old prisoner started talking. Whether from naivety or for a more cynical reason, he appeared to break from the normal code of silence adopted by those immersed in the Irish criminal underworld, providing a rare insight into the origins of a feud that had been raging since the summer of 1997 between two warring factions of the same gang, with one side led by Declan 'Deco' Gavin and the other by Brian 'King Ratt' Rattigan. The two officers were left feeling somewhat sceptical when their suspect, Frederick Thompson, informed them that the previous two years of gun attacks and violent assaults had started because of a motorbike.

Thompson, from Loreto Road in the Maryland area of Dublin's south inner city and who, according to one former investigator, once had aspirations of becoming a garda, was no stranger to violence:

Many of us knew him and when he used to see the uniformed lads on the street he would often say: 'When I grow up, I'm going to join the guards.' The other kids used to laugh at him and, because he was bulky when he was younger, he wasn't afraid to dish out a few beatings. He showed zero interest in school and was only interested in getting home to play outside with his friends or help his family on their stall. It's been strange to see him grow from a young troublemaker who was involved in damaging phone boxes and the odd joyriding incident into one of the country's most dangerous criminals.

The Thompson family were market traders, dealing on Meath Street in Dublin's south inner city, and were well respected in the area. No criminals were involved in their stall and it was the family's main source of income. Showing little interest in school, the young Freddie often worked in the family business. He also developed a passion for boxing but mainly did his training at home and wasn't aligned to any gym. However, as his criminal career kicked off, he spent less and less time training and instead found himself roaming the streets with a gang of like-minded young men, engaging in anti-social behaviour.

Thompson's childhood dreams of joining the gardaí soon evaporated when he earned his first conviction, aged sixteen. He was bound over to keep the peace for six months at Dublin's Children's Court on 22 April 1997, after he was convicted of a public-order offence for making 'indictable general comments' and 'threatening behaviour'. The case related to him and other young thugs harassing residents around his neighbourhood in the south inner city and shouting abuse as families went about their daily business. Before this incident he'd spent time selling newspapers and had started work as a butcher's apprentice, but he soon abandoned any plans to earn a living through legitimate means. His first conviction as a teenager would not be his last.

A few weeks later, on 8 May 1997, Freddie was bound over to keep the peace once more, and again on 5 August 1997 for a similar offence. Less than a year later, on 29 June 1998, he was convicted of threatening behaviour for the fourth time.

On 12 January 1999, the now eighteen-year-old received a six-month suspended sentence, again for threatening behaviour. Tried as an adult for the first time, Thompson received the suspended sentence at Dublin District Court for threatening Rattigan associates who were simply walking in the Cork Street area of Dublin's south inner city.

A former neighbour, who did not want to be named, said the people in the area weren't surprised to see the path that he had chosen:

> He was always a bit of a bully boy as a child and was in trouble from when he was no age, but no one can answer why he would go on to become centrally involved in murder. He seemed to thrive on it as he got older and most definitely seemed addicted to it.

Less than two years after his first conviction, Thompson had been arrested by detectives from Crumlin Garda Station yet again. He was sitting in the interview room being interrogated about a gun attack on the home of a rival gangster and key Rattigan associate, Noel Roche, at Kilworth Road, Crumlin, on 13 March 1999. The eighteen-year-old was arrested twelve days after the drive-by shooting, in which two shots were fired through the front door of the property. Thompson, along with his best friend and mentor, 'Deco' Gavin, had emerged as the chief suspects for the attack. Gavin and Freddie Thompson had grown up together and were best friends in their teenage years. Gavin introduced Thompson to crime and Freddie was one of his enforcers in the early days of his career. Despite being just a few months older than Thompson, Gavin was already one of the capital's most prominent drug dealers. After the shooting a resident had also heard Noel Roche shouting: 'If anyone's interested, it was Deco Gavin.'

It was the second time Roche had been targeted by Thompson as the up-and-coming gangster was keen to make a name for himself in the criminal underworld. He was also suspected of firing a shot through Roche's front window nine days earlier, at 11.55 p.m. on the night of 4 March.

In a file compiled by gardaí, as part of their investigations into the growing tensions between the Gavin and Rattigan gangs and their associates, detectives said:

> Most of the original members of both gangs grew up together in a small area of Drimnagh. Sometime in 1997 a dispute arose between various members over drugs and money, causing a split. Different members of both gangs were assaulted and a series of tit-for-tat assaults and criminal damage to cars belonging to them occurred. Friends, relatives and associates from other areas including Freddie Thompson, and Paddy Doyle, from the north inner city, were also brought into the dispute.

Paddy Doyle had already earned a fearsome reputation for violence. He was introduced to Thompson through a mutual friend, and the pair struck up a relationship after Doyle offered his services as an enforcer. Doyle was also someone who was trying to make a name for himself in the underworld and he soon informed Thompson he was prepared to kill.

As gardaí interrogated Thompson about the shooting at Noel Roche's house, 'Fat Freddie' outlined how the dispute had accelerated. According to the eighteen-year-old, it all began with Derek Lodge burning a motorbike belonging to Declan Gavin. In retaliation Gavin then attempted to petrol bomb Lodge's house. The detectives noted that it was one 'of the best accounts' of the origins of the feud.

Garda intelligence established that Derek Lodge was a small-time drug dealer from Dublin's south inner city who was involved in a row with 'Deco' Gavin over an unpaid drug debt. When Gavin didn't pay up, Lodge was accused of burning Gavin's motorbike. Lodge had friends in the Rattigan faction and was regarded as someone who wasn't afraid to use violence.

As well as being surprised at Thompson's admission, gardaí such as Detective Superintendent Gabriel O'Gara, now retired, were sceptical:

Here you had this cocky teenager who had grown up idolizing people like Martin Cahill being arrested for a very serious offence and telling detectives it was all to do with someone's motorbike being torched. It may have been a contributing factor to the ongoing tensions between the groups but at the heart of it was money, drugs and power. A number of veteran criminals were doing time around the 1999 and 2000 mark and he was determined to step into their shoes. If only we'd known then what he was capable of. It was all about ego for him. He was a very violent individual and it wasn't long before the people of the south inner city experienced this.

Another retired detective, Dessie Brennan, spent forty-one years working in the gardaí's 'A' District. Home to some of Ireland's most violent criminals, 'A' District's territory covers swathes of Dublin's south inner city, including Thompson's home ground, Kilmainham and Inchicore. Its territory also extends to areas of Crumlin and Drimnagh which are covered by Sundrive Road and Crumlin Garda Stations. Brennan remembers Thompson as an 'arrogant teenager':

> Freddie Thompson was just a cocky young man who was try-ing to make a name for himself. He was very nice to gardaí when he was stopped and questioned but beneath this façade there was a steely determination for him to become the main man. He was cute and streetwise and knew not to get too aggressive with gardaí. He was at the heart of serious crime in the 'A' District and this lasted for many, many years, with many people suffering.

When detectives interviewed Thompson over the Roche incident it was clear he was displaying a co-operative façade. He was questioned for a day before being released.

The gardaí's subsequent report contained Thompson's claim that the feud had 'escalated' after a car belonging to 'Deco' Gavin's mother, who had no involvement in crime, was 'burnt with acid'.

Completing their investigation into the shootings at Noel Roche's home, gardaí concluded: 'While both Declan Gavin and Freddie Thompson were arrested for these incidents no charges will be preferred due to insufficient evidence.'

Throughout the summer of 1999 the tit-for-tat attacks diminished, with both sides agreeing to a fragile peace. The two factions managed to work together on drugs shipment, using criminals on the payrolls of both sides as intermediar-ies. The arrangement did not last for long.

According to the gardaí investigators' file, the feud re-ignited after Gavin was caught up in two major drugs seizures:

> The fact that Declan Gavin was arrested on 11 August 1999 in a Garda National Drug Unit (GNDU) operation in which a large quantity of ecstasy tablets, worth €1.5 million, were seized, and again on 10 March 2000, when a large quantity of cocaine and ecstasy were seized, also impacted on the dispute.

After escaping justice on the first drugs capture, due to lack of evidence, investigators were convinced it was Gavin's involvement in the second seizure of 1.7 million euros' worth of cocaine and ecstasy at the Holiday Inn Hotel in Dublin's Pearse Street that sealed his fate. Two fellow gang members Phillip Griffiths and Graham Whelan had gone to two rooms they'd rented in the busy hotel to break up and bag two kilograms of cocaine and 49,000 ecstasy tablets. They had informed staff that they did not want to be disturbed, but the hotel became suspicious when the young men never left their rooms and refused to allow cleaners in.

The hotel contacted Pearse Street Garda Station and five officers were dispatched to the Holiday Inn. Led by Sergeant Seamus Boland, the officers forced their way into the room. They found the huge stash of drugs and caught Graham Whelan throwing a blue holdall bag out the window. The bag was later recovered and gardaí noted that it contained the cocaine the gang had spent two days cutting up and placing into bags for sale on the streets of Dublin. Weighing equipment and other drug-mixing paraphernalia were also discovered. Gavin, who was in another hotel, kept ringing Griffiths' phone and trying to get through to the room. Gardaí kept the line engaged and he stormed into the room thinking his cohorts were out of it. That's when he was arrested.

Questioned over a two-day period, Gavin was later released without charge. A file was prepared by gardaí for the Director of Public Prosecutions (DPP), and Gavin's two friends, Griffiths and Whelan, were later charged with possession of drugs with intent to supply. As news of the charges and Gavin's subsequent release spread to the south inner city, the young dealer was branded a 'rat' by Brian Rattigan and his associates.

Rattigan, who was suspected of contributing €35,000 to pay for the drugs shipment, demanded his money back. Gavin refused to hand over any cash, describing the seizure as an 'occupational hazard'. Rattigan vowed revenge and, despite Gavin's pleas of innocence, the gang fractured. According to detectives in one file on the dispute, 'each side was blaming the other for "ratting" to gardaí'.

On the one side was the faction led by Rattigan and his associates, who were convinced Gavin was a garda informer. On the other, Gavin had secured the support of Freddie Thompson and others, including Daniel and Christopher Kinahan, the sons of the drugs godfather Christy 'Dapper Don' Kinahan, and of Freddie's cousins, Liam Byrne, his brother David and Liam Roe.

As gardaí continued to keep a special eye on the feuding gangs, they pulled over a car in July 2000. Inside were Thompson, Declan Gavin and David Byrne, whose execution years later would lead to a bloodbath between the Kinahan cartel and Gerry 'The Monk' Hutch's gang. They had all clearly been in a fight. With the gangland battle lines drawn, it was only a matter of time before the hostilities escalated.

Gardaí were fully aware of Thompson's potential for violence. A few months earlier, on 12 February 2000, he'd attacked a man with a screwdriver outside the Garda Members' Club on Harrington Street, in inner-city Dublin. On that occasion Thompson had been arguing with his partner when an innocent bystander asked him to calm down. 'Fat Freddie' then twice stabbed the man in the arm, before fleeing from the area. He was arrested and later charged with assault causing harm, but it would be almost three years before he appeared in court in connection with the offence.

Around the same time, Thompson was forging links with criminals in the north inner city, including young criminals such as Christopher 'Bouncer' Hutch, a nephew of Gerry Hutch. On one occasion, on 17 October 2000, Thompson was stopped in a car along with Christopher Hutch and Barry Finnegan, a member of the Hutch gang. According to gardaí: 'This crew were heading towards a house on Ballyfermot Road. Another associate was hanging around the area. Search was negative. All are active criminals.'

Thompson also had other issues on his mind when his then girlfriend, Vicky Dempsey, gave birth to the couple's only son, Bradley, on 7 November 2000. However, the nineteen-year-old was still heavily involved in tit-for-tat attacks during the feud and seemed to place more emphasis on this than on becoming a father. Thompson was repeatedly caught driving with no insurance, and he was stopped on other occasions in 2000 and in 2001 with known criminals, including David Byrne and another young criminal, who later emigrated to Australia.

Tension mounted as both sides continued to issue threats and brand each other as 'rats' when they crossed paths in their rival territories. Thompson in particular was running a campaign of intimidation which former Detective Superintendent O'Gara said made it hard for the garda forces to put an end to the cycle of violence:

The problem for gardaí at the time was that people were afraid to come forward because of what might happen to them or their families. From 2001 onwards, Freddie Thompson was behind what can only be described as a reign of terror, but things would get even worse once he came under the control of the Kinahan Organized Crime Group, who were beginning to flex their muscles at home and abroad. I've also no doubt that if the resources available to gardaí now in the fight against organized crime were available as Thompson was beginning his career things could have been a lot different for him.

The Rattigan gang made the next move in the ongoing war. On 5 June 2001, the home of a key Thompson associate, Darren Geoghegan, on Galtymore Road in Drimnagh, was targeted in a drive-by shooting. For Gavin and Thompson the attack was a declaration of war as Geoghegan was regarded as a senior member of their gang. Geoghegan was also responsible for laundering cash for criminal gangs across the capital and had been linked to a drive-by shooting in west Dublin a few months earlier. During the gun attack an elderly relative narrowly escaped injury and, vowing revenge, Geoghegan, Thompson and Gavin placed Rattigan at the top of their hit list.

Three months after the drive-by shooting, gardaí stopped Thompson as he was driving his car. While nothing was found during the search, gardaí noted the tax disc had a different registration to the vehicle itself and Thompson was 'obnoxious and aggressive'. Surveillance operations on the two factions by garda intelligence at the time revealed the Rattigan faction had 28 gang members and 53 associates, compared to 27 trusted foot soldiers in the Gavin and Thompson faction, along with 52 associates. However, according to gardaí, it was the Gavin and Thompson faction's links to forty associates of a veteran criminal, Martin 'The Viper' Foley, including James 'Jaws' Byrne, the father of Thompson's cousins and future Kinahan cartel lieutenants Liam and David Byrne, that gave their side 'a slight advantage'. An aspiring hitman for hire, Eric 'Lucky' Wilson, had also offered his services to Thompson and his allies.

Wilson was a young criminal from the Ballyfermot area who was also earning a reputation for violence. Martin 'The General' Cahill was a relative. He, like Paddy Doyle, had made it clear he was willing to kill in return for cash.

Both sides had sought help from outside the capital, with the Rattigan faction joining forces with the Keane/Collopy gang in Limerick, while the Gavin and Thompson side forged an alliance with the McCarthy/Dundon gang, the Keane/Collopy's arch rivals, also Limerick based. Just as in Dublin, the Limerick gangs had once worked together before greed and paranoia swept through their ranks, leading to bloodshed.

During their investigations into the capital's warring factions, gardaí noted:

All were associates of main gang members at one stage or another and inevitably there could be crossovers. A worrying link has now emerged with the differing sides in the Drimnagh feud aligning themselves with feuding gangs in Limerick. These associations are believed to have originated from their associations while in prison.

While gardaí classified the Gavin and Thompson faction as the stronger of the two opposing drugs gangs, both sides continued to issue threats. It was Rattigan's actions on 25 August 2001, however, that led to a declaration of gangland war and to the loss of sixteen lives over a fifteen-year period in what would become one of Ireland's deadliest gangland disputes – the Crumlin–Drimnagh feud.

On the evening of 24 August, Brian Rattigan and his associates had gathered to celebrate the eighteenth birthday of his brother Joey. The gangster and his friends enjoyed a marathon cocaine and booze session into the early hours of 25 August. 'King Ratt' then decided he wanted some food so he ordered his associate John Roche, Noel Roche's brother, to get some extra supplies at the Abrakebabra fast-food outlet in Crumlin.

Arriving at the restaurant, Roche noticed Rattigan's one-time friend and now bitter enemy – Declan Gavin. He immediately launched into a tirade of abuse, calling Gavin 'a rat'. Gavin protested his innocence and retaliated by saying that Roche was a garda informant. As other clientele looked on, Gavin then claimed that he would soon be charged over the Holiday Inn drugs seizure and would also be going to prison. Roche dismissed these claims and continued to hurl abuse at 'Deco'.

Roche's friends dragged him away from the restaurant and they all returned to the party. When they told Brian Rattigan about the heated exchange with his former friend, the gangster was raging. He armed himself with a knife, got a balaclava and ordered his associates to drive him to the restaurant.

Arriving back at Abrakebabra around 3.30 a.m., Rattigan and his friends saw Gavin and started shouting 'rats' from the car. Brian Rattigan pulled on his balaclava and ran towards his former friend. As a group of young people who had just returned to the area after a night out ran for cover, Rattigan plunged a knife into Gavin's chest. Seriously injured, Gavin stumbled into Abrakebabra in a desperate attempt to flee from his attacker, his one-time friend and ally. A security guard acted quickly and locked the door, blocking Rattigan from following 'Deco' into the restaurant to finish the job. The rival gang then fled the scene as Gavin's close associates, Darren Geoghegan and Paddy Doyle, arrived.

A number of people in the restaurant tried to help Gavin before he was transferred to St James's Hospital at around 4 a.m. He was immediately rushed to the operating theatre, having suffered a single stab wound to the heart. Despite their best efforts to save him, Thompson's best friend was pronounced dead shortly afterwards.

It wasn't long before news of Declan Gavin's death and the identity of his murderer reached the Thompson faction. The confirmation that Brian Rattigan was responsible for the killing spread throughout the south inner city. According to security sources, Freddie Thompson vowed revenge and put plans in motion to target members of the Rattigan faction.

In the meantime, Gavin's family were in the sights of Rattigan's gang. Gardaí received intelligence that Rattigan had instructed his enforcers to bomb the home belonging to Gavin's mother, Pauline. Declan's older brother Aidan, who distanced himself from Thompson after the killing, later stated that he'd been told he had a €50,000 price on his head and that there had been attempts on his life. He claimed a detective from the Emergency Response Unit (ERU) had advised him to arm himself with some type of weapon for protection. Aidan Gavin also said he was living a life under threat and had been forced to sleep in different safe houses across Dublin to avoid being killed.

Following Gavin's killing, more of Thompson's associates distanced themselves from the gang, often at the request of their families. Liam Greenhalgh, ex-captain of the Irish under-16 football team, and a close friend of Declan Gavin, fled to

Australia a year after the killing, making a new life for himself. Just a year before Gavin's killing, he had received a four-year suspended sentence for pointing a gun at gardaí during a motorcycle chase on 18 July 1998. Along with Thompson's first cousin Liam Byrne, Greenhalgh had pleaded guilty to possessing a weapon with intent and to robbery of a shop in the Liberties area. Unlike many of his friends, a former neighbour explained, Greenhalgh was one of the lucky ones:

> Liam was an intelligent young man and had simply got caught up with the wrong people. Once his friend Gavin was killed, he knew he had to leave otherwise he would end up dead or in prison. He made the decision to leave his family behind and create a good life for himself. The only time he comes back to Ireland is for funerals. He's not involved in anything now and has put his associations with Byrne and Thompson firmly in the past.

Immediately following Gavin's death, a major murder investigation was launched by detectives from Sundrive Road Garda Station in Crumlin, south Dublin. Gardaí received a crucial piece of evidence early on, when a palm print was taken from the window of the restaurant. It was later established that the palm print matched Rattigan's left palm. An analysis of blood found next to Rattigan's palm print was also discovered to match Gavin's DNA. The gardaí had their number one suspect – as did Freddie Thompson, who was now the gang's leader.

Detective Sergeant Joe O'Hara and a number of other gardaí called to Rattigan's family home to arrest him on 28 August, but he was not there, as he was staying at a safe house. They knew he was due in court on 4 September 2001, but he fled when they approached. He was later arrested that day in a pub on James's Street. However, he was released soon afterwards due to lack of evidence. He was also arrested on suspicion of possessing firearms, but again was later released without charge. The investigating team had no choice but to allow Rattigan back on the streets as files were prepared for the Director of Public Prosecutions.

Thompson's number one priority was to avenge the death of his best friend, but he was biding his time until the huge garda response to the feud died down. He was also attending to the organization of more drug deals. The tensions between the two rival factions had led to increased garda activity, but they still managed to carry on business as usual. Both Rattigan and Thompson had their own customers and suppliers and they flooded the south inner city with batches of heroin and cocaine.

As Thompson and his allies regrouped over the coming weeks and months, it was the Rattigan faction who launched another attack. On 15 November 2001 they fired shots for a second time at Darren Geoghegan's home in Galtymore Road, Drimnagh. No one was hurt in the attack but Thompson was coming under pressure from his gang to hit back. In a preemptive strike, gardaí from the Kevin Street and Sundrive Road Stations swamped the south inner city over December 2001 and into 2002. They knew the threat of violence from both sides remained at a very high level and they were preparing for the worst.

Former Detective Superintendent O'Gara, who was a detective inspector at Kevin Street Garda Station between 2001 and 2007, recalled:

It was an extremely difficult period for gardaí in the weeks and months after the killing of Declan Gavin. Gavin was a serious player and it was clear there would be no end in sight to the violence because both factions were intent on causing as much damage as possible. The gardaí did everything they could to keep a lid on the violence because it was always simmering in the background; the targeting was continuing on a daily basis. Thompson and Gavin were like brothers and Thompson was determined to strike back after his killing. Thompson had filled the void left by Gavin's death and he was clearly out for blood. Thankfully no one lost their lives for the remainder of 2001, but we knew that wouldn't last.

This is also a view shared by former Detective Garda Brennan:

It was a very tense time for gardaí trying to keep a lid on things and resources were certainly stretched. Everyone knew what we were dealing with and there was this underlying fear that things would only get worse because of the calibre of criminal we were dealing with. They were both vying for the top position in the world of organized crime in the south inner city. The killing of Declan Gavin made it personal to Thompson and I thought the feud would only end with either of them being arrested or killed. I had absolutely no idea this thing would go on for as long as it has.

In the early months of 2002, gardaí braced themselves for more violence. On 15 February 2002, Rattigan embarked on another mission to murder his rivals. His gang had received information on Thompson's possible location, but the shooter was unable to locate him. It was a lucky escape for the 21-year-old.

Around midnight on St Patrick's Day 2002, Rattigan decided

to make another move. He received information that senior members of the Thompson faction were socializing at Judge Darley's pub in the Parkgate Street area of the city centre. Arming himself with a handgun, Rattigan travelled to the bar with an accomplice and fired a number of shots. The garda report stated: 'Brian Rattigan did a drive-by shooting at this pub as a number of the opposite gang were drinking there. This happened at 1 a.m. in the morning. Rattigan was later arrested but there wasn't enough evidence for a charge.' Unbeknownst to Rattigan, his enemies had been meeting to discuss the execution of 'Deco' Gavin's killer and they wasted no time in putting their plan into action.

Just three hours after the shots were fired at the city centre pub, Thompson and Paddy Doyle, along with two other gang members, made the trip to Rattigan's family home in Cooley Road, Drimnagh. Brian Rattigan was still living there, along with other innocent members of his family, who were not involved in crime. As they approached the house, Rattigan's younger brother Joey spotted the two gunmen. Unable to wake his older brother, who was in a drunken stupor, he warned Brian's then girlfriend, Natasha McEnroe, to 'get up quick' as there were 'fellas outside with ballys and guns'. Joey then ran out to the back garden and hid until it was all over.

According to a subsequent garda file on the attack:

Following the incident at Judge Darley's pub, Freddie Thompson and Patrick Doyle organized a gang to go to Rattigan's house at 4 a.m. in the morning. They shot their way into the house, discharging a number of bullets. At least four people were involved. Brian Rattigan was shot in the stomach by Freddie Thompson.

McEnroe ran to an en suite bathroom, where she watched one of the gunmen shoot her sleeping boyfriend. He was later rushed to hospital and, although left with serious injuries, managed to survive.

Fleeing from the property, the two gunmen went straight past McEnroe as she yelled: 'Come back here you dirty bastards.' One of the men pulled up his mask and smiled as Rattigan was left lying in a pool of blood. Natasha told gardaí that the man under the mask was 'Fat Freddie' Thompson.

Thompson and Doyle were arrested at the beginning of August but were later released without charge and a file was forwarded to the Director of Public Prosecutions. When told that he had been identified as one of the gunmen, Thompson warned gardaí: 'Mark my words, she won't go to court with that.'

Having escaped justice for the gun attack on the Roche family home, Thompson had luck on his side once again when the DPP subsequently ruled there would be no prosecution.

With Rattigan lucky to be alive and recovering from his injuries, Thompson's gang had the upper hand. The gardaí continued to keep up the pressure, however, and Thompson found himself before a court the following day. He had been arrested on suspicion of dangerous driving and received a fine.

The violence was unceasing, and two months later another young man linked to the feud was killed. On 22 May 2002, Derek Lodge, one of Thompson's former associates and the man accused of starting the feud by burning Declan Gavin's motorbike, was shot dead outside a portable cabin on the Kenilworth Road in Rathgar, south Dublin. While he may have been involved in the origins of the feud, gardaí believed Lodge was targeted by a hitman, Shay Wildes from Tallaght, because he had threatened another man. Lodge would have known all the main players in the feud and often socialized in the same pubs as Freddie Thompson, who was a suspect, but gardaí further said that:

It's not known if Lodge was involved with the Roche and Rattigan gang but someone had put his name up for burning Gavin's motorbike. In any event Lodge moved well away from this gang shortly afterwards and was not associating with them at the time of his murder.

As tensions continued to mount on the streets of Dublin's south inner city, an innocent man had a lucky escape when he was targeted by the Thompson faction on 28 May 2002. The resident, who wasn't involved in crime or linked to any of the feuding factions, was targeted at his Crumlin Road home after Thompson's enforcers wrongly linked him to their enemies. Detectives reported:

This man answered a knock to his front door at 3 a.m. A gunman discharged a .38 round through the front door hitting the man in the chin. He refused to co-operate and didn't make a complaint. Information was that the man saw Declan Gavin at Abrakebabra and then made contact with Brian Rattigan who went down and killed him. There was no link ever made to this in the Gavin killing. No arrests were made in the shooting but it's believed to be part of the Freddie Thompson gang.

Gardaí braced themselves for more violence and knew they wouldn't have to wait long for further retaliations, as former Detective Superintendent O'Gara described:

With Freddie Thompson leading one gang and Brian Rattigan the other, the potential for violence was huge. We were dealing with two young men who were extremely violent and volatile. We were trying to disrupt the activities of two of the most violent criminals this country has ever seen. They didn't care that the actions of their associates were destroying the communities they called home. Gardaí were out there every night putting their lives on the line trying to protect communities from criminals who were hell-bent on death and destruction. Paranoia was rife within the gangs and they were under serious pressure. If gardaí had access to the type of anti-gangland legislation used by the courts today, then things might have turned out differently.

The required legislation would not be enacted for another seven years. In the meantime, a killing spree orchestrated and masterminded by Thompson would soon be under way.

2. Target Practice

> I'm going to be the next big thing and youse are
> going to be busy then.
>
> Freddie Thompson

By the summer of 2002, Freddie Thompson had become a key target for gardaí across Dublin, and particularly in the Crumlin and Kevin Street Garda Stations. He epitomized the new breed of ruthless criminal on the Irish gangland scene. Almost a year after taking control of his best friend's criminal organization, Thompson's gang was still immersed in a feud with the faction led by Brian Rattigan. At the same time, he was continuing to run a successful business distributing drugs around the capital, working with gangs in the south and north inner city. Former Detective Superintendent Gabriel O'Gara, a detective inspector in Kevin Street at the time, was aware of Thompson's growing reputation in the underworld:

> I was working with some fantastic investigators who had watched Freddie Thompson grow up, and it was no surprise to them that he was at the heart of this feud. Everyone knew in the community – knew who Freddie Thompson was at that time because he had already earned a fierce reputation for violence that would remain with him for the rest of his life. Thompson, along with his associates, was a major priority for us at the time.

Thompson's main supplier was the gang run by Christy 'Dapper Don' Kinahan and his right-hand man, John 'The Colonel' Cunningham. Freddie used his childhood friendship with Kinahan's sons, Daniel and Christopher Jnr, to forge links with the gang, who were smuggling drugs into Ireland through their contacts in Holland and Spain.

Gardaí were under no illusions about the threat posed by Thompson and his associates. One security document outlined how the gang's 'activities centred in the south inner city and south-west regions of Dublin, controlling most of the drugs trade. This group appears to be well established in the drugs trade, with no shortage of drugs, cash or firearms.'

In order to tackle them, gardaí had increased patrols in the south inner city. This was designed to disrupt the movements of drugs and weapons but also to prevent murders and gun attacks. Detectives were also continuing to build intelligence on the movements of the key players. Other responses included arresting some of the key members for drugs searches. A subsequent security report noted:

They are all too aware of the efforts being made to apprehend them. They do not flaunt their wealth, only driving average cars, having average accommodation, regularly changing their cars and more often than not will hire cars. This gang is probably one of the most vicious in the country. The gang members are also aware of efforts to kill them by rival gang members and are regularly wearing bulletproof vests, changing accommodation and will never be alone.

Senior detectives who investigated Thompson maintained that behind his façade 'lies a violent and dangerous criminal'. In the words of one investigating Garda:

He was reckless. If you were selling drugs and you wouldn't sell for him you could expect to be sliced across the face. They were also cutting addicts up who owed them just €200. If they couldn't get to the addicts, they would get to their families. There have been many occasions over the years where decent families have become caught up in the drugs world and have had to remortgage their homes just to pay off their debts. As Thompson's reputation for violence grew, so too did the intimidation. He was thriving on it and didn't care about the families living in his community.

The threat Freddie Thompson and his associates posed to gardaí and to the innocent people of Dublin was summed up by the same security report: 'This group are largely involved in drug dealing with serious connections to groups in Britain and continental Europe. They have ready access to firearms and have no hesitation in using them.'

While Thompson's gang, thanks to the backing of the Kinahan clan and members of the Hutch group in the north inner city, had secured a strong position in the drugs trade, avenging their former leader's death remained high on their agenda. Brian Rattigan, however, was in self-imposed exile after the attempt on his life and they couldn't find him. 'Fat Freddie' was leading the hunt, but 'King Ratt' continued to evade them, hiding out in safe houses around Dublin as he recovered from his injuries.

With both the Rattigan and Thompson factions on high alert, planning and waiting for further attacks, Thompson was obsessed with keeping one step ahead of his enemies. His methods included wearing a wig around Dublin, dressing as a woman and wearing glasses to disguise himself. When he was stopped by gardaí while in disguise, he would often make smart remarks, pull down his tracksuit bottoms or attempt to

flee. When he was stopped by gardaí on 16 April 2002, officers noted how Thompson was 'very nervous' and spoke about
'the threat of death constantly hanging over' him. During
another garda search, however, 'Fat Freddie' boasted about
his criminal credentials and told the officers: 'I'm going to be
the next big thing and youse are going to be busy then.' It was
a promise he would keep for the next fifteen years.

As the drug dealing continued, so too did the targeting
from the feuding gangs. On 13 June 2002, the Thompson
gang were linked to the shooting of two brothers at a property in Park Terrace, near the Coombe area of central Dublin.
Thompson's associates wrongly believed the men were
linked to the Rattigan faction and fired five shots from a
semi-automatic weapon at them. Both men were hit in the
attack, which investigating gardaí described as 'indiscrim-
inate'. The men were lucky to escape with their lives. Three
members of the Thompson faction were later arrested before
being released without charge.

The gun used in the failed double-murder bid, a Smith &
Wesson .38, would be put to use again just over a month
later – and this time the target was personal. Thompson had
selected Rattigan's younger brother Joey for execution. As
one former investigator explained: 'Thompson and his gang
knew that Joey Rattigan had information on the Gavin killing and to them the murder was justified.'

Brian Rattigan was still staying in safe houses on the outskirts of Dublin and also in Limerick. As he got fit again, he
was using the contacts he had built up and was importing
drugs into Dublin's south inner city, using the Basin Street
Flats complex as a stronghold. His eighteen-year-old brother
was one of the few people the gang leader could trust. The
teenager's role in the gang, a former investigator said, was to

distribute small amounts of ecstasy and cannabis, as, unlike his older sibling, Joey Rattigan was not a man of violence:

> Joey was just in awe of his brother and looked up to him because he had made money from drug dealing and had survived a murder bid. Joey enjoyed the trappings of wealth, but there was no way he was going to become a major player in the criminal underworld – he just didn't have it in him. He would sell some pills and cannabis and collect some of the debts from his friends but that was it. He wasn't even a major player in the feud and wouldn't have been involved in taking up firearms against his brother's enemies. Joey wasn't a threat to anyone and was simply a naïve young man. The only way he would have been targeted was because of his name. Brian Rattigan had high hopes for his younger brother, but deep down he knew he didn't have it in him to kill people or use violence. Joey would have a role in the gang but it would be very minimal.

The eighteen-year-old didn't seem to realize that he was a potential target or that his relationship to Brian would inevitably earn him a top spot on Thompson's hit list. Instead of taking precautions, said one detective, Joey Rattigan continued to live his normal life:

> He had been socializing in the centre of Dublin in his brother's absence, was regularly seen on visits to the shop and was still meeting with friends in Drimnagh and Dublin. If he had thought that he was in any type of danger, then he wouldn't have been staying at his family home.

On the evening of 16 July 2002, Joey Rattigan was relaxing at home in Cooley Road, Drimnagh, with his girlfriend. Some time that night, he received a phone call from his friend Paul

Warren, asking him to come for a drink at the now closed Pimlico Tavern in the south inner city. As Warren had known Rattigan for some time, with the friends keeping in close contact during the feud, the eighteen-year-old decided to join him at the busy pub. It was a decision that would cost Joey Rattigan his life.

What Joey Rattigan didn't realize was that while Paul Warren was maintaining links to both sides during the feud, as it progressed, his loyalty settled with the Thompson faction. Freddie knew that Warren had not yet come under suspicion from the Rattigan gang members and that he could use him to set up Joey Rattigan.

In *Cocaine Wars*, the journalist Mick McCaffrey explained how paranoia was rife among the feuding factions:

> Friendships were cheap and a person you thought was on your side one minute could suddenly turn against you the next. Joey Rattigan thought that Paul Warren was on his brother's side, but in gangland there is no such thing as real friendship, and loyalty is not a commodity that is rich in supply. Unbeknownst to Joey Rattigan, Paul Warren was a turncoat.

As the night wore on, Warren and Rattigan were joined by two other friends. Rattigan's girlfriend also arrived at the pub at around 12.15 a.m. After dropping his girlfriend back to Cooley Road, Joey Rattigan and the three men drove to an apartment in the Inchicore area. They spent a few hours drinking there and then Warren gave Rattigan a lift home, dropping him just metres from his house in Cooley Road at around 2.05 a.m. As he approached his front door, a gunman who had been lying in wait shot Joey Rattigan once in the head. The shooter then fled as Rattigan collapsed.

Hearing the shot, Rattigan's neighbours phoned the emergency services. As the eighteen-year-old clung to life, the paramedics arrived within minutes and rushed him to the nearby St James's Hospital. However, just a few hours after being admitted, the teenager was declared brain dead and passed away when his life support machine was switched off.

As investigators from Sundrive Road Garda Station held a meeting the following day to discuss the second murder associated with the feud, Brian Rattigan was plotting his revenge. According to one former investigator:

> There was no way Brian Rattigan was going to let this go. He doted on his younger brother and was livid when he received the news that he had been shot dead. To him, his brother was an easy target and he also knew the murder was aimed personally at him.

The intensive Garda investigation continued over the following weeks and detectives were soon convinced that Thompson had played a key role in the hit. In one intelligence file, gardaí classified Thompson as one of their chief suspects:

> Joseph Rattigan was shot dead at point blank range on Cooley Road having been dropped off by a number of people whom he was drinking with. Paul Warren and two other men were arrested the following day but subsequently released without charge. Freddie Thompson and Patrick Doyle are suspects for carrying out this murder in retaliation for the killing of Declan Gavin.

Gardaí would later establish that the murder weapon, a Smith & Wesson .38 revolver, recovered during a house search in August that year, was the same weapon used in the attack on the two brothers on 13 June. Despite being arrested for the murder after the discovery of the firearm, Thompson and Doyle were later released without charge due to lack of evidence.

A file was sent to the Director of Public Prosecutions over Paul Warren's involvement in the killing but he too escaped justice due to lack of evidence.

As the Garda investigation hit a brick wall, everyone knew that Thompson and Doyle remained the chief suspects. This intelligence added fuel to the simmering feud as 'King Ratt' struggled to deal with the loss of his brother and with the Thompson faction's ascendancy. He turned to cocaine and alcohol as a way of coping and instructed his gang to target anyone who had been involved in luring his younger brother to his death. At the top of his kill list was Paul Warren.

Brian Rattigan moved back into his heavily fortified family home in Cooley Road, Drimnagh, to direct operations. He also stayed at safe houses and kept moving around to avoid detection as he knew the Thompson gang were still trying to kill him.

Rattigan remained a major target for gardaí across the capital as well, including officers from the Bridewell Station in Dublin's north inner city. Detective Inspector John McMahon, now retired, and Detective Sergeant Pat Lordan, now a Detective Chief Superintendent at the Garda National Economic Crime Bureau, had received intelligence of Rattigan's involvement in the drive-by shooting at Judge Darley's pub on St Patrick's Day 2002 and were intent on questioning him. But their first attempt was abandoned as, in an odd coincidence, Joey Rattigan was murdered on the day of the planned operation. Gardaí did not want to arrest the deceased's brother when tensions were running so high. However, four weeks after the second killing of the feud, gardaí made their move.

Arriving at his family home on Cooley Road on the morning of 14 August 2002, officers were stunned to find the door of the Rattigan stronghold open. Detectives believed the reason for this abnormal behaviour was that an innocent relative had left the property to help a neighbour jump-start their car.

Officers rushed in and made their way to a bedroom upstairs, where they found Brian Rattigan asleep. After waking him up, detectives told him he was being arrested for the drive-by shooting the previous St Patrick's Day.

During the subsequent search Rattigan was very polite and was trying to give the impression that he had nothing to hide. A member of the investigation team's suspicions were raised by Brian Rattigan's unusually polite behaviour: 'Freddie Thompson is out to get him and he's being very calm and co-operative. This isn't the Rattigan we know. There was something not right about his behaviour.'

The search of the bedroom continued and the detective's instincts were proved correct. The team found heroin worth €27,000 hidden in a sock inside Rattigan's duvet. 'King Ratt's' co-operation had been a ruse to try to protect his drugs business, which he was clearly still running successfully.

The discovery was a huge result for gardaí and a major blunder by Brian Rattigan. For the first time in the feud one of the key actors was facing a lengthy spell behind bars. With the high value of the heroin, Rattigan knew he would soon be off the streets as, under the legislation, anyone caught with drugs worth over €10,000 could be charged with 'possession with intent to supply' and face a strong prison sentence. For someone who had been involved in organized crime for a number of years, a former officer later said, Brian Rattigan had made a rookie mistake:

Rattigan had been involved in the drugs trade for at least five years, had already claimed his first victim and yet here he was holding on to a large quantity of heroin. This was something Thompson would never have done – he was too cute for that. Rattigan had made a fatal mistake by keeping the drugs in his bed and had simply handed his rival the upper hand in their ongoing dispute. He was off the rails at the time with drink and drugs and this undoubtedly affected his judgement.

Brian Rattigan was immediately arrested and brought to Store Street Garda Station for questioning. Over a twenty-four-hour period he was first interrogated about the drive-by shooting and then about the drugs found in his bed. Gardaí knew there was not enough evidence to get a conviction on the drive-by shooting so they focused on the drugs charge instead. He was brought to Dublin District Court, where he was charged with possession of heroin with intent to supply. However, despite the objections of former Detective Superintendent Cormac Gordon and the then Detective Sergeant Pat Lordan, who told the court that Rattigan was a dangerous criminal currently involved in a feud which had claimed two lives, Rattigan received bail and walked free.

With Rattigan's behaviour spiralling out of control after his arrest, Thompson appeared to have the advantage in the gangland war. However, he too showed his reckless nature a few days later, when he drove his car straight at a garda officer in Rathmines, south Dublin. The gardaí had an associate of Thompson's in custody and the gang leader was trying to help the man to escape. It didn't work and Thompson was arrested and charged with endangerment. However, he received bail so, like Rattigan, was back on the streets.

With his trial date for the assault set for early 2003, gardaí received intelligence that Thompson was holding secret meetings with his associates in hotels across Dublin. On one occasion in the run-up to Christmas 2002, gardaí received information that Thompson and four of his gang members had met with Martin 'The Viper' Foley at a Dublin hotel. One report speculated: 'Possible Thompson is trying to secure more support for his feud with the Rattigan faction.' In former Detective Superintendent O'Gara's view:

> When you look at Freddie Thompson's convictions in his early years they range from public order to threatening and abusive behaviour, assault and driving offences. It's only when he has a firm grip on his gang that he's brought before the courts on more serious offences. It was no surprise he tried to help some-one escape because for all his bravado he was also reckless. They were simply young men who had gotten ahead of them-selves and believed in their own hype. It was only a matter of time before he had more serious convictions to contend with because he was obsessed with power, money and control.

As 2002 drew to a close, at a sitting of Carlow District Court, Thompson was banned from driving for twenty years after he was repeatedly caught speeding and driving with no insurance. His trial date on the endangerment charge was also just around the corner. Thompson's reckless behaviour was finally catching up with him.

At the beginning of February 2003 he received a two-year sentence for driving his car at the unarmed garda officer the previous August. The charge also coincided with a six-month jail term he'd received a few weeks earlier, on 20 January, for criminal damage. After the hearing, the 22-year-old Thomp-son was on his first trip to Mountjoy Prison.

Inside the prison he forged alliances with many criminals, including those connected to the Hutch gang in Dublin's north inner city. While he was serving his sentence for driving the car at the garda, Thompson also received a concurrent three-year sentence for assaulting the innocent bystander outside the Garda Members' Club on Harrington Street in February 2000. The endangerment trial ran alongside the assault trial as the assault was a more serious offence. Thompson was also ordered to pay €1,500 to the injured man, but the compensation was never paid.

Gardaí later discovered that Thompson showed his softer side during his imprisonment, penning letters to his childhood sweetheart, Vicky Dempsey, who had been left alone with the couple's two-year-old son. In one letter, found by gardaí during the search of an apartment used by Thompson, Freddie promised to abandon his life of crime following his release from prison:

> I swear to God baby it's just you and me and our boy. When I get out of here I will be there for you and our son. I'm doing ok in here but I miss you so much. It's not the same when I'm not with you. I want to put all this behind me when I get out and we can get away somewhere. Just the three of us. I want to get out.

A former investigator claimed gardaí were shocked to see Thompson in a different light:

> The search of the property was for evidence into drug-dealing activity, but the team were surprised to see his letters from jail. You had this extremely dangerous and volatile criminal who was moving through the ranks of the underworld at a rapid pace, a criminal who had been linked

to a murder and someone who had fostered a strong reputation for violence showing a completely different side to his personality. This wasn't the Freddie Thompson the people of the south inner city knew. It appeared as if he was going to go on the straight and narrow but deep down we all knew this was just a ruse for him to keep his partner onside.

In the early days of his prison sentence, an investigator explained, gardaí received intelligence that Thompson had sent orders to his gang to kill anyone who attempted to befriend the mother of his child:

Thompson was very jealous and if he thought for one second that someone was trying to make advances towards his girlfriend he wouldn't have hesitated for a moment to have them killed. It was like he had a split personality. He showed a caring nature to his family and those close to him, and then showed extreme levels of violence to those he considered his enemies and those who owed him money.

With Thompson serving his first major sentence, Rattigan, who remained out on bail, seized the opportunity to strike at his rivals. Around 11.30 p.m. on 15 February 2003, Rattigan and fellow criminals Wayne Zambra, Wayne McNally and another unidentified male armed themselves with a pump action shotgun, and set out to target members of the Thompson faction. However, the trio's plan unravelled when a garda patrol car from Kilmainham Station noticed a Nissan Sunny acting suspiciously at 11.50 p.m. on La Touche Road in Bluebell. Failing to stop, the car sped off as the garda patrol car and another garda vehicle, containing Detective Garda Brian Hearne and Detective Garda Jim Mathews, gave chase.

In their subsequent file to the Director of Public Prosecutions, gardaí stated:

> While pursuing this vehicle, the rear-seat occupant, Brian Rattigan, discharged a number of shots in an effort to evade arrest. This car was abandoned on Bluebell Road and all four occupants were pursued on foot. Rattigan levelled a pump action shotgun in the direction of gardaí. Detective Garda Hearne discharged a shot from his official issue firearm and Rattigan was overpowered and arrested and firearm recovered. Later Wayne Zambra and Wayne McNally were also arrested.

The fourth man escaped and was never charged, but Brian Rattigan was not so lucky. He was brought to Cloverhill Prison, where he was held on remand and charged with unlawful possession of a firearm with intent to endanger life. This time 'King Ratt' would not receive bail . . .

Just three months later, Rattigan appeared at Dublin Circuit Court and received a six-year sentence for possession of drugs with intent to supply. Rattigan's decision to store them in his home had proved to be a costly mistake. He also received a concurrent four-and-a-half-year sentence for the Bluebell shotgun incident, with the result that he would be in prison for seven years.

Rattigan suffered a further blow on 18 September 2003 when Detective Sergeant Joe O'Hara and Detective Inspector Tom Mulligan walked into his cell in Cloverhill Prison and charged him with the murder of his former friend Declan Gavin. The gang leader was remanded in custody on this charge as he continued to serve his sentences for the drugs seizure and for his clash with the gardaí in Bluebell.

Rattigan's somewhat bizarre reply to the murder charge was: 'No, dirty fucking rat.'

With Thompson and Rattigan both behind bars, the rest of 2003 passed off relatively peacefully. However, as this former investigator knew, it was still business as usual in terms of the day-to-day drug-dealing operations:

> Thompson and Rattigan had both been locked up early on in the year and it looked as if the rival factions were happy to focus on the business side of their criminal enterprises. They were both making a lot of money, but we all knew this relative calm wouldn't last for long.

3. Payback

Youse have opened up gang warfare and your boys
could get shot in their beds without their guns.
Freddie Thompson to officers of the
Emergency Response Unit

At the beginning of 2004, rival gang leaders 'Fat Freddie' Thompson and Brian 'King Ratt' Rattigan were still off the streets serving out their sentences. It was a development welcomed by gardaí who had established increased patrols to prevent further loss of life in the communities of Crumlin and Drimnagh. Senior officers, however, like this former detective, were deeply concerned about both Thompson's and Rattigan's ability to orchestrate attacks from their prison cells:

> Two of the country's most violent criminals were off the streets but that didn't mean the threat had diminished. They may have been in prison but they still had influence and support. They were both determined to keep the feud going because Thompson still wanted revenge over Gavin and Rattigan had promised to avenge the death of his younger brother.

Just fifteen days into the New Year, Thompson's gang were the first to strike. At 1.35 a.m. a number of shots were fired through the window and door of a property in Westcourt Apartments in the Basin Street area of the south city

centre. Two women in the property, including Brian Rattigan's cousin, as well as her ten-month-old son, had a lucky
escape. In their investigations into the shooting, gardaí came
to the conclusion that Thompson's associate Paddy Doyle
had carried out the attack and that the women, who had no
involvement in crime, had been targeted because of their
association with Brian Rattigan.

Hearing about the attack in his cell in Cloverhill Prison,
Rattigan ordered his gang to increase their efforts to target
members of 'Fat Freddie' Thompson's faction. One of the
key members of Thompson's gang to still feature high on
Rattigan's hit list was his 'fixer' and money launderer, Darren
Geoghegan. Shots had already been fired at Geoghegan's
family home, and on 30 January 2004 officers from the gardaí's
Crime and Security branch received intelligence of another
credible threat to his life. Like many of his contemporaries,
however, Geoghegan showed contempt when Detective Sergeant John Walsh, now retired, informed him of the threat,
as outlined in one garda report:

> A threat to the life of Darren Geoghegan was received and
> communicated to Sergeant John Walsh. He subsequently
> met and gave advice to Darren Geoghegan on 3 February
> 2004. Geoghegan laughed when given the advice and
> remained in Sundrive Road Station for all of thirty seconds.
> Threats were obviously from the Rattigan group.

One week later, intelligence from informants on both
sides of the feud was continuing to flood into the gardaí's
Crime and Security branch. At the same time, phones belonging to gang members were being tapped. In just one day,
10 February, investigators received intelligence of serious
threats to the life of Rattigan's associate Joseph 'Joey' Redmond

and to the life of Thompson's friend Michael Frazer, the car dealer who would cheat death on six different occasions over the years. Frazer was another young man from the south inner city who had grown up with Thompson. The pair would remain close during the feud, maintaining their friendship.

Under legislation, gardaí are obliged to pass on information to an individual if they receive intelligence of an imminent threat to their lives. This is officially known as a Garda Information Message form, and one was issued to Michael Frazer. The purpose of the message is to inform the individual to take necessary security precautions to prevent such an attack. According to one report on the threats to Frazer's life:

> Michael Frazer called to Sundrive Road Garda Station and he was spoken with and given the crime prevention advice. He refused to acknowledge the fact that he was involved in any group and expressed surprise that anyone would want to do anything to him. However, when pressed further, he did say that if anything were to happen to him it would be because of the Drimnagh feud and his former friendships with persons like Freddie Thompson, Brian Rattigan and others.

Just six days after his meeting with gardaí, three shots were fired at Frazer's home in Knocknarea Avenue in Drimnagh. As he fled one of the gunmen shouted: 'Tell Mickey, he's gonna get it.'

As the tension mounted, the targeting continued. Brian Rattigan had not forgotten about the man who had lured his younger brother Joey to his death almost a year and a half earlier. In the interval since the killing, Paul Warren had distanced himself from Thompson's faction by telling people that he had only met Joey Rattigan for a drink. Despite

Warren's pleas of innocence, 'King Ratt' had identified his brother's 'friend' as a key target, and a hit team was assembled to assassinate him.

Working as a glazier for Hennessy Glass, on 25 February 2004 Warren finished his shift for the day. He went to Gray's pub, on Newmarket Square in the city centre, for a few drinks with two friends. They were playing pool and watching a Champions League match on the TV when, at around 8 p.m., a former cellmate of Brian Rattigan's, Jonathan Mooney, walked into the pub with his girlfriend. After taking a look around Mooney made a call on his girlfriend's mobile and then received a call back ten minutes later. The man at the end of the line was Brian Rattigan, calling from his cell in Cloverhill Prison. Throughout the course of the evening, Rattigan would make a series of calls asking for details about Paul Warren, such as what clothes he was wearing and where he was sitting in the pub.

At the same time, a Rattigan associate and gun for hire, Gary Bryan, was on his way to Gray's pub. Bryan was a drug addict from the south inner city whose main crimes up to this point had been burglaries. During his time in prison, however, he'd developed associations with the Rattigan faction. Bryan had offered his services as a hitman after his release in return for cash. Working alongside the contract killer was a Rattigan gang member, John Roche.

After confirming that their target was in the pub at 10.47 p.m., Bryan and Roche stormed into Gray's just before 11 p.m. Warren took one look at the armed men, whose faces were covered with balaclavas, and made a desperate attempt to escape by hiding in the men's toilets. Within seconds, Bryan had forced open the door and opened fire with his

Magnum revolver, hitting Warren in the face. As they left, the gunman was reported to say: 'I got him. Let's get out of here.'

Arriving at the pub minutes later, gardaí found Warren lying in a pool of blood. He was pronounced dead at 11.55 p.m. The Rattigan faction had claimed the third victim of the feud.

Former Detective Superintendent Gabriel O'Gara, who led the murder investigation at the time, believes Warren was just one of many young men used by Thompson and his gang during the feud:

> In terms of gangland, Paul Warren wasn't a major player. He was a petty criminal who got way in over his head when he agreed to help Thompson and his gang target Joey Rattigan. Warren was a nobody who only had a few convictions for possessing drugs. He was from the south inner city and would have known members on both sides of the feud. He was typical of the young men in the south inner city who were exploited by people like Thompson. He would have been promised all sorts but all along he was simply expendable to people like Thompson and when people like him get involved in organized crime it can only end two ways – prison or death. Everyone knew he had been arrested for the Rattigan murder and there was no way Brian Rattigan was going to forget about it. It appeared Warren had become complacent because he still continued to drink in bars in the south inner city. In the months before his death his actions would indicate that he was someone who didn't believe they were under threat.

The next move in the feud was on 27 February, when four members of the Thompson gang attacked a completely innocent man with baseball bats. Thompson's associates had linked him to the Rattigan faction after he was spotted helping Seamus 'Shay' O'Byrne, the partner of Rattigan's sister, Sharon, push-start his car. In their report on the incident, gardaí later stated:

> This man is unconnected to either gang. He was seriously assaulted by four men with baseball bats. He received a good hiding which required hospital treatment. Before the assault finished one of the culprits was heard to say, 'He's not one of them.' All the man had done was push start O'Byrne's car. Initially one of the four culprits had shouted at him 'You're dead!' but after giving him a hiding, and realizing he was not connected, they left him there injured.

It would not be the last time an innocent bystander would find themselves caught up in the feud.

Just days after Warren's killing, the murder investigation team received a breakthrough when an informant named Bryan as the gunman. A huge surveillance operation was initiated to track Bryan's movements, with his flat in Dublin's south inner city being monitored on a 24/7 basis.

On the evening of 9 March 2004, Bryan, who was clutching a white Puma bag, and his girlfriend, Valerie White, were observed leaving his apartment. Gardaí followed them to Valerie White's sister's house and watched as they returned to the flat without the bag. Bryan was arrested in Tallaght, south-west Dublin the following day on suspicion of committing another burglary. During a search of his apartment on 11 March, investigators recovered a Taurus .357 Magnum handgun and six rounds of ammunition. His girlfriend was also questioned by gardaí before being released without charge.

Elaine White's apartment was searched by a team of detectives, led by one of Ireland's most prominent gangland investigators, Detective Sergeant Adrian Whitelaw. During the search officers recovered the white Puma bag and discovered it contained four live rounds, a black balaclava, a mobile phone and twelve spent cartridges. Elaine White told gardaí she wanted no involvement with Bryan's actions and had been forced to hold the bag after he threatened her. She was released without charge.

Two days later, on 13 March, detectives had another boost when Bryan's girlfriend, Valerie White, came forward. She was furious that her family had been dragged into the investigation and provided a full account of her partner's involvement in the murder. She was able to give gardaí specific details as Bryan had confessed his involvement in the hours following the killing. The hitman had no knowledge of his girlfriend's statement to gardaí as he was still in custody.

The detectives continued to build their case against Bryan and also focused on Rattigan's spotter, Jonathon Mooney. He was arrested on 7 April 2004, before being released without charge on 9 April as a file was prepared for the Director of Public Prosecutions. Mooney would later receive a five-year sentence for assisting an offender and withholding information.

The investigation team received more proof to support their case when fingerprint evidence discovered on the white Puma bag was confirmed as belonging to Bryan. On 21 April, with their evidence completed, the detectives made their move and the gun for hire was finally arrested. Two days later, he appeared at Dublin District Court, where he became the first person connected to the Crumlin–Drimnagh feud to be charged with murder.

With one of Rattigan's contract killers safely off the streets, Thompson and his gang were in prime position to continue their offensive against anyone connected or related to the imprisoned gang leader. The gardaí's Crime and Security section received regular intelligence on each side's ongoing targeting of the other in the feud. From his cell in Mountjoy, Thompson was understood to be pestering his gang to step up their campaign against Rattigan's associates over the course of the summer and autumn.

On 24 September 2004, the experienced gangland investigator Detective Inspector Brian Sutton, now a Chief Superintendent, met with Rattigan's older brother Richard and his mother, Christina, both of whom are not involved in criminality, at their home in Drimnagh. The senior officer explained that gardaí had received information that they were in danger of being 'shot or injured' and advised them to review their personal security. Richard Rattigan replied that he had received a phone call just the day before warning him there was a price on his head and that there was a contract out on him. According to a garda report: 'He refused to divulge who had contacted him but only said it was to get at Brian. He further said he would be moving to Ballyfermot with his pregnant girlfriend.'

Following the senior garda's meeting it wasn't long before Brian was told about the threat to his relatives. A former prison guard revealed Rattigan's reaction at the time:

> He was incensed with rage that his older brother and mother had been dragged into the feud. He was constantly mouthing off in the prison that if something happened to another of his family members Freddie Thompson's family would also pay a huge price.

Brian Rattigan wasted little time in retaliating to the threats made against his family. A few weeks later two gang members fired two shots into the front window of Freddie

Thompson's family home in Loreto Road in the south inner city and two shots into a Nissan van parked in the driveway. Thompson's mother, Elizabeth, who is innocent of any involvement in organized crime and has been targeted purely because of her son's actions, had a lucky escape. Gardaí later recovered four spent cartridges from the scene.

Neighbours were horrified by the shooting but not surprised, with one local saying:

> Everyone felt sorry for her because she wasn't involved in anything. She tried everything she could with Freddie but she just couldn't stop him from choosing the path that he did in the end. It was a disgrace for a mother to be dragged into something as horrible as this. People in the area were terrified of her son but they still had a lot of time for Elizabeth.

With innocent family members of both factions seen as 'legitimate targets' and being drawn into the feud, hostilities were reaching a new level. Thompson walked out of prison just in time for Christmas 2004 and gardaí braced themselves for a fresh wave of attacks. They knew he'd had plenty of time to plan his revenge.

Before launching an offensive on the Rattigan faction, however, Thompson had some personal business to take care of. A few days after his release he was suspected of assaulting a young man after accusing him of attempting to befriend his girlfriend, Vicky Dempsey. The man was hospitalized and had to get twenty-seven stitches after the attack.

Thompson's next move was against an associate of Rattigan's – Joseph 'Joey' Redmond. On 23 December 2004, the front door of an apartment in the Lansdowne Valley Apartment complex in Drimnagh was kicked in. Gardaí believed the incident was an attempt by Thompson's gang to kidnap Redmond, who had been staying there with his girl-friend, a first cousin of Brian Rattigan. Redmond's girlfriend was reported as being 'terrified and frightened' after the incident.

With Freddie Thompson now back on the streets, gardaí believed that the gang leader had instructed his fellow gangsters to increase the levels of violence, as one detective described:

> He was livid over the attack on his mother's house and there is a suggestion his gang planned to abduct Redmond, torture him and murder him as a warning to others who were still on the side of the Rattigan faction. It was all about increasing fear in the south inner city.

At the beginning of 2005, keeping up the onslaught against the Rattigan faction remained a key priority for Thompson. To finance his campaign the drug dealing continued, with Freddie's fellow gang members forging allegiances with other gangs in the north inner city and in west Dublin to increase their market share.

Thompson's gang made its next move on 1 March 2005 when one of their hitmen fired a number of shots with a semi-automatic pistol at a close associate of Rattigan's. It happened outside his home in Cooley Road and the victim fled into an adjoining garden. Gardaí thought that he was lucky to escape with his life.

On 9 March 2005, despite being out of prison for just a few months, Thompson again showed his propensity for violence. He led a hit team against John Roche, one of Brian Rattigan's key associates, as payback for his involvement in the murder of Paul Warren. Thompson also hadn't forgotten that Roche had told Rattigan about Gavin's whereabouts on the night he was killed. Freddie also held John Roche responsible for playing a key role in the murder of his best friend.

Along with Thompson's money man, Darren Geoghegan, a low-level Thompson associate and a UK-based criminal, who would go on to become a key member of the Kinahan cartel, Thompson set off to attack Roche at his apartment in Irwin Street, Kilmainham. Unbeknownst to John Roche, members of Thompson's faction had rented an apartment overlooking his property and had spent weeks monitoring his movements. During the surveillance, Thompson's spies established that Roche left in his car most evenings before returning around midnight. His routine was no different on 9 March and he got back home at around 12.15 a.m. As he approached the doorway, a gunman emerged from the shadows and opened fire. Roche was hit three times in the chest, with a stray bullet entering the window of a nearby flat – luckily no one was home at the time. The Rattigan gang member was pronounced dead at the scene.

During their investigation into the killing, gardaí from Kilmainham concluded that John Roche had been shot in retaliation for the murder of Paul Warren. Even though Warren had distanced himself from both factions, and was not an active member of the gangs, Thompson still regarded him as a close friend and had appreciated his efforts in helping them to target Joey Rattigan. Detectives believed, said a former detective, that an unidentified gang member had pulled the trigger, with Thompson and Geoghegan acting as 'spotters':

> There was intelligence at the time that Thompson was orchestrating every aspect of the murder, from start to finish, and that when Roche was shot, he watched and laughed.

There was also intelligence that the gang celebrated the shooting by going on a session. Thompson was never charged over it because there just wasn't enough evidence or people willing to come forward, despite everyone in the community knowing who was behind the murder.

While Thompson was intent on waging war against Rattigan's gang, he was also carrying out a personal vendetta against Joey 'The Lips' O'Brien. Joey was a small-time local drug dealer who would go on to become a key witness in a feud-related murder. O'Brien emerged as a target after Thompson received information in prison that Joey had been seen socializing with Freddie's girlfriend, Vicky Dempsey. Thompson had also wrongly received information that O'Brien, who had a 'loose association' with the Rattigan gang, was selling drugs on Freddie's patch. Just three days before John Roche's murder, at around 4.40 a.m. three members of the Thompson gang had chased after O'Brien in the south inner city. O'Brien managed to escape but he knew he was a marked man.

As Thompson took command of his gang once again, he was extremely paranoid and found it hard to trust people, constantly looking over his shoulder. The attack on O'Brien and Roche's murder were just two examples of the 24-year-old's campaign to reinstate himself. He was constantly roaming the streets searching for Rattigan associates, but also for those who owed his gang money over unpaid drug debts. It was a full-time occupation identifying targets and trying to stay one step ahead of his enemies and the gardaí, and sometimes it was an obvious strain. In one instance, on 30 March 2005, Geoghegan and Thompson were stopped in a car by gardaí in the Kildare Street area of Dublin city centre.

They were arrested on suspicion of possessing drugs and officers noticed that Thompson was 'extremely nervous and agitated'. He was wearing a bulletproof vest, while Geoghegan was wearing a stabproof vest. According to gardaí, on this occasion Thompson, who regularly wore women's clothing, and glasses, and painted his toenails pink as part of his disguise, was also wearing a 'Noel Gallagher lookalike' wig. Geoghegan was later charged with a road traffic offence but Thompson was released without charge.

'Fat Freddie' remained on the warpath and wasted no time in organizing another murder. This time his gang's target was the 26-year-old Terry Dunleavy, a well-known drug dealer from the north inner city area of Dublin. On 14 April 2005, at around 10 p.m., Dunleavy had driven to his girlfriend's apartment at Croke Villas, on the north side of Dublin city centre. As he approached the property, a gunman confronted him on the stairs of the apartment block, hitting him once in the chest, before finishing him off with three shots to the head.

When gardaí searched Dunleavy's Volvo, they found cannabis worth €110,000. At the time, gardaí suspected the murder was linked to a dispute between rival drugs gangs on the north side of the capital, where the Kinahans would have been the main suppliers. Thompson, because of his connections to Daniel Kinahan, was also acting as an enforcer, chasing people who owed them money. If the debtors didn't pay up, then Thompson dealt with them. Terry Dunleavy had no apparent connections to either the Thompson or the Rattigan factions, but, as the garda investigation continued, it was soon established that the motorbike the gunman had used was owned by an associate of Thompson's just three weeks before the murder. Gardaí then discovered the motorbike had been taken as part payment for a drug debt owed to the Thompson gang. The owner of the bike was later arrested and, although he admitted owning the motorbike, refused to name the people who had taken it.

The investigation into Dunleavy's murder has remained open over the years, but detectives were unable to bring anyone before the courts due to lack of evidence and the unwillingness of people to come forward. They suspect the gunman was Jason O'Driscoll, a well-known gun for hire from north Dublin. Detectives believe he was personally recruited for the hit by Freddie Thompson himself, after Dunleavy's failure to pay a drug debt.

Dunleavy's father, James, was also convinced of Thompson's involvement in the murder of his son. In an interview with an *Irish Sun* journalist, Gary Meenely, in 2018, Dunleavy's father talked about how Thompson has destroyed countless lives through his violent actions:

> The police told me that Thompson was involved in Terry's death. He has done away with a lot of people. Families are wrecked but life is nothing to him. Terry was naïve, he was only a young lad and fell into the wrong crowd. I was always saying 'My God' there are an awful lot of cases. It wasn't just Terry. There were an awful lot of innocent people. It's what he said. I'm glad the police said that Thompson was involved in Terry's murder. They said he ordered it, he was behind it.

On the reasons why his son may have been murdered, Mr Dunleavy said:

> Money went missing but I'm not exactly sure. Terry got into some stuff he shouldn't have. When you look back at all them young lads, they are gone. Thompson thought he was

untouchable. All he had to do was get someone to do it. They don't think of the consequences when someone is killed – the family, the friends. Freddie's involvement in the murder came up at the inquest, the police mentioned it. Life is nothing to him.

In response to the Roche and Dunleavy murders, the then Justice Minister, Michael McDowell, introduced 'Operation Anvil' in May 2005. A former Garda Commissioner, Noel Conroy, was given extra resources to combat the growing threat of violence in Dublin's south inner city. Operation Anvil was devised to 'target specific suspect criminals, their associates and travelling criminals involved in serious crime'. In practice, it meant more obvious garda patrolling in Crumlin and Drimnagh, including extensive checkpoints, supported by armed patrols. Intelligence-driven covert operations were also undertaken by a combination of specialist garda units.

The State's response to the growing cycle of violence did not seem to affect Thompson. He still roamed the streets looking for victims. Around 4 p.m. on 5 May 2005, the wife of a close associate of Brian Rattigan's contacted gardaí and claimed she was being followed by three men in a blue Ford Mondeo. Shortly afterwards, the car was stopped by detectives and they discovered Thompson was the front-seat passenger. He was wearing a wig and glasses and, as officers approached the car, Thompson ate the SIM card from his mobile phone. In the rear of the car was Paddy Doyle, Thompson's hitman of choice. The driver of the car was a young associate who came from a well-known crime family and who would go on to become a key member of the Kinahan cartel. During a search of the car, detectives recovered a leather belt for shotgun ammunition, a Bord na Móna firepack, a balaclava and gloves.

The trio were later brought to Sundrive Road Garda Station before being released. Although there were no weapons in the car, gardaí were convinced they were on their way to collect arms for a hit on a Rattigan associate. Shortly after their release from custody, an innocent relative of Rattigan was attacked by three men, with one of them wielding a hammer. Although refusing to make a complaint, the injured man described how one of the men was wearing a black curly wig – a favourite disguise of Freddie Thompson's.

In the weeks that followed, the game of cat and mouse between the warring factions and gardaí played out. Thompson knew he was a major target for gardaí, but he continued to spend his days being driven around the streets of Dublin looking for enemies. In one incident he was stopped by gardaí in the city centre and taunted detectives about the ERU's killing of two criminals, Colm Griffiths and Eric Hopkins, on 26 May, after they had robbed a post office in Lusk, north County Dublin: 'Youse have opened up gang warfare and your boys could get shot in their beds without their guns.'

The following month, there was surprise among some of the gang members and gardaí alike when an article appeared in the *Evening Herald* claiming that the gangs had called 'a truce'. The article referred to ongoing negotiations between senior gardaí, clergy and some of the mothers of the main participants. The majority of the people involved were convinced talks between the mothers would prove futile because the feud was now personal.

Any chance of a peace deal ended on 22 July, when Thompson ordered his associates to keep on with their offensive against innocent members of Rattigan's family. At around 10 p.m. that night, five shots were fired into a house in Grand Canal Bank on Dublin's southside. The owner of the house was a cousin of Rattigan's who was confined to a wheelchair, and was not involved in crime.

At the same time, gardaí also received intelligence from an informant that Thompson and his associates had recruited 'two shooters from Limerick' to target members of Rattigan's gang. The informant also outlined how 'King Ratt', who was incensed by the attack on his sick relative, had offered a €30,000 bounty to anyone who claimed the life of Freddie Thompson or one of his associates.

The following month, Joey 'The Lips' O'Brien was once again in Thompson's sights. On 18 August 2005, he was forced to hide near a garda station to escape the clutches of Thompson, Geoghegan, David Byrne and another gang member, Eoin 'Scarface' O'Connor. A loyal friend of 'Deco' Gavin's, O'Connor was another young member of Thompson's gang who had built up a reputation for violence since the start of the feud.

As the four young criminals hunted O'Brien, Byrne's older brother, Liam, later described by gardaí as a 'top-tier member' of the Kinahan cartel, was spotted nearby in a Honda HRV jeep. Gardaí believed Thompson's plan was to kidnap, torture and kill O'Brien as a warning to others who were selling drugs without his permission. For 'Fat Freddie' it was also personal, as he was determined to target anyone who he thought was trying to befriend Vicky Dempsey. A garda report on the incident detailed how:

On witnessing persons getting out of vehicles wearing bulletproof vests, O'Brien made good his escape and hid in the front gardens of houses backing on to Sundrive Road Garda Station. While hiding in bushes, Joey O'Brien observed Freddie Thompson standing nearby with a gun in his hand.

O'Brien remained hidden until he thought it was safe to go to Sundrive Road Station and report the incident.

The following day another man who had been linked to Vicky Dempsey was pursued by her jealous partner. The man, who had previously been attacked by Thompson, rang the vicious thug to ask why he was being targeted and to say he had done nothing wrong. Thompson replied that he was 'going to cut his throat'. Freddie subsequently attacked the man with a baseball bat as he walked along Windmill Road in Crumlin but his victim was too afraid to report the matter to gardaí.

Around the same time as the failed attempt on Joey O'Brien's life, gardaí in Portarlington, Co. Laois, searched a house and arrested Eric 'Lucky' Wilson, who would go on to become one of Ireland's most notorious hitmen. During the search they discovered a list containing the personal details of eight of Rattigan's closest associates, his girlfriend, Natasha McEnroe, and family members. The list detailed the cars driven by Rattigan's sister and girlfriend, with a note that they were 'easily got'. Also on the list was the name of Rattigan's innocent brother Jason, who suffered from spina bifida and was confined to a wheelchair. Another file earmarked the possible location for the shooting of a Rattigan associate, with the chilling note: 'Front room downstairs definite.'

Remaining silent when questioned, 'Lucky' Wilson was later released without charge. The people on his list were warned their lives were in danger while Wilson remained Freddie Thompson's top choice of guns for hire.

Due to the mounting body count on the Rattigan side and Thompson's growing reputation in the underworld, he was arrogantly convinced that his gang would win the war. He also remained paranoid, however, as he knew Rattigan's gang members had made him their number one target. In Thompson's world the best form of defence was attack, and with the gang leader on the warpath not even his most trusted associates were safe from his bloodlust.

4. Killing Machine

The simple message is don't get involved because
it will destroy you. There is paranoia, there is
mistrust and there is pressure.
Valerie White, whose partner, Gary Bryan,
was murdered by Thompson's gang.

By September 2005, Freddie Thompson was regarded by gardaí as a one-man 'killing machine', fighting a war on many fronts. Thompson's propensity for violence and lust for murder were well known in garda circles and in the streets he terrorized. Detectives had watched him grow from a joy-rider into a serious player in the Dublin drugs trade. Although not yet twenty-five, 'Fat Freddie' was now being investigated as a prime suspect in a series of savage murders. Gardaí were also aware that the mayhem which had followed his release from prison at the end of 2004 – his feud with the Rattigan mob, his obsession with targeting small-time drug dealers who owed him cash and his attacks on anyone he thought had tried to befriend his girlfriend during his time in prison – was unremitting.

On 9 September 2005, gardaí were called out to deal with a typical example of the war being waged by Thompson. The gang leader and an associate had called to a house in Crumlin Park, the home address of Joey 'The Lips' O'Brien, and threatened Joey's father over a so-called outstanding debt. In a statement to gardaí, Joey O'Brien claimed he had paid the gang €30,000 but they were 'seeking further payments'. He also told officers how he had been confronted by Thompson earlier that day and had defended himself by producing a sword. When Freddie and his associate returned to the property, they warned O'Brien's father, who had no involvement in crime, he could 'expect a grenade attack on his home' if their demands weren't met.

Thompson was still intent on destroying the Rattigan gang, but he was also focusing on becoming a supplier for other drugs gangs in the capital. With the pressure mounting from every side – the gardaí, the Rattigan faction, rival drug dealers – the gang leader turned to cocaine and became increasingly paranoid. Freddie loved his family and felt they were the only people he could truly trust. Unlike Christy Kinahan Snr, however, who had his two sons working for him, Freddie had no immediate family member in his gang. His only relatives in crime were his cousins Liam Roe and David and Liam Byrne, whom he did trust, but other gang members and some of his closest friends were becoming targets of Thompson's mounting paranoia.

At the time his closest confidant, the contract killer Paddy Doyle, was one of the few people Thompson fully trusted. As one investigator explained: 'During that period of the feud Thompson and Doyle did everything together and were often stopped in cars together. They were inseparable because Thompson knew Doyle was loyal and would have done anything for him.'

Another associate stopped with Thompson on many occasions was his personal financier, Darren Geoghegan, who was still in charge of 'cleaning' the gang's cash, which he did by purchasing commercial premises in Dublin and investment properties in various countries, including Spain and Bulgaria. He was regarded as extremely intelligent by gardaí, and his services had also been utilized by other criminal networks operating across the capital.

Geoghegan had grown up in Drimnagh and had been a close friend of Declan Gavin's from childhood. He'd worked as a painter before turning to a more lucrative career in organized crime. He was also good friends with Thompson growing up and got to know Doyle when he later joined the gang. Surrounded by people he'd known since childhood or who he thought he could trust, Geoghegan had no idea of the danger he was in.

On 13 November 2005, Geoghegan, along with a fellow gang member, Gavin Byrne, travelled to the Carrigwood estate in Firhouse, south Dublin. Byrne had been keeping a low profile during the feud and was widely regarded as Geoghegan's assistant. Investigators later believed the two money launderers were instructed by Thompson to travel to the area to meet with a senior associate to talk about a planned attack on the Rattigan faction. Unknown to Geoghegan and Byrne, however, other members of the gang had voiced concerns about their access to large amounts of cash and Geoghegan's business arrangements with other criminals. They suspected Geoghegan was attempting to use the money-laundering networks for other gangs.

Driving into the quiet housing estate in a silver Lexus, Geoghegan and Byrne parked and waited for the senior associate to arrive. Both men were wearing bulletproof vests because they were terrified of being shot by Rattigan's associates. Just two minutes later, a BMW, which had been stolen in Northern Ireland, pulled up alongside them.

The passenger in the BMW emerged and got into the back seat of the Lexus. Within seconds, the man in the back seat opened fire with a SIG Sauer pistol, hitting both Geoghegan and Byrne twice in the head and killing them instantly.

As the garda investigation swung into action, detectives initially suspected members of Rattigan's gang were behind the double murder. They knew Geoghegan had survived previous attempts on his life, and he had also been officially warned by gardaí his life was under threat because of his links to Thompson. But detectives were soon following a different line of inquiry. After further investigations they were of the firm belief that Paddy Doyle had been ordered by Thompson to carry out the hit in a row over drugs money. Another investigator said:

> The initial suspicion fell on the Rattigans because these were two senior members of the Thompsons who had been taken out of circulation. But when informants within the Rattigan gang told gardaí it was nothing to do with them, and because Geoghegan would never have met anyone he didn't trust, suspicion fell on his own gang.

Garda investigators heard many other theories going around, but they also suspected that Geoghegan would only have allowed a trusted associate into his car. The team's suspicions were confirmed when informants within the Thompson faction came forward and passed on intelligence that Doyle was the hitman. In the words of a security source:

> Life was cheap to people like Thompson and Doyle. This incident showed just how callous they were because it was clear they were prepared to wipe out their friends to protect their own selfish interests. Geoghegan was popular among

many criminals and Thompson was lucky he didn't have another feud on his hands. People were mad to consider someone like Thompson as a friend because he could turn on them over the slightest thing. Friendships mean nothing in the world of gangland.

Following the murders of Geoghegan and Byrne, detectives from the gardaí's Organised Crime Unit (now the Garda National Drugs and Organised Crime Bureau) established 'Operation Steel' specifically to target Thompson. Although detectives in Crumlin and Kevin Street Stations were conducting their own investigations, garda management felt a separate operation was needed to tackle Thompson because of the growing cycle of violence.

The 'Steel' team never fully established why Geoghegan and Byrne were executed, and no one was ever brought to justice over the double murder. However, the main theory is that Thompson found out that Geoghegan was planning to relocate to Spain and establish his own drug-dealing network, with the major north Dublin drugs lord Marlo Hyland as his main supplier. One senior security source insisted that Geoghegan was leaving because he had become 'tired' of the gang war with Rattigan, explaining: 'There's a strong suspicion that Geoghegan was planning on cutting all ties with Thompson. Only Geoghegan and Thompson had access to the gang's money, so Thompson was concerned his best friend would leave him with nothing.'

Gardaí also received intelligence that Thompson had been in the area of the shooting in a Mercedes just an hour before the double murder. The case was one of fifteen unsolved gangland murders listed for re-examination by gardaí and is still under investigation at the time of writing.

Just two days after the double murder, Thompson's assassins were dispatched once again. This time their target was a Rattigan loyalist, Noel Roche, whose brother John had been shot dead a few months earlier. The key Rattigan associate knew he was a major target for the Thompson gang, but he continued to socialize in bars and clubs around Dublin. The night of 15 November was no different when he made the life-changing decision to go to the Phil Collins concert at the 3 Arena, in Dublin's north inner city. During the concert, gardaí believe Roche spotted a rival gangster and decided to leave early. Outside the venue, Roche and his girlfriend were collected by a friend in a Ford Mondeo before driving to her apartment in Coolock, north Dublin. Unbeknownst to them, two men, who have never been identified, were waiting in a Fiat Punto. They followed the pair until Roche managed to lose them. At the same time, a phone call was made to Paddy Doyle, detailing Roche's movements. The contract killer then rang a low-level gang member, twenty-year-old Craig White, and told him to come and pick him up.

After dropping off his girlfriend, Noel Roche and his driver made the fateful decision to return to the Temple Bar area of the city centre for a late drink. The Thompson faction knew Roche had a safe house in the Coolock area so White and Doyle were driving towards it when they got lucky and spotted Roche's Mondeo on the Clontarf Road at around 10.25 p.m. As Roche and his driver attempted to flee, White drove in front of them and forced them to stop. Doyle stepped out of the car and fired three shots into Roche's head.

Fleeing from the scene, the killers drove to south Dublin before abandoning their car. White then made a schoolboy error and forgot to destroy the evidence. It wasn't long before gardaí had recovered his fingerprints and DNA from the vehicle. He would later become the first person to be convicted of murder in the feud. Around the same time, gardaí received intelligence that Doyle had claimed his third life in two days.

Struggling to cope with the pressure from gardaí and discovering Rattigan had placed a €60,000 bounty on his head, a week after the murder Paddy Doyle called to Crumlin Garda Station and told a detective he wanted a way out. When the officer suggested the contract killer admit to his crimes in return for a favourable deal from the DPP, Doyle laughed and walked out of the station.

It would be the last time Doyle would be seen by gardaí in Ireland. Fearing for his life and now one of the country's most wanted men, Doyle spent weeks living in safe houses and disguising himself as a woman before fleeing to the sanctuary of the Costa del Sol.

With Doyle's relocation to Spain, Thompson had lost his trusted sidekick. He refocused on the gang's drug-dealing business and, throughout the remainder of 2005 and into 2006, they continued to earn huge amounts of money. However, the feud was never far from Thompson's thoughts. On 15 April 2006, he was at Dublin Airport on his way to Amsterdam with Eoin O'Connor and another young associate, who would go on to become a hitman for the Kinahan cartel, when they met Rattigan's girlfriend, Natasha McEnroe, and a group of her friends, who were en route to a music festival. Thompson and McEnroe were soon exchanging insults, but when airport police were forced to intervene, both sides backed off, claiming it was just 'banter'.

As the summer of 2006 approached, Thompson began spending more and more time with members of the Hutch gang in the north inner city. When he was in prison, he had built up a relationship with Gary Hutch and he used this useful contact to meet with other Hutch associates.

Gary Hutch had been introduced to crime at a young age. His first conviction was on 10 April 2000, aged eighteen, when he received a three-month sentence for theft. This was followed on 12 July 2000 by a €100 fine for animal cruelty, after he dressed a sheep in clothing and threw it over a wall into a garden in Sherrard Street in Dublin's north inner city where it was mauled by three dogs. In the years that followed he was mainly involved in car thefts, before progressing to aggravated burglaries. On 4 October 2001 he received a three-year sentence for aggravated burglary. It was during his time in prison for this conviction that he was introduced to Thompson and the pair quickly established a working relationship. At the same time as Gary Hutch was forging an alliance with Thompson and the Kinahans, his brother Derek 'Del Boy' Hutch was also working closely with the cartel, often dishing out beatings to people who refused to pay their drug debts.

On the May Bank Holiday Monday, Thompson met Hutch at a Chinese restaurant in Dublin's Dame Street. Gary Hutch was on temporary release from prison and was due to finish his sentence the following year. During the dinner the pair were also joined by a Thompson associate, who remains on the run, and the Hutch gang's loyal supporter James 'Mago' Gately. The dinner was used as a cover for Thompson and Gary Hutch to discuss their plans for working together after the armed robber's release.

The following month, the members of both gangs were among the 250 guests attending the champagne reception at the wedding of Thompson's brother, Richie, at the Stillorgan Park Hotel in south Dublin. Throughout the celebrations, members of the gardaí's Organised Crime Unit were also in attendance, amid concerns the Rattigan gang would attack the wedding party.

Thompson's unrelenting campaign achieved an unexpected boost when the Rattigan loyalist Wayne Zambra was shot dead on 19 August 2006. As with the Geoghegan and Byrne murders, gardaí soon established that a killer for hire from Rattigan's gang had accepted a contract for internal housekeeping. With Thompson's gang no longer in the frame for the murder, detectives had identified Gary Bryan, the man who'd shot Paul Warren, as the chief suspect.

Unfortunately for Bryan, he wouldn't live long enough to face justice over the murder. In February 2006, Bryan had gone on trial for the murder of Paul Warren two years before. Gardaí were left frustrated, however, when Bryan's girl-friend, Valerie White, withdrew her initial statement, citing concerns for her safety, and the case collapsed. The hitman had remained in prison on another charge relating to him being caught with heroin worth €10,000 and was not released until July 2006. Bryan had kept a low profile since then, until he emerged as a suspect for the Zambra murder. He was Rattigan's number one hitman and, despite narrowly avoiding a life sentence, remained loyal to his boss. But within five weeks of Zambra's murder Bryan's work for the Rattigan faction would be over for ever.

On the night of 26 September, Bryan and his girlfriend made a visit to Valerie's mother's house in Bunting Road, in Dublin's south inner city. Checking outside, Bryan became agitated when he saw a blue Volkswagen Golf drive past the property. He'd seen a key Thompson associate, Graham Whelan, in the car.

Bryan told his girlfriend: 'I'm in danger. There's a fella that's going to make a phone call. I have to get out of here.'

Thompson and Whelan had grown up together and were very close in their teenage years, moving into the drugs trade at the same time. Following Gavin's killing, Whelan had been elevated to number two status in the gang, reporting directly to his childhood friend. Bryan knew that Whelan had been released from Wheatfield Prison on 19 June 2006 after serving his sentence for being caught with the drugs at the Holiday Inn, back in March 2000.

In her attempts to calm her partner down, Valerie persuaded Bryan to wait for a cup of coffee and to finish working on the couple's car outside the house. However, at around 6.35 p.m. that evening when she went back inside, a masked gunman approached Bryan as he sat in his car and shot him three times in the back. Despite his injuries, Bryan managed to stagger from the car. The shooter then fired another three shots into his head as he lay on the ground, killing him instantly. As Valerie rushed outside, she shouted at the fleeing gunman before trying to comfort her partner of six years.

Bryan's death was a crushing blow to the Rattigan faction – their leader was behind bars and now their main contract killer was dead. 'Fat Freddie' Thompson and his gang clearly had the upper hand in the persisting feud.

The murder was a stark reminder of the likely consequences faced by those involved in organized crime. In a rare interview, Bryan's partner, Valerie White, took the brave step of pleading with young men to ignore the advances and the offers of cash from criminal godfathers:

I'm just worried there are still people like Gary – who was an addict – that will get sucked into feuds. Gary is a prime example of what drugs and the world of gangland can do to someone. I can still remember his killer leaning over him and emptying the chamber into his head. The smell of the gun that day will be with me until the day I die.

A lot of young men lost their lives in that feud and I was caught up in it. I know there are young lads out there who may want to get involved because of the easy offer of cash, but it's just not worth it. Before they know it, their whole family could be dragged into it and they will be the ones going to prison. If me telling people the trauma I experienced being with a contract killer and living in constant terror stops one young lad getting involved then it will have been worth it. The simple message is don't get involved because it will destroy you. There is paranoia, there is mistrust and there is pressure.

Bryan, who was a heroin addict, was involved in burglaries from a young age and in the course of his adult life had been in prison seventeen times. He had received sentences for car theft, drink driving, possession of a firearm and aggravated burglary. His most serious conviction had been in April 2004 for possession of heroin. Valerie described how during his time in prison he forged close links with the Rattigan faction:

> Gary was involved in burglaries, but he came out of prison as a hitman. I know for sure he was involved in one murder because he told me, but I don't know about others. I have lived through a feud and it's a nightmare, including for the families of those involved. Once you're in, there's no way back.

Valerie White still has regrets about withdrawing her statement in the Paul Warren murder case because she was terrified of the possible consequences:

I wish I had got up in the witness box for the Warren family. I feel more guilty about the Warren family than I do about not getting Gary put away. I feel I have let them down. When Gary told me what he did I was shocked – I did not want to be in this world. I retracted my evidence because I was worried about my life and the lives of my family.

No one was ever charged for Gary Bryan's murder, but investigators believe it was orchestrated by Thompson and his first cousin David Byrne.

Just three days after the murder, investigators also received a fresh insight into the inner workings of Thompson's gang when his first cousin Liam 'Bop' Roe, another member who would go on to play a key role in the Kinahan cartel, was stopped by officers manning a checkpoint under Operation Anvil. Roe's relationship to Thompson meant that he was held in high esteem by the rest of the gang. His role was to provide transport to senior gang members and also to provide safe houses during the feud with Rattigan. By this stage of the feud, every interaction between the rival gangsters was recorded by gardaí. On this occasion Roe claimed that he was focusing on his fitness at a gym in the Coolock area and was 'trying to stay away from Freddie's gang' because he had 'lost his taxi licence' and couldn't 'drive the lads around' any more. Gardaí also noted Roe had insisted Thompson was 'paranoid', that the Zambra and Bryan murders were 'terrible' and that he had no idea where Thompson was based.

Gardaí were searching for Freddie Thompson's location as they were trying to keep tabs on him to pre-empt any further attacks. Freddie, however, had decided to concentrate on his gang's drugs business. Drug dealing was still their number one priority and Thompson was determined to make more money and to assert his position as one of the dominant forces in the drugs trade in the south inner city. The feud could wait.

Towards the end of October 2006, Freddie travelled to Holland to personally oversee a drugs and weapons shipment. At the time, the Netherlands was the main go-to spot for Irish criminals to purchase ecstasy, heroin, cannabis and cocaine, with automatic weapons often thrown into the shipments as part of the overall package. Thompson's contact in Holland was Christy Kinahan's right-hand man, John Cunningham, previously convicted of kidnapping Jennifer Guinness. While he was in Holland, Thompson also had the advantage of forging a stronger relationship with Daniel Kinahan. With Daniel marked as the heir to his father's throne, it made perfect sense for the two young drug dealers and friends to do business together. The Kinahan gang were already Thompson's main supplier, but Freddie knew Daniel's father had amassed a huge contact list from all around the world and he wanted in. To gain access all he had to do was declare his loyalty to the Kinahans – this was no problem as Thompson was happy to be known as an associate of the powerful cartel.

Unbeknownst to Thompson, however, from the moment he arrived in Holland, he was under surveillance by Dutch police. Investigators in Amsterdam had received a tip-off from gardaí in Kevin Street in Dublin that Thompson was in Rotterdam to oversee a drugs and arms shipment to Ireland. Following a number of days of surveillance, on 27 October 2006 Dutch police moved in and arrested Thompson outside a house in Sionstraat, Rotterdam. Inside, police found several kilos of cocaine, worth an estimated €300,000, and six handguns. Three other Irish nationals, a man and two women, were also arrested. Two of the suspects had been recruited by Thompson to bring the drugs back to Ireland from Rotterdam through the English port of Hull.

Back in Ireland, the cautious approach adopted by Dutch police had left detectives frustrated. Instead of moving in when Thompson was inside the house, the Dutch team had feared a shoot-out and had waited until he'd left it so they could arrest him outside. As a result of this decision, four months down the line Thompson was able to wriggle out of the charges when he convinced a court that the drugs and guns did not belong to him. Freddie had slipped through the net once again and happily headed back to Dublin. One investigator explained the Irish team's frustrations over the arrest:

> Everything was given to them on a plate and the intelligence was of a very high value. If Thompson had been caught inside the house with the drugs and guns, then things would have been better for the communities where he was causing all the damage. It was a wasted opportunity.

The Dutch drugs seizure was the second blow to Thompson's organization within a week. A few days earlier drugs worth €11 million had been confiscated by gardaí in an operation in Clondalkin, west Dublin. Gardaí had established that a number of criminal groupings in the city had worked together to arrange the huge shipment and that a proportion of it belonged to Thompson.

Despite these losses, by the beginning of 2007 Thompson's gang still had the upper hand in the feud. Rattigan remained in prison on remand for Declan Gavin's murder, Bryan was dead and one of Rattigan's main enforcers, Wayne McNally, narrowly survived a murder bid on 20 February, when he was shot in the face in the Gray Square area of Dublin's south inner city. Another close associate, Trevor Brunton from Cabra in north Dublin, had been caught with a gun just before New Year's Eve. A subsequent search of Brunton's apartment had led to the seizure of drugs worth over €150,000. He would later receive an eight-year sentence for the offences. During his time in prison, and similarly to other gangsters over the years, Brunton switched sides, declaring his loyalty to Thompson and his bosses in the Kinahan cartel.

Thompson was still wary of an attack from the Rattigan side, but he continued to move freely around Dublin. In one encounter with gardaí, on 7 April 2007, Thompson and his close associate Graham Whelan were stopped in the Cork Street area of the south inner city. During their interaction with the officers, Thompson showed his sinister side when he asked them if their stab vests would 'take a bullet' and if gardaí would be 'getting bulletproof hats'.

A number of weeks later, on 24 April 2007, he was spotted by officers coming out of a Spar shop in the Dame Street area of the city centre. However, before they approached, he ate the top-up slip for mobile phone credit.

He declared: 'I did this to stop you checking me phone.'

When stopped in a red Golf GTI being driven by Graham Whelan in Crumlin two days later, he referred to Liam Keane from Limerick being spotted in the company of Rattigan's associates: 'He won't last long, he'll get plugged,' was his stark warning.

The feud with Rattigan's gang showed no sign of ending and gardaí remained on the streets, trying to prevent further bloodshed. In another encounter with gardaí on 2 May 2007, Thompson, who had four Nokia 2310 phones in his possession, mentioned that the Dublin criminal Alan 'Fatpuss'

Bradley had rung RTÉ radio's *Liveline* programme. Freddie raged: 'He's only a Finglas rat.'

During the conversation, Thompson also boasted of his links to Dublin City Council: 'I'm not worried about the car getting clamped because I have loadsa friends in Dublin City Council. I'm going to the Forum bar to watch Man United because it has loads of cameras there.'

Despite the ongoing feud, Thompson and his associates still enjoyed a busy social life, especially in the heart of Dublin. Freddie and his crew, however, were banned from the Sin nightclub in Dublin's Temple Bar in June 2007 after threatening staff. During another night out, on 24 June 2007, Thompson also exchanged 'insults and taunts' with the aunt of the murdered criminal Darren Geoghegan. According to a garda report, she became 'very wound up and had to be calmed down by friends'. Another example of Thompson's bravado was recorded by gardaí on 6 September 2007, when he asked officers to join him for a drink 'so you can keep monitoring me'.

Many of the city's top venues were all too aware of Freddie and his gang, with some other venues following Sin's example and issuing bans to the gangsters. A head doorman at one of the capital's premier venues spoke to gardaí about his concerns at Thompson's regular visits to his club. Detectives monitoring Thompson's movements established that many bar owners were afraid to confront 'Fat Freddie' and his associates, as this report detailed:

A head doorman had noticed gardaí speaking with Thompson and Liam Roe before they entered a club. Said he wants to bar them but is concerned about repercussions. Aspires to deny them entry and doesn't want any of his staff becoming 'pally' with them. He knows exactly who they are and calls them 'scum'. Said he doesn't want the heat on the club these guys inevitably bring. However, he did say they were as 'good as gold' once they were inside.

The security staff had cause for concern. On a previous occasion earlier that year Thompson's cousins Liam Roe and Liam Byrne had threatened to return to the City Bar on Dame Street in central Dublin and 'shoot the door staff and burn down the premises'. Although Roe was questioned over the incident, he never faced justice as the Director of Public Prosecutions ruled there was insufficient evidence to charge him.

Throughout 2007, Thompson worked closely with gangsters based in north Dublin, including the gang boss Eamon 'The Don' Dunne. According to a garda report, Thompson 'colluded with Eamon Dunne, Paddy Doyle and another criminal, to target John Daly'. Daly hit the headlines when he contacted the RTÉ radio's *Liveline* from his prison cell. He was shot dead on 22 October 2007 and gardaí insisted: 'Thompson paid €10,000 to have John Daly murdered at the behest of Eamon Dunne who was worried about Daly selling drugs on his patch. Dunne appears to have convinced Thompson it would be best to have Daly out of the way.'

While Freddie Thompson and his associates continued to enjoy the spoils of their drugs trade and their victories over Rattigan's gang, the relative calm didn't last for long. A new, more serious threat emerged in the form of the INLA and the group's leader in Dublin, Declan 'Whacker' Duffy. The Republican terrorist group had often funded its activities by 'taxing' local drug dealers. Duffy was well used to identifying criminal gangs for extortion and the Thompson gang's dominance on the Dublin gangland scene meant that it quickly moved to the top of his list.

Hailing from Co. Armagh, Duffy had joined the INLA as a thirteen-year-old in 1987, following the shooting of his brother by the British Army. Five years later, he was part of an INLA unit who travelled to Derby, England, and murdered a British Army recruitment officer, Sergeant Michael Newman. Following the murder, Duffy returned to Northern Ireland, where he was actively involved in targeting members of the security forces until the INLA followed the Provisional IRA's decision to declare a ceasefire in 1994. Duffy then moved to Dublin, where, like Freddie Thompson, he soon earned a fierce reputation for violence. In 2001, he'd received a nine-year sentence for leading the INLA gang involved in the 'Ballymount Bloodbath'. On 6 October 1999, four criminals had called to the premises of a Walkinstown warehouse looking for IR£600 in compensation from a businessman, John Creed. They'd accused one of his relatives of being behind an arson attack on their van. However, Creed was one step ahead of the criminals and had called Duffy and the INLA for protection. The criminals were stripped naked, beaten and told to leave the country. Events spiralled out of control when twelve associates of the criminals then arrived. In the ensuing melee, an INLA man, Patrick 'Bo' Campbell, was stabbed to death. Duffy was later jailed for false imprisonment and arms possession.

Following his release from prison in early 2007, Duffy hadn't wasted any time. He'd approached Thompson and demanded cash in return for the INLA's 'protection' but Freddie told him to 'Fuck off'. Furious, Duffy had immediately placed Thompson at the top of an INLA hit list. Thompson remained in Dublin and seemed too arrogant to care that he had been threatened by a paramilitary group with access to a large supply of weapons.

On 11 September 2007, Thompson showed he had no concerns over cash either when he was stopped by gardaí in Dublin city centre with €1,000 in his possession.

A few weeks later, detectives received intelligence that Freddie had spat in the face of an INLA representative when another demand for cash was made. A group of INLA members later tried to get into a Dublin nightclub to target Thompson but were refused entry.

'Fat Freddie' still didn't go into hiding and on 22 November 2007 the INLA made their move. Their plan ended in failure, however, when gardaí seized an AK47 rifle from a man who was walking up a city centre street in Dublin. Based on intelligence, the high-powered weapon had been removed from an INLA arms dump for an assassination attempt on Freddie Thompson. Aware of the number of weapons at the disposal of the INLA and mindful of his enemies in the Rattigan faction, Thompson temporarily left the city.

Over the next few weeks, as 2008 approached, he moved between Dublin, Holland and the UK. He'd hoped to attend the Ricky Hatton fight in Las Vegas around this time, but he was refused entry to the US because of his previous criminal convictions.

Struggling to cope with the mounting pressure, Thompson was offered temporary sanctuary by the Kinahans. Just after Christmas 2007, he headed for their luxury Spanish headquarters in Estepona on the Costa del Sol.

5. On The Run

> I'm feeling paranoid because all the gardaí are
> pulling back and nowhere to be seen. Isn't that what
> happened to Cahill? Look what happened to him.
> There's at least ten people who want me dead.
>
> Freddie Thompson

At the beginning of 2008, Freddie had put such a target on his back, he was spending as much time out of Ireland as possible. He'd had another narrow escape from the INLA after the AK47 seizure and flitted back and forth to Dublin from Birmingham, Holland and Spain, ducking and weaving in his usual manner.

During his secret trips to Dublin, Thompson used the name 'Sean Byrne' and stayed in the capital's hotels, as the INLA and Rattigan's gang continued to hunt him. Both organizations had orders to kill Freddie on sight. In one hotel in Dublin's Temple Bar, detectives launched a search after receiving information that members of Thompson's gang were using it as a base. Although there was no sign of Freddie Thompson, during the search officers recovered a bulletproof vest. The vest and the first aid boxes were important features of life on the run for 'Fat Freddie' as he fought to stay alive.

A few weeks into the New Year, the 27-year-old again showed there was no loyalty in crime when he was tasked by the Kinahans with arranging the murder of the veteran criminal Martin 'The Viper' Foley. Once named as one of Thompson's ninety-one closest associates, Foley, who has survived numerous attempts on his life over the years, including an attempt by the Provisional IRA to kill him in 1984, was targeted by Thompson's associates on 26 January 2008. A fitness fanatic, Foley was shot four times as he sat in a car outside the Carlisle gym in Kimmage, south Dublin. Investigators believed the hit was ordered by Christy Kinahan because of a row over €100,000.

Thompson was trying to make a name for himself in the cartel and organized the shooting, despite his long-standing friendship with the once feared criminal. He emerged as a suspect when gardaí found his passport in the home of the alleged gunman. The shooter remains on the run, after he was linked to another botched hit by the Kinahan cartel. In the words of one investigator:

> On this occasion Thompson was simply following orders. He did what he was told because he knew how big the Kinahans were becoming. Foley and Thompson were once very close and it was just like the Darren Geoghegan case all over again. Foley had introduced Thompson to some key contacts when he was trying to get weapons and Foley would also have looked out for him, but none of this mattered to Thompson – even the lives of his close friends meant nothing . . . Foley knows who tried to kill him but he left it alone because he just wanted to get on with his life.

Around the same time, gardaí received intelligence that the INLA, led by Duffy, were still intent on killing Thompson. Sources claimed that the paramilitary group had been backed in their plans by Republicans from Dublin and Dundalk and that they had a hitman from Dundalk on standby, waiting to receive the green light to target Freddie. Gardaí also suspected Duffy had orchestrated hoax bomb calls to test garda response times. Detectives were concerned that the INLA would use explosive devices to target Thompson.

Thompson was aware of the danger but persisted in secretly visiting Dublin. On 11 May 2008, during one of his trips home, gardaí were given an insight into Thompson's links with the Hutch gang from the north inner city. Back then, the Hutches and Kinahans were drug-dealing allies and Thompson moved easily between them as he had contacts in both gangs. On that occasion, Thompson and Derek 'Del Boy' Hutch were at the Boomerang nightclub with a 'very well-spoken girl', who would go on to become one of Ireland's top models. In his conversations with gardaí outside the club, Hutch said he and Thompson had been out dancing.

Thompson was continuously on the move, evading the open kill order that was out on him. One of his many bolt-holes was in Birmingham in the UK. Thompson had maintained close ties there with many of his associates who had moved over from Dublin. Freddie also spent a lot of time in Holland trying to organize drugs shipments. However, the place he felt safest was in southern Spain and he returned to the Kinahan stronghold whenever he got the chance.

Down on the Costa del Sol, Christy Kinahan and John Cunningham had expanded far beyond the limited Irish market. They were now running a truly global drugs- and arms-smuggling empire, with accompanying money-laundering services on offer for anyone who wanted them. The Kinahans were now drugs wholesalers, who imported drugs worth millions from South America and Morocco and sold them off in smaller amounts to Irish and UK gangs. Due to their international connections, Kinahan and Cunningham were arranging vast amounts of shipments. The money earned from these drug deals was then being used to buy properties in Spain and Brazil. Businesses, including dry-cleaning companies, were also established to launder cash.

Both men were so preoccupied with sourcing new contacts and establishing connections that they left the day-to-day details of organizing the thousands of euros' worth of drugs shipments to Kinahan's oldest son, Daniel. He increasingly needed more manpower, in the form of both couriers and muscle, and, as Freddie had known Daniel since childhood, he was welcomed with open arms. Gerry Hutch's nephew, Gary Hutch, was already a trusted lieutenant within the Kinahan operation, and Thompson's old comrade-in-arms Paddy Doyle was also on the scene, if not part of the Kinahan inner circle. The three settled in Estepona, near the Kinahan gang's base.

For three young men from poor working-class backgrounds in Dublin, the Costa del Sol was like another world. Estepona and its environs had year-round sunshine, an eternal party atmosphere, due to the never-ending influx of tourists, and no shortage of good-quality hard drugs to abuse.

Most importantly, the three criminals felt relatively anonymous there. While Freddie's problems were mainly other criminals and the INLA, the other two had even more pressing reasons to keep their heads down. Doyle was actively being sought by gardaí after the Darren Geoghegan, Gavin Byrne and Noel Roche shootings, over the three-day period in November 2005. The failure of White and Doyle to burn out the car following the Roche hit meant that Thompson's best friend risked a murder charge if he returned to Dublin. Gary Hutch was in a similar situation. He was a suspect in the murder of Derek Duffy, a drug dealer who had been lured to a meeting in Finglas before being shot five times in the head.

Living in Spain was the safest option for both men, and when Thompson was in town, they would hit the bars and nightclubs. The trio would stay up until dawn, on a diet of cheap cocaine and alcohol. Their days were spent hanging around the gym or attempting to organize drugs shipments with other criminals.

But the good times would not last. Although Doyle had been the first of the three murderers to move out to Spain, he was the least trusted of the three in the Kinahan gang's eyes. This was largely due to his volatile personality – at 6 foot 3 inches, Doyle had an intimidating physique and no qualms about using it. Fights in nightclubs were a common occurrence, often with other criminals. The extra attention did nothing to win him favour in the eyes of Christy Kinahan or John Cunningham, for whom keeping a low profile was all-important. The two veteran criminals knew that violence brought more attention from law enforcement agencies. Doyle had also moved into drugs trafficking himself and travelled regularly to Amsterdam, throwing his weight around for whoever was willing to hire him. Investigating gardaí, still searching for Doyle, learned that at one point he beat another drug trafficker, Michael 'Roly' Cronin, to within an inch of his life in the Dutch city in a dispute over drugs.

On one of his regular trips to Holland, Doyle had met a fellow fugitive from the law, the British criminal Simon 'Slapper' Cowmeadow. In 2002, Cowmeadow and his gang had been caught unloading 100,000 ecstasy tablets hidden inside a consignment of frozen chips and he'd been on the run ever since. Sentenced to eighteen years in absentia, Cowmeadow, like Doyle, was now working at arm's length with the Kinahans.

In November 2007, the association between them had

ended, when Cowmeadow was found dead on an Amsterdam street, shot through the eye by unknown assassins. A broken leg, inflicted post-mortem, indicated he'd been shot elsewhere and that his body had possibly been pushed from a moving vehicle.

Over the following months, Doyle seemed unconcerned about what had happened – enough to continue to go about his daily routine. It would be a fatal mistake, and one which would have far-reaching consequences for all of them.

On 4 February 2008, Hutch, Doyle and Thompson were making their way back from the gym to the house where Doyle and Hutch lived in the Bel Air estate on the outskirts of Estepona. Thompson stayed there as well on his frequent trips to Spain. Hutch was driving and Doyle was in the passenger seat, with Thompson sitting behind them. The BMW X5 SUV in which they were travelling was a familiar sight to locals, who used to regularly see it going back and forth to the town centre.

That morning, the vehicle had taken its usual route, turning off the Autovía del Mediterráneo onto the Camino de Brijan. After passing by a childcare centre, Hutch took a right onto the Calle Mejorana, which starts off as a curved street with room enough for just one car to pass. Anyone travelling up that way comes to a small crossroads, where they have to stop to see if any traffic is coming from either side – making it the perfect place for an ambush. As the BMW emerged into the roadway where Calle Mejorana widens, a car pulled up opposite them and a gunman fired five shots into the passenger side windscreen and window. Hutch, in a panic, drove into a lamp post, jumped out and fled. Freddie did likewise, while Doyle ran back down the narrow street from which they had just emerged.

The gunman knew his target. He ran after Doyle, firing as he went, hitting his target a number of times in the back. Halfway down the thoroughfare, Doyle fell to his knees, unable to go on. His pursuer caught up with him and finished him off with two shots to the head.

Spanish authorities launched a widespread investigation, consulting the gardaí for background on some of the people involved. As their investigation developed, it emerged Hutch and Thompson were both suspected of being complicit in their old pal's death. Gary Hutch, in particular, is believed by gardaí to have tipped off the assassin about their movements. Intelligence soon indicated that the hitman was Eric 'Lucky' Wilson and both Hutch and Thompson left Spain days after the murder. Before he left Hutch had turned himself in to local police for questioning and was released without charge.

In the weeks that followed, various garda theories began to make their way into the media. Doyle was said to have either beaten up a Russian gangster in a nightclub or to have given two fingers to a Turkish drugs syndicate who threatened him after one of Paddy's shipments was seized and he refused to pay them. Dutch police, however, had different information. Their intelligence, passed on to the Spanish authorities, was that 'the killing in Holland of Simon John Cowmeadow coincided with the disappearance of €400,000 or €500,000. It appears Patrick Doyle and Cowmeadow were responsible for the disappearance of this money, which belonged to the Kinahan organization.'

Returning to Ireland in March 2008, Thompson didn't seem unduly concerned by his former confidant's death. He was regularly seen frequenting nightclubs in Dublin's Temple Bar over the coming months, as he kept an eye on his gang's affairs. He had another lucky escape, however, when gardaí arrested two suspected hitmen they believed were plotting to kill Thompson. Informed of the threat to his life, 'Fat Freddie' immediately flew back to his bolthole in Spain.

Thompson returned to Ireland in June and cheated death once again. On 16 June 2008 gardaí received intelligence that a lone masked gunman had entered the Central Bar in Aungier Street in Dublin's city centre, searching for Thompson. Freddie's brother Richie was in the bar, but there was no sign of the gunman's intended target and he left immediately.

The threat against Thompson was still hanging over him – and over his family. On 24 June 2008 three shots were fired at his grandmother's home. The shots were fired by three gangsters from a red Citroën car. No arrests were ever made, but Thompson was reportedly raging. The chief suspects were members of Rattigan's gang who were also working with associates of Declan Duffy at the time. The attack happened just a day after Freddie returned to Dublin from a trip to Prague with seventeen members of the gang. Gardaí suspected they had travelled to the region for firearms training.

Doyle's murder had just been business for all concerned, and Hutch and Thompson clearly had no fear of falling to the same fate, but that would not be the end of it. Two days after the murder, gardaí had made a €3.5 million cannabis seizure in Kildare, netting the Kinahan gofer and former League of Ireland goalkeeper Eddie van Boxtel in the process. The massive shipment had belonged to the Kinahan cartel. British police were also increasingly concerned about Kinahan drugs trafficking into the UK and the discovery in London of a large cache of arms sent by Daniel Kinahan. The Dutch authorities were anxious about Kinahan activity escalating on their patch with the murder of Cowmeadow, and the Belgians were quite familiar with Christy Kinahan, thanks to his attempts to launder money via property deals in Antwerp.

All of this illegal activity was emanating from the south of Spain, but until now the Kinahans had avoided fouling their own doorstep. The shooting of Paddy Doyle in Estepona changed all that. On 7 July 2008, a top-level meeting was held in The Hague between members of An Garda Síochána, Spain's Policía Nacional, Belgium's Police Fédérale and the Dutch Korps Landelijke Politiediensten (KLPD). The Spanish agreed to begin round-the-clock electronic and physical surveillance on the Kinahan cartel members – including Freddie Thompson.

Committing to such an expensive and resource-draining operation indicated how seriously the problem was being taken. 'Operation Shovel', as it was codenamed, was now underway. Freddie, of course, knew nothing about this. He was busy trying to ensure his supremacy in his native south inner-city area and, more importantly, to just stay alive.

Thompson returned to Ireland for a brief period on 27 September 2008 and was stopped by gardaí as he made his way furtively up Dublin's Grafton Street. Freddie was co-operative as gardaí went through the motions of yet another search. In his pockets were €35, his passport and a 'crumpled up piece of paper' with a name and an address of a man in Ballyfermot. Asked what it was for, Freddie grinned.

'We're just old friends. Have to catch up, you know how it is.'

Thompson also told gardaí how he was doing, half in jest, half in ire: 'I'm feeling paranoid because all the gardaí are pulling back and nowhere to be seen. Isn't that what happened to Cahill? Look what happened to him. There's at least ten people who want me dead.'

The reference to Martin 'The General' Cahill and the alleged conspiracy with the IRA to murder him was archetypal Thompson. Ignoring Freddie's attempted digs, the detectives thought it obvious that the strain was getting to him.

Thompson left Ireland again shortly afterwards and intelligence reports could not establish his exact whereabouts. Often, over the next few months, he would disappear, briefly re-emerge and then vanish again.

Around the same time, gardaí also received intelligence that a Republican serving a sentence in Portlaoise Prison had agreed to take on a €100,000 contract, after his release, to kill Thompson. The contract had been offered by Rattigan and other criminals, including one from Kildare, who wanted 'Fat Freddie' out of the way because of the threat he posed to other drugs gangs. Thompson was made aware of the threat and arranged a meeting with David Byrne and his father, James 'Jaws' Byrne, in an attempt to get information on the contract killer's identity.

Another report, on 22 April, detailed that gardaí had received intelligence that a hitman from the Cabra area of north Dublin had been recruited by Declan Duffy to target Thompson.

Despite these serious threats on his life, Thompson began making regular trips back to Ireland in March 2009 to oversee drugs shipments and to perpetuate his eight-year-long war with Brian Rattigan. Just days after his return to his home city, Thompson's gang once again targeted Rattigan's family. On 13 March 2009, 'Shay' O'Byrne, the long-term partner of Rattigan's sister, Sharon, was shot dead outside his home in Rossfield Drive, Tallaght. O'Byrne was shot five times in front of his son. During the incident, Rattigan's sibling was shot in the leg as she attempted to retrieve the weapons from the killer who said: 'Let go of the gun, you tramp.'

Investigators believe the gunman was Garret O'Brien, from Bray, Co. Wicklow. He was recruited by Thompson's gang to shoot O'Byrne as payment of a drug debt. O'Brien, along with gang member Gary Flynn and Thompson's close friend Eugene Cullen, would receive life sentences for their roles in the murder. Cullen would later die in the Midlands Prison from a drug overdose.

Within weeks of O'Byrne's killing, as one senior officer said, investigating gardaí had received intelligence that Thompson had sanctioned the murder:

> Thompson wasn't involved in the murder himself but there was intelligence to suggest that he played a role in identifying O'Byrne as a target. The murder sent another message to Rattigan that no one in his family was safe. O'Byrne and Brian Rattigan were very close, and Thompson was determined to wipe out his entire gang.

Over the course of the next few months, Thompson was feeling relatively safe around Dublin and started socializing in the city centre again. On 7 May, he managed to start a row with a man in a wheelchair by pouring a drink over him in a Temple Bar nightclub. Thompson's cousin Liam Roe had to carry the man to safety upstairs.

A month later, however, Thompson was back in Spain again following a shooting at a relative's house. No complaint was made to gardaí and there were no injuries, but the incident proved his feud with Brian 'King Ratt' Rattigan was very much alive.

Just four months after the O'Byrne killing, Thompson again prioritized his list of targets in the feud. His gang were focusing on Rattigan's enforcer and number two – Anthony Cannon, from Robert Street, in Dublin's south inner city. Cannon was regarded by gardaí as a serious criminal who was heavily involved in both gun attacks and drugs trafficking. Just two years before, he had threatened to kill two men outside a pub because they had wolf-whistled at some women who were in his company. The wolf-whistlers were too terrified to make a complaint and Cannon was never charged. The enforcer had been involved in the feud from the very beginning because of his long-standing friendship with Rattigan. As it escalated, and with Rattigan in prison, Cannon helped to oversee the Rattigan gang's drug-dealing enterprise.

The enforcer was suspected by gardaí of firing shots into the home of an innocent relative of Thompson's in 2008, and he had also called to Thompson's family home brandishing machetes. Cannon's fate was sealed, however, when he'd spat into the face of an innocent female relative of Thompson a few weeks earlier. On 17 July 2009, the Thompson gang made their move. Cannon was shot twice in the head in the Ballyfermot area of Dublin and died instantly.

During their investigation into the killing, which remains unsolved, gardaí suspected gun for hire Eric 'Lucky' Wilson had been recruited by Thompson for the hit. The shooting was a further blow to Rattigan, with another of his closest associates murdered by the Thompson gang. By one investigator's assessment:

Cannon was ruthless and was Rattigan's main enforcer. Once Cannon was identified as the man who targeted Thompson's family there was no way he was going to survive. He was the man continuing the feud for Rattigan while he remained in prison, and with Cannon out of the way the feud was essentially over. Thompson may have been out of the country most of the time, but Cannon's killing made it easier for him to slip home.

Gardaí still kept tabs on Thompson on his frequent trips back to Dublin. He stayed in hotel rooms around Camden Street to avoid being shot and officers would regularly stop and chat to him, enduring his mouthiness and exhibitionist antics in the hope of gleaning some intelligence. 'Fat Freddie', who couldn't keep his mouth shut, regularly obliged. All his information had to be vetted, however, to ensure it wasn't an attempt to give them a bum steer.

With Cannon out of the way, Thompson was feeling more secure than he had in years. Rattigan was on remand for sentencing over Declan Gavin's killing and the Crumlin–Drimnagh feud was all but won. Despite this, Thompson was still conscious of security. On 15 November 2009, his solicitor wrote to gardaí in Sundrive Road Garda Station in Crumlin asking what measures they were taking to protect his client. The solicitor had previously written to gardaí on 29 April 2009, expressing similar concerns for his client's safety.

Thompson seemed to have gotten over his fears a few weeks before Christmas, when he joined a group of associates, including Liam and David Byrne, members of the INLA, Eamon 'The Don' Dunne and gangsters linked with Limerick's McCarthy/Dundon gang at the National Stadium in Dublin. He was also celebrating Brian Rattigan's conviction that same month for the murder of 'Deco' Gavin.

Gardaí watched as the twenty-strong group, clearly all on their best behaviour, laughed and joked as the boxer Matthew Macklin defended his title against Rafael Sosa Pintos. The gathering, arranged by Christy Kinahan, had been organized to bring all of the main players in Ireland's drugs business together to spread the message that violence was bad for business. It was a message that would fall on deaf ears.

Gardaí passed the information that the meeting had taken place along to the Spanish, who saw it as further proof of the Kinahan gang's clout. The Spanish team had got their surveillance operation up and running the month before. Operation Shovel was a no-holds-barred effort to bring down the Kinahan cartel, and the mobile phone of every gang associate was tapped, no matter how minor a role they played. For the Policía Nacional, however, the operation was a slow process. Predictably, the golden rule that business should not be discussed on the phone had been drilled into all of the experienced criminals in the cartel. They were supposed to either use their mobiles to set up face-to-face meetings or to talk in code about 'computers' (handguns), 'waiters' (assault rifles) and 'cars' (drugs).

Christy Kinahan and John Cunningham were aware of the security risks mobiles created and had been making active enquiries about the use of encrypted PGP (Pretty Good Privacy) devices. PGPs were priced on the black market at Stg£2,000 per phone as they used a secure server that ensured nobody could listen in. They have since become standard issue to cartel members, but back in 2009 their use was in its infancy and their price meant they were unlikely to be dished out to the dozens of subordinates the Kinahans had around their Estepona power base. So it was a case of saying as little as possible, which everyone understood. Except Freddie.

Thompson's first indiscretion came in December, when he rang Gary Hutch. As they called each other several times a day, and generally talked about which drugs they had taken or which hookers they had slept with, the police listening in weren't expecting much. This time, however, Thompson was a little more excited than usual and wanted to know where Hutch was as he had something for him 'in his pocket'.

Obeying the usual rules, Hutch said he would see him in a couple of minutes.

But Freddie could not wait and missed the inherent warning.

'Now it's not that big,' he continued, leading Hutch to respond: 'I can fucking imagine.'

'No, seriously, it's not that big,' Freddie replied eagerly.

'It'll work though, right?' asked a clearly perplexed Hutch.

'Yeah, probably. It'll probably just spit out one bullet and that'll be it,' Freddie laughed.

'Hang up the phone,' Hutch ordered, and the line went dead.

Police surmised that Hutch did not inform the Kinahans about Thompson's indiscretion because Freddie wouldn't stop letting his mouth run away with him.

A couple of weeks later, investigators recorded Thompson receiving a late-night call from an unknown man on a Spanish mobile. The caller asked repeatedly whether Freddie would be 'back before the morning', and sounded frustrated with Freddie's vague answers. Pressed, Thompson again broke the golden rule of silence, eventually disclosing: 'We're on the way back but . . . we're about fifty from Algeria and I don't think we'll arrive until four in the morning.'

Listening police could only assume he was returning to somewhere in Spain from a drugs-smuggling operation, but they had no way of pinpointing where he was or where he might land. There was too little intel for them to do anything about it.

The 'Shovel' team was beginning to build up a picture of

the cartel hierarchy at this stage. They concluded that Gary Hutch had effectively become Daniel Kinahan's right-hand man, with Freddie slightly below him in the pecking order. Liam Byrne was tasked with running the Dublin end of things and was treated almost as an equal by Daniel, as was his brother David. The Spanish ranked Thompson as an 'arms supplier and bodyguard', noting that humiliatingly, on occasions he was treated as a 'messenger' by Christy Kinahan, who saw Freddie as a 'gofer'. Daniel treated Thompson as an equal, but it was Hutch who seemed to be trusted with organizing drugs shipments and he, in turn, had his best pal carry them out with him.

The cartel now had over thirty core members, each with a defined role. Daniel headed up the 'hard' faction in charge of drugs and arms trafficking, while his younger brother, Christopher Jnr, was in charge of the money-laundering end of things.

The investigation team was making no effort to hide its surveillance. They regularly set up roadblocks and pulled over the gang's cars, asking the drivers explicitly if they were Irish. The 'in your face' policing was having the desired effect – the members of the cartel were becoming more and more paranoid. On 21 January, Daniel Kinahan was recorded ringing his then wife, admitting to her he was becoming freaked out because there was a 'big police checkpoint' on a bridge leading into Estepona. Before that, he had spotted them near the Auld Dubliner, the Irish pub in the town centre that the gang controlled and used to launder money.

Daniel's nerves were not eased by a phone call from Freddie, who told him that he was stuck in the Irish consulate in Málaga, an hour down the road, because the 'cops are everywhere'. Thompson said he was on his way somewhere else, but had diverted to the consulate because 'the pigs are blocking everything'. In another call, Daniel's wife later tried to calm him down, telling him the controls were 'routine' and that they were 'always there', but Daniel – correctly, as it turned out – was adamant that a message was being sent. Unaware of the extent to which himself and his family were being fully observed, he insisted: 'I have the feeling they are planning something.'

Kinahan became obsessed with the idea of surveillance, and it was no coincidence that he was the main mover behind a series of counter-intelligence war games the cartel members were involved in four days later on 25 January. The training would consist of shooting practice, martial arts and street exercises, all under the watchful eye of a former special-forces soldier who ran a firm specializing in covert operations. Convinced his phone security was already up to the task, Daniel wanted his minions to be fully versed in handling arms, how to identify tailing police and – most importantly – how to shake them off.

Daniel was taking it very seriously. Investigators recorded him ringing his secretary, asking her to check online for local shops that sold false beards, wigs and 'that kind of thing'. 'Something like for Freddie who has no hair,' he added. The secretary duly texted him the address of a shop in Málaga which sold hairpieces made of real human hair.

The Kinahan heir had decided that only certain members of the cartel hierarchy were allowed to participate in the training, and the fact that it was going on at all was supposed to be kept tight – except that didn't happen. In a call to Freddie, an irate Daniel Kinahan fumed down the line that he was 'pissed off' because someone he referred to as 'The Scout' knew about the course and Daniel wanted to know 'how word had leaked out'. 'The Scout' 'would love to do this course, but how do they know we're doing it?' he went on, adding that he already had one suspect who he thought had 'ratted'. Daniel then asked Freddie to tell 'the team' to keep their mouths shut, and Thompson promised he'd get the message across.

Daniel was extremely excited about the course and rang one of his pals back in Dublin to brag about how 'brilliant' it was the night before it began. Freddie and Gary Hutch were rather less worked up, though. Gary rang Thompson late that evening, stoned once more and providing details of the prostitute he had just hired, a blonde he had been with before. Nor were other gang members grasping how seriously the whole thing was meant to be taken.

Freddie and two others were dispatched to the wig shop in Málaga to pick up some disguises. One of them rang Daniel back to ask if a black hairpiece with green stripes would suffice.

The training exercise the following day was set for Manilva, a small coastal town, just twenty minutes' drive from Estepona. Daniel was all business and couldn't wait to get started. When one unidentified member of 'the team' called him that morning to tell him he would be unable to make it because his car had broken down, the elder Kinahan boy was incandescent: 'This is fucking ridiculous,' he spat down the line. 'When I ask you something, I want you to do it!'

The exercise went ahead with just Daniel, Freddie and two other trusted cartel members, Davin Flynn and Ross Browning, taking part. Gary Hutch had not even made it to the session.

Spanish police could see the gangsters were engaging in some sort of surveillance training, but they were not sure about the aim of the exercise and what it was supposed to achieve.

The police couldn't follow communications between the four-some either, as they had switched to walkie-talkies. An insight was provided when Daniel switched back to his phone and rang Browning to inform him that a cop had arrived nearby.

'Get out of there,' he instructed.

Flynn was seated somewhere else in the complex and was told to stay put because another policeman was at the end of the street.

Browning himself was hiding in some shrubbery and Daniel asked him to tell Freddie 'not to come near the place'.

Another war game was scheduled for a few days later and that morning, the ex-special-forces trainer rang Gary Hutch's mobile and Freddie picked up. The man explained things would start at 1 p.m. and the aim was to follow anyone they came across within a set apartment complex without being noticed. It would 'require vigilance', he said, and the gangsters would have to 'get information' on anyone they tailed. But the training went no better that day for the wannabe spooks. Gary Hutch rang Daniel to say someone was following him in a van and then Freddie checked in to announce he had 'security all over' him.

Spanish police could hear that Daniel was becoming increasingly frustrated at how things were going. He called the whole thing off after receiving another call from Browning, who was laughing uncontrollably. The convicted armed robber had dressed in drag for the day, but had attracted the attention of a passing small child who shouted: 'That woman is a man!'

Daniel rang Gary Hutch to tell him: 'The operation is over.'

However, the surveillance training and further outings did gradually have the required effect. The gang had already been switching cars regularly as a security measure, but now they began to dramatically increase their anti-surveillance activity. Spanish police noted in their investigative file: 'They drive at high speed, carrying out evasive manoeuvres, circling several times around roundabouts, stopping abruptly, and carry out counter-surveillance when they are on their way to important meetings.'

Thompson had no idea at the time how important these efforts would be in saving the necks of him, Hutch and possibly the cartel as a whole. At the beginning of February 2010, Thompson and Hutch met with Daniel Kinahan, his father, Christy, and the cartel's second-in-command, John Cunningham, on the premises of a now-defunct gift shop outside Marbella. The police suspected the shop was another cartel-owned money-laundering front.

The Spanish investigators had no way of monitoring what was going on inside, but they could tell this was not a casual get-together. It was one of the few occasions the cartel's top tier had been spotted in the one place since Operation Shovel began.

Christy Kinahan would be in regular contact with Daniel and with Cunningham, who favoured golf course chats to ensure privacy, but the duo rarely talked to other cartel members. For them to deign to meet those lower down the food chain meant something was afoot, but the question was what they were planning.

The answer came a couple of days later, on 3 February, when Thompson and Hutch set out in convoy, heading west along the A49 motorway towards the Portuguese border. Their anti-surveillance training quickly came into play, with Freddie taking point and Hutch following. The pair maintained a constant distance of four to five kilometres between their cars, driving at high speed to flush out any tails. Police could have easily pulled them over for speeding, but they had a bigger goal in mind than dishing out penalty points – not that either man had a Spanish licence or would have cared anyway. The cartel had their own workshop and it was known that this was used to alter the structure of cars and vans to include secret compartments to transport drugs and weapons. The police knew that the Algarve coast, just across the Spanish border, was an established location to land illegal shipments, either on shore or using buoys equipped with GPS.

The 'Shovel' team thought it looked like a real chance to nail both Thompson and Hutch red-handed and potentially link the pair to the meeting with Daniel, Christy and John Cunningham two days earlier. But it was not to be. Although the Spanish team set up roadblocks aimed at trapping the pair on their return and searching the vehicles, the two couriers never arrived.

Thompson and Hutch, presumably on instructions, returned by a different route. The 'Shovel' investigators had missed their opportunity to nab them in the act.

6. Under the Radar

I will never be driven from my house. I had my
car damaged and my windows smashed and I think
this is all because of my nephew's feud with
Freddie Thompson.

Anne Rattigan

Operation Shovel rolled on throughout 2010, but with little
more concrete in the way of evidence emerging, at least at
the Spanish end. The cartel members were becoming better
and better at avoiding surveillance, both in person and on
the phone. Even Thompson seemed to have cleaned up his
act and he had largely eliminated his mobile-related gaffs,
possibly because he was spending less time on it. As part of
his work for the Kinahans, Freddie was back in Dublin over-
seeing shipments into the country.

Spanish police did what they could, mapping out the com-
plicated money-laundering apparatus that the Kinahans were
using to hide their money in Brazil, Cyprus, the Far East and
elsewhere. Freddie wasn't involved in this side of the organization but he was financing his life from his share of the
huge shipments. The money was allocated by the Kinahans
and he would have received different amounts depending on
the amount of drugs involved.

The hugely expensive round-the-clock monitoring by the
Spanish police forces could not go on for ever. Eventually, at

the end of April, a decision was taken that it was time to move in. Following international consultations between the police forces involved, a date was set for a simultaneous operation on 25 May 2010.

The cartel knew the authorities were on to them, but they had no idea just what was coming. In the early hours of 25 May, co-ordinated teams battered down the front doors of Christy Kinahan's, Daniel and Christopher Jnr's, and John Cunningham's houses, along with all the other cartel members on the Spanish watchlist. When the 'Shovel' team moved in, Thompson and Gary Hutch would have been two of their top targets, but the surveillance team had been powerless to stop the two lieutenants leaving Spain before the raid.

The rattled gangsters had no idea how to react to the raids. Christy Kinahan, who spoke several languages, including Spanish, claimed he didn't understand the warrant being read out to him. Cunningham resisted arrest and received a black eye. Shell-shocked, Daniel and Christopher Jnr put up little resistance and were led from their homes into the dawn darkness.

There were consecutive raids on other properties in Ireland, but no senior cartel members were arrested in Dublin as the Byrne brothers were lying low. Forty-five separate searches were made, leading to just one arrest. Eleven cartel members were detained by London's Metropolitan Police officers in the UK, bringing the total held under Operation Shovel to thirty-four suspects – twelve of whom were Irish. There were two notable absences, however, with both Thompson and Hutch away in Holland on separate operations. Freddie had been sent by Daniel to organize a drugs shipment to Ireland, while Hutch was apparently there on his own business.

The two criminals had a lucky escape. Investigators had gone to the gangsters' apartment, smashing the windows and breaking down the doors. Hutch later rang a pal who'd checked the place and was informed it had been thoroughly ransacked – the sofa was 'destroyed', the air con dismantled and, crucially for Hutch, his bedroom safe had been cleared out. A flurry of anguished calls were made between the stranded pair in Holland and their various contacts back in Spain and Dublin as they tried to comprehend the scale of what had happened.

'They're all over us, buddy,' a panicked Thompson told Hutch in one call. 'Keep your head well down because there are at least twenty-nine people arrested in Spain, England, Ireland and Seville.'

'They got the boss and four others too,' Hutch responded. 'I've no idea what's going on. I'm dizzy.'

In an attempt to calm down, Hutch went 'to buy a bag of weed'. But these troubles could not be smoked away. Isolated from their bosses in the Kinahan cartel, who remained in Spanish custody as the investigation into their billion-euro drugs empire continued, Thompson and Hutch decided to remain in Holland. They were under the protection of the Moroccan mafia – a favour which would be reciprocated by Thompson six years later. While Thompson was arranging the drugs shipment, using one of the many contacts cultivated by Kinahan senior over the years, investigators believe Hutch had travelled to the country to cultivate his own contacts. He was also spotted meeting with an associate of his Uncle Gerry, which investigators suspected was to discuss the possibility of an arms shipment.

Although Daniel Kinahan had orchestrated Thompson's trip to the Netherlands, the only person who had known about Hutch's trip was Thompson as the pair travelled together to Amsterdam from Málaga airport. With Thompson and Hutch evading capture by the Spanish authorities, the rest of the cartel were asking questions about them. One investigator elaborated:

> It wasn't long before many of the cartel's main associates questioned why Thompson and Hutch had not been arrested, considering the amount of time they had spent in Spain and the key roles they held within the organization. The upper echelons of the Kinahan leadership were in custody while Thompson and Hutch remained free men. The only thing that saved Thompson was that he was ordered to Holland by his boss, and because someone like Gary Hutch came from criminal royalty, he was given the benefit of the doubt. The belief was that Hutch had also convinced Thompson that he was in Amsterdam to arrange a weapons shipment that would clearly benefit the cartel. Due to the nature of their work, it was only natural that their associates would question why they weren't in Spain when the raids happened, but in the end it was all just down to coincidence and luck. However, there would always be suspicions of Thompson and Hutch because they weren't family. They were trusted associates but, like many in the Kinahan cartel, they were also expendable.

In the months following the 'Shovel' raids, Thompson's main base was in Amsterdam, and he also spent time in the UK and Dublin. He had no intention of returning to Spain while there was still a chance he would be arrested. Ireland wasn't a safe place to be either. Freddie had the upper hand in his incessant war with the Rattigan gang, but he was very aware of the new anti-gangland legislation that had been introduced in Ireland the previous July, which made it possible for an individual to be convicted on a senior garda's evidence of facilitating the activities of a criminal organization. One former officer recalled: 'Thompson was terrified of this legislation. He was convinced that he could be sent to prison on the word of a guard and would often return to Dublin for brief visits, wearing a disguise and travelling on a fake passport.'

Despite Thompson's self-imposed exile, he was still intent on targeting innocent members of Rattigan's family, eventhough Brian Rattigan had been convicted of the murder of Declan Gavin in December 2009. In one of Freddie's fleeting visits back to Dublin in the summer of 2010, the Dublin home of Rattigan's aunt, Anne Rattigan, was petrol bombed. The innocent woman vowed to remain at her home in the Coombe area of Dublin:

> I will never be driven from my house. I had my car damaged and my windows smashed and I think this is all because of my nephew's feud with Freddie Thompson. The only reason we were being singled out is because of my surname. We've done nothing wrong. I haven't seen my nephew in years. I know he's an enemy of Freddie Thompson but this has nothing to do with me. I love living in this area. The local community have been fantastic and they know life has been hard for us. I can't thank people enough for supporting us. It's a small minority of people attacking me and the only thing I can do is improve the security of my home and pray it stops.

Gardaí believed that, like many of the feud's victims before her, she had been targeted simply because of her name. According to one investigator:

Anne Rattigan is another example of the innocent people targeted by Freddie Thompson. Thompson knew Rattigan's family members weren't involved in anything, yet he still terrorized them. He was intent on destroying anyone connected with Rattigan and making their lives a misery because his own family had been targeted. These types of attacks were an example of his obsessive and controlling personality. He just lived for chaos, death and misery – they were the factors that fed his addiction to violence.

With Thompson's protracted absence from Spain and focus on operations in Holland, he turned to one of his associates, a heroin dealer, Greg Lynch, to fill the void in Dublin. Lynch, whose father was a childhood friend of Christy Kinahan, was given responsibility for supplying drugs into the south inner city. Thompson was arranging shipments in Holland and Lynch would then distribute the drugs in Dublin as the cartel struggled to get the organization back up and running.

Gardaí were determined to crack down on Thompson's gang and the cartel's most lucrative business. Coinciding with the launch of Operation Shovel, gardaí in Dublin's South Central Division had established 'Operation Goldeneye' to run alongside it. On 24 June 2010, the 'Goldeneye' team had their first major success. Gardaí seized cocaine worth €8.5 million, a Colt semi-automatic pistol, a 9mm handgun and five .45 calibre rounds of ammunition from a house in Tallaght, south Dublin. Michael Fitzgerald, a builder with mounting financial difficulties, had been recruited by Thompson's associates to store the drugs and firearms to earn a 'modest profit'. The builder would later receive an eight-year sentence for his part in the massive haul.

Operation Goldeneye was run by officers who had spent

years investigating Thompson and it was classed as a specialist Organised Crime Unit within the gardaí's South Central
Division. Under the command of former Detective Superintendent Gabriel O'Gara, former Superintendent Thady
Muldoon and Superintendent Joseph Gannon, the aim of
the initiative, O'Gara said, was to 'specifically target' Thompson's associates and the gangs of young drug dealers controlled
by his representative, Lynch:

> 'Goldeneye' was an initiative designed to infiltrate and dis-
> rupt the activities of organized criminals who were aligned
> to the Kinahans. The Kinahan cartel had a major network
> of criminals within the south inner city who they used as a
> distribution chain in the sale and supply of drugs. The net-
> work had its leading lights in the form of David Byrne,
> Freddie Thompson, Liam Byrne and Greg Lynch.

The senior detective considered the seizure in Tallaght a
'huge success' and also 'evidence of the drugs and weapons
at the disposal of people like Freddie Thompson and Greg
Lynch':

> We were targeting people like Freddie Thompson, his asso-
> ciates in the Kinahan cartel and others like Greg Lynch
> who were fast becoming major players in organized crime at
> that time. Thompson may only have been sneaking into the
> country from time to time but he still had influence because
> he had over a decade of involvement in organized crime
> already under his belt by that stage.

The 'Goldeneye' team's capture had identified how Thompson, although mainly based outside Dublin, still had 'influence'
and associations with 'ninety-one' of the country's most serious criminals. At the same time, investigators established that

Thompson was suspected of working with Lynch in controlling sixty young dealers across the south inner city.

As part of their remit, officers attached to 'Goldeneye' were also tasked with prosecuting the gang members who were preying on vulnerable children and their families in Dublin's south inner city. During their investigations, officers established that associates of Thompson and Lynch were forcing families to remortgage their homes over unpaid drug debts incurred by their children, some aged just thirteen. The drugs enforcers often used 'Fat Freddie' Thompson's name when collecting debts to ensure families knew the calibre of gangster they were dealing with. Daily threats were also a common occurrence for investigating officers at the time. The intimidation included threats to burn cars and homes belonging to gardaí, and to shoot users for failing to pay debts. Thompson was careful to have others issue threats on his behalf.

In one file sent to the Director of Public Prosecutions, 'Goldeneye' detectives insisted they were targeting a gang:

> whose sole area of expertise was the importation, sale and supply, and distribution of controlled drugs within the greater Dublin area. The unit was deployed with a specific remit of targeting organized crime and all the persons associated with this prominent criminal gang who live and operate this illegal enterprise within the Dublin Metropolitan Region, South Central Division.

With Operations Goldeneye and Shovel running in tandem throughout the summer of 2010, detectives in the south inner city remained alert, waiting for Thompson's possible return to Dublin. They also continued to identify those who were moving drugs and weapons for his gang, both in and outside the city. In another file sent to the DPP, gardaí explained that the organized-crime gang were also 'involved in the importation of firearms which are used as "tools of the trade" to enforce and copper-fasten their criminal enterprise within the area of this illegal drugs trade operating within the South Central Division'.

The 'Goldeneye' team were often backed by the Emergency Response Unit, and they maintained a covert and overt presence on the streets of the capital. The scale of the weapons available to Thompson and his fellow gangsters became all too apparent when officers arrested Paul O'Neill a few weeks later. An acquaintance of Thompson's, O'Neill had only one previous conviction, in July 2010, when he had been cautioned for refusing to pay his motor tax. Lacking the criminal pedigree of his associates or their list of arrests, he was the perfect candidate as far as Thompson was concerned. Using the leverage of O'Neill's cocaine and gambling addiction, the cartel offered the 39-year-old a payday in return for hiding drugs and firearms for them. O'Neill accepted, but he didn't realize that gardaí had received a tip-off about his involvement in the scheme. They quickly established a surveillance operation and moved in on 22 September 2010.

Leaving his place of work at around 5 p.m. that day, the forklift driver was immediately intercepted by members of the ERU. When his home was searched after his arrest, investigators recovered a black laptop bag containing two Ingram sub-machine guns, two silencers, four loaded magazines and a large quantity of 9mm ammunition.

The following morning, Detective Sergeant Adrian Whitelaw, a lead investigator with the 'Goldeneye' team and one of the few officers who has investigated Thompson since his introduction to organized crime, returned to O'Neill's place of work.

Detective Sergeant Whitelaw recovered another two Ingram weapons, two silencers, four loaded magazines and more 9mm ammunition. Gardaí also discovered cocaine, with an estimated value of €31,500, hidden in a metal cabinet used to store maintenance tools. In return for his loyalty, Thompson's associates had paid O'Neill just €200 for each successful drugs drop he'd made in the weeks before his arrest.

In their prosecution file to the Director of Public Prosecutions, gardaí stated that O'Neill had made 'full and frank admissions' but the forklift driver had refused to name names. Investigators commented that O'Neill 'holds a genuine fear of the repercussions he would face if he were to disclose the identity of those persons'. Gardaí were in no doubt that O'Neill was living in fear of Thompson, his associates and Greg Lynch, and that these were the people O'Neill had refused to name during his interviews. As part of their file to the DPP, detectives also outlined O'Neill's role within the gang:

> It is obvious Paul O'Neill plays an active part in the mechanism of this organized criminal enterprise. He can be considered a vital cog in the wheel of this criminal enterprise as he knowingly facilitates the transportation, storage and preparation of firearms and controlled drugs for these persons. O'Neill was not at the higher echelons of this criminal organization but through his willingness to accept responsibility for the transportation of weapons and drugs, this made him a valuable asset to the criminal gang. He continued to feature in the criminal organization because he was below the garda radar. There are many people like him who would have been used by criminal organizations to feed a drugs habit or if they had encountered financial difficulties.

Gardaí believed that Thompson and his gang had been behind a spate of killings since the murder of Brian Rattigan's brother Joey in 2002, but the discovery of the Ingram sub-machine guns was a major breakthrough for investigators. It was the first time these powerful weapons had featured on the gangland scene in Dublin. Often used by Mexican drugs cartels and gangs in America in drive-by shootings, the weapons were considered 'particularly lethal' because of their ability to fire at a rate of 1,200 rounds per minute. Investigators believed, as one officer explained, the weapons had been sent to Ireland from Thompson's Dutch base:

At the time of the seizure Freddie Thompson was moving around Europe and he would have had the contacts in Amsterdam to arrange such a shipment. He already had experience of importing arms to Ireland and this enterprise had his fingerprints all over it. He was one of only a few criminals who would have had the expertise in introducing these weapons into Ireland. The weapons could have been used by Thompson for further attacks on people associated with Rattigan, against the gardaí or on anyone who stepped out of line. It was serious firepower. Thankfully they were caught just in time; otherwise there would have been further bloodshed on our streets.

Concerns over the weapons were also shared with the DPP. In their report on the case, gardaí regarded it as 'a very worrying development':

The Ingram firearm is an extremely deadly weapon and it is the firm belief of investigating gardaí that should these firearms have been deployed on public streets, the consequences of discharging such a weapon in a public place would have been devastating, not only to the intended target but also innocent bystanders alike. It is clear these firearms were destined to be part of the gang's arsenal and were to be used to intimidate and control the workings of their illicit drugs trade.

During O'Neill's trial the following year, Detective Garda, now Sergeant, Linda Williams told Dublin Circuit Court it was her belief the weapons were to be used by a major organized-crime gang in the south inner-city area of Dublin. In his summation Judge Martin Nolan told the court the defendant had been 'sucked into' a criminal enterprise and was 'used by a criminal gang because of his addictions'. O'Neill received a five-year sentence for his involvement.

The pressure again mounted for Thompson in December 2010 when, seven months after their arrest, Christy, Daniel and Christopher Kinahan Jnr were released from custody on bail. To celebrate their freedom, the gang threw a lavish fancy dress party on the Costa del Sol. Thompson and Hutch were two noticeable absentees. The Kinahans had told them to keep away from Spain in case they got arrested and until the cartel was fully operational again.

Thompson remained outside Ireland for the rest of the year as the garda investigations into his criminal enterprises went on. Alongside 'Goldeneye', the gardaí also launched 'Operation Flint' to target the up-and-coming dealers who were supplying drugs in the Dolphin's Barn and Fatima areas of Dublin's south inner city. The 'Flint' officers targeted the street dealers, including some as young as thirteen, who were on Thompson's payroll. As part of their efforts to seize drugs in these areas, which had been terrorized by Thompson and his gang over the years, officers seized heroin worth €500,000 and cocaine worth €50,000, forcing the young dealers to go out of business or to move elsewhere.

Feeling homesick at the start of 2011, Thompson used a fake passport in the name of John Roe to make secret trips to Dublin. One such occasion was on 17 February, when he was spotted by gardaí entering his mother's house in the Maryland area of the south inner city. As gardaí approached, Freddie fled through a series of back gardens. He was convinced he would be arrested if they caught him. However, his belief that a European Arrest Warrant had been issued for him was unfounded, as the Spanish authorities were still in the process of completing it.

In a follow-up search of a Dublin property linked to Thompson, detectives recovered €2,000 in cash hidden in a washing machine. They also received an insight into Thompson's character when they recovered letters he had sent to his partner, Vicky Dempsey, during his time in prison in 2003. Detectives had previously gained similar insight into Thompson's enemy Rattigan when they uncovered a series of Valentine's poems he wrote to his now ex-partner Natasha McEnroe. In one of the letters to Vicky Dempsey, Thompson expressed his love for his partner:

> I am in the cell looking at the TV but there's fuck all on and I am thinking of you I miss you so much. I have been thinking of all the good time. I know we have had some bad times. When I am in good times are the best baby. I hope you love me the way you say you do because I will love you till the day I die. You and me will be happy babes when I get out and I don't give a fuck what it takes. We can get on with life and will make it till the end. I hope to see you soon and if you see 'Bop' [Liam Roe] tell him I said hello.

In another letter to his childhood sweetheart, Thompson showed his softer side again when he asked Dempsey to 'wait for him' and said he was spending 'every day in the gym' ahead of his release, adding:

When I get out, I'm not going back to the way it was. Tell our son I want him to be a boxer like his da. You are my baby and I am yours. I am going to take every day as if it is our last. I want you to be my wife hun. If it's what you want I know you are the one for me. I am in the cell hun thinking of you and it's all good.

Thompson also offered some parental advice to his partner:

Tell the baby I love him and make him go to school – I don't want him to grow up to be like me hun I will not let him be like me. I don't give a fuck he is a good boy. I would like you to get him into the boxing and we will be ok. Can you also try and get the *Sunday World*? I am going to bed hun so I will let you go. Don't be upset hun I love you more than life. I will not let you or him down again. Me and you will not let them get to us hun. Fuck them all, we don't need them. I need you and you need me. I am sorry again love.

One of the detectives explained that officers were 'surprised' to see a different side of Thompson's character:

It was very unusual to see someone who was behind such mayhem and misery talk about love and devotion. Thompson was a gangland hard man yet here he was telling his partner the only thing that mattered to him were his partner and child. But in the end this was all just for show because once he was released from prison he was back to planning murders. Organized crime was the real love of his life.

Later that month gardaí in Kevin Street Station received intelligence Thompson was considering a new life for himself, his partner and their son in the Far East. According to one detective:

> There was a suggestion at the time that Thompson was considering moving his family to the Philippines because they had no extradition treaty with Ireland. He was under a lot of pressure at that time and was struggling to cope with the investigation in Spain and also because he was paranoid that he could be killed at any time by his enemies and those he considered friends. The only people he seemed to trust were his family.

A few days after his close encounter with gardaí, however, Thompson again left Dublin – without his son or Vicky Dempsey. In his absence, a small group of supporters from the Basin Street area, who had remained loyal to Brian 'King Ratt' Rattigan, orchestrated a campaign of intimidation against Thompson's family. In the first incident, on 12 March 2011, Thompson's older brother Richie suffered a broken leg after he was attacked in the Karma Stone pub on Wexford Street in Dublin city centre. The four individuals involved in the row were led by Rattigan's enforcer Gerard Eglington.

Two months later, on 15 May, with Thompson still in exile, Rattigan's gang continued their offensive by leaving a homemade bomb at the rear of Freddie's family home. The device, which included gunpowder filled with petrol and a plastic substance, luckily failed to ignite. If anyone had been near the bomb when it exploded they would have suffered serious injuries or worse, as the crude make-up of the device meant that the plastic component would stick to the skin of the target. Thompson was furious when he heard about the failed bomb attempt and he immediately placed Eglington at the top of his gang's hit list.

Thompson couldn't risk returning to Dublin but his gang made their move on 25 June 2011. They had recruited a contract killer, who would later be used by the Kinahan cartel, to target Eglington. Investigators believed a Thompson gang member spotted Rattigan's enforcer drinking at the Blackhorse Inn in Inchicore, south Dublin, and sent a message to the hitman giving the target's location. Eglington, however, had left the pub by the time the killer arrived.

In a bizarre twist, gardaí were at the premises just eight minutes before the hitman walked in. They had been called to the pub after two men stormed inside, waving a firearm and yelling: 'Where are the rats?' It has never been established who these two men were or why they were in the pub. The main theory is that they may have been looking for someone else.

Wearing a mask, surgical gloves and plastic covers on his feet, the Thompson gang's hitman opened fire, fatally injuring Darren Cogan who was enjoying a drink at his local pub. Just as in many other cases associated with gangland hits, the shooter had murdered the wrong man. Gardaí believe the innocent 22-year-old, who was not involved in crime, had been targeted simply because he was wearing a similar jumper to Eglington's. Investigators later received intelligence that when the hitman was told by Thompson's gang that he'd shot the wrong man, he replied: 'So what.'

Rose, the murder victim's mother, expressed her pain in a subsequent interview:

> I cry in the morning and I cry at night because I just miss my beautiful son so much. Darren was just such a popular boy and he was the life and soul of the party. He used to do

things for old people in the area and we've just been robbed of a special person in our lives.

The feud which had started in 2001 had claimed its fourteenth victim when Darren Cogan was murdered in a case of mistaken identity. The young man was totally innocent and was murdered simply because Thompson was hell-bent on avenging the attack on his brother Richie, where he'd ended up with a broken leg.

The tragic murder of Darren Cogan didn't deter Thompson from his determination to strike back at Rattigan's family and his number one target – Gerard Eglington. In one of his attempts to target Eglington in August 2011, a hit team for the Thompson gang was mobilized in the south inner city when they heard that the enforcer would be making a trip into Dublin city centre to renew his passport. However, Thompson's associates aborted the plan after gardaí swamped the city centre when they received intelligence about the murder plot.

Thompson was getting tired of moving between Holland and the UK and he had pressing reasons for returning to Dublin. On 22 September 2011 he arrived in Ireland to attend the funeral of the drug dealer Michael 'The Panda' Kelly, who had been murdered a week earlier.

During his time in the UK and Holland, Thompson had maintained his long-standing relationship with Kelly, widely regarded as one of Ireland's major drugs importers. The northsider had no convictions, but he was a major target for the Criminal Assets Bureau (CAB) over unpaid tax issues. Established in 1996 in the aftermath of the murder of the journalist Veronica Guerin, the CAB's remit was to strip criminals of their wealth and illegal gains. In his early criminal career, Thompson's gang had worked closely with Kelly's associates in north Dublin, with the gangs often coming together to pay for drugs and weapons shipments. On other occasions, Kelly had been recruited by Thompson to provide logistics and transport for shipments coming into Ireland. In return, Thompson, with the Kinahans' sanction, facilitated Kelly's recruitment of contract killer Eric 'Lucky' Wilson. Both Thompson and Kelly, however, had been dealt a huge blow when Wilson received a twenty-three-year prison sentence in Spain in the summer of 2011 for the 2010 murder of a UK national, Daniel Smith. Regarded as one of Ireland's most prolific contract killers, Wilson had been linked to ten gangland assassinations over the years. The hitman was also the chief suspect in the disappearance and murder in Spain of the killer Christy Gilroy on 21 January 2009.

On that occasion, Thompson's close friend Gary Hutch was the last person to see Gilroy alive on the Costa del Sol. Gilroy had fled to Spain after he was identified by gardaí as the main suspect in the double murders of the drug dealers Michael 'Roly' Cronin and James Moloney in Dublin, on 7 January 2009. The heroin addict was ordered to receive treatment at a clinic on Spain's southern coast. However, the contract killer's boss, Eamon 'The Don' Dunne, had then asked the Kinahan cartel to help Gilroy to 'disappear', amid concerns he would speak to the authorities as he struggled to cope with his guilt.

According to Spanish police files, Hutch, who was living with Thompson in Spain at the time, is suspected of paying for Gilroy's treatment in the drug rehabilitation centre before agreeing to drive him there. However, Gilroy never arrived at the clinic and has not been seen since. Investigators believe he was driven by Hutch to a remote location, shot by Wilson and buried in a shallow grave. A former investigator believes Thompson also knew about Gilroy's execution:

> Hutch would have earned the trust of Gilroy and offered him all sorts of help when all along he was plotting to have him killed. There's no question Thompson would have known of the plot because Hutch told him everything and the pair were inseparable.

The investigation into Gilroy's disappearance carries on and authorities in Spain have been unable to recover his remains, despite numerous appeals. Gilroy's sister, Glenda, has urged anyone with information to come forward:

> I accept that Christopher did very bad things, but he was threatened into those murders because he was soft, like a child trapped in a man's body. But justice has been done for that. He's been murdered, so let us have him home to bury him. I don't want arrests and trials. An anonymous tip-off, a note in a church, anything that will end this nightmare.

'Panda' Kelly's funeral brought many of Ireland's major gangland figures together, including Thompson and other senior members of the Kinahan cartel. The drug dealer had been living on borrowed time when he became a target of Alan Ryan, a young dissident Republican terrorist who was running a Real IRA unit in north Dublin. In the first week of September 2011, Ryan and his gang were demanding a tax from drugs gangs in the north inner city, warning them that they had to hand over a slice of their profits if they wanted to stay in business. Thompson had once had the same problem with the INLA's boss, Declan 'Whacker' Duffy, in the south inner city and Kelly had adopted a similar policy, telling Ryan there would be no cash. Determined to send a message to the main players in Dublin's gangland scene, Ryan's gang made their move on 15 September.

As 'Panda' Kelly walked to a friend's car, parked close to his girlfriend's home in Marrsfield Avenue, Clongriffin, north Dublin, he was hit five times in the head and chest by a gunman armed with an AK47 assault rifle. His killers finished him off by driving over his head as he lay in a pool of blood. The murder would also lead to growing tension between Alan Ryan's Real IRA and a drugs gang in north Dublin run by a man known as 'Mr Big'.

After the funeral, Thompson was needed in Dublin and he decided to stick around. He planned to set himself back up in Ireland on a full-time basis – it was a decision 'Fat Freddie' would come to regret.

7. Anglo-Irish Relations

> Do you understand how these people work? If they
> can't get to me, they get to the people you love. They
> kill the people you love.
>
> James Mulvey, drug dealer

Setting up a Dublin base again, Thompson intended to make good use of the relationships he'd forged during his exile in Holland and the UK. He'd made some particularly valuable new contacts in Birmingham – and top of the list was Thomas 'Bomber' Kavanagh.

Like many of the UK's major cities, Birmingham has become home to generations of Irish families. As the city's industrial power grew in the nineteenth century, so too did the number of people who left Ireland, both north and south of the border, looking to build a better life there. However, when a Dublin businessman and car dealer, Thomas 'Bomber' Kavanagh, left his hometown in 2008, it was for very different reasons.

Kavanagh, whose wife, Joanna, is the sister of the senior cartel figures Liam and David Byrne and also Thompson's first cousin, was never involved in the feud with Rattigan. 'Bomber' was feeling the pressure from other quarters – namely the gardaí. By 2008, he had already amassed a string of convictions for assault, threats to kill, possession of firearms and assaults on garda officers. When investigators from the CAB, however, started to delve into his affairs and his growing property portfolio in Ireland and Spain, Kavanagh knew it was time to leave.

Settling in the leafy suburb of Solihull, just outside Birmingham, Kavanagh soon established contacts with major players from the UK's organized-crime scene. As part of their investigations into his criminal network, CAB investigators established how he had a 'direct role in the directing' of the cartel. Investigators also claimed Kavanagh was 'one step above Liam Byrne in the gang'. He had also been arrested by the UK's National Crime Agency (NCA) and charged with possession of a stun gun, as part of a wider probe into international drugs trafficking.

As a result of his senior position within one of Europe's most dangerous drugs gangs, it was no surprise that Thompson had been invited to join 'Bomber' following Freddie's exile from Spain after the 'Shovel' raids. Thompson had to keep moving between the Netherlands and the UK and that required help, as one investigator explained:

> If criminals want to remain on the run from the authorities then they have to have the support network and logistics in order to achieve this aim. Thompson was ordered to keep away from Spain as the 'Shovel' investigation continued so he spent his time in the UK and Holland. When he needed somewhere to stay in Birmingham he turned to Kavanagh because he had the support to help him. He may have spent his days in pubs and going to the gym, but Thompson also realized that he had to be available to assist Kavanagh at the drop of a hat. During his time in the UK, there was intelligence to suggest that he was acting as an enforcer and used to intimidate people who owed his employers cash. Authorities in the UK also received intelligence of Thompson's visits to

the UK and they were concerned the violence could follow him because of the sheer amount of murders he had been involved in over the years.

During his time in the UK, Thompson also used the opportunity to establish contact with a businessman, Maurice Sines – a friendship that would remain intact for many years. Investigators believe Sines, who once clashed with the music star Elton John over a planning application to install caravans close to the singer's home and lost, was first introduced to Thompson and the Byrne brothers around 2009. A business-man involved in the leisure trade before moving into the horse-racing industry, Sines was also involved in the car trade, which is where he was introduced to 'Bomber' Kavanagh. Through Kavanagh's introductions, he then forged close links with Thompson and the Byrne clan. Sines, identified by the CAB as being 'linked to a larger organized-crime network in Birmingham', welcomed his new friends with open arms.

During Thompson's frequent visits to the UK, Sines would often host parties at his luxury home in Solihull and entertain his new business partners in Birmingham's top res-taurants. According to a security source in the UK:

> Sines is a big player in the UK but for some strange reason he loved socializing with people like Freddie Thompson and other Irish criminals who were renowned for their vio-lence. He often needed muscle for protection and that's why he remained close to Thompson.

Another major UK criminal introduced to Thompson by 'Bomber' Kavanagh was the drug dealer James Mulvey. A UK native, Mulvey was a cousin of 'Bomber' Kavanagh's Dublin-based cousin, Gerard 'Hatchet' Kavanagh. Mulvey was also a close associate of Daniel Kinahan and worked with the cartel on many of the drugs shipments they smuggled into the UK and Ireland. When Thompson arrived in Birmingham, Mulvey used him as an enforcer.

Mulvey had been behind a huge drugs- and gun-smuggling operation which began in 2006. His associates used to hide the huge blocks of cocaine and cannabis inside industrial metal pipes and then transport them to a warehouse in Belgium. From there, they were transported to Inkberrow in Worcestershire in England before being distributed to other cities in the UK and to Dublin. The enterprise ran successfully for three years before it was eventually smashed by the gardaí and the NCA in 2009. Mulvey would go on to receive a thirty-two-year sentence in 2018 for conspiring to import cocaine and cannabis worth €80 million into Ireland and the UK. The scheme was only foiled when an observant employee at the warehouse in Belgium noticed that the same metal pipes kept returning to the facility.

In the same operation, gardaí recovered metal pipes at an industrial unit in west Dublin, before twenty-two kilograms of cocaine and 392 kilograms of cannabis were seized in Belgium in February 2007.

During their investigations, officers established that before he was finally identified Mulvey's gang had smuggled drugs on fourteen different occasions into the UK and Ireland. Two of Mulvey's associates were arrested in 2009, but he went on the run. He spent his time with Thompson and other cartel associates at his €1.4 million villa on the Costa del Sol and at bases he had in Eastern Europe. One investigator stated that:

> Mulvey and Thompson were very close and there was intelligence that they were often socializing together in Spain.

When Thompson went to the UK, Mulvey still had business interests there and would have used Thompson on certain occasions as muscle. Mulvey also had a string of properties in different names that Thompson would have used during his time in England. There's no doubt there were people in the Kinahan cartel who would have helped him evade capture after the seizure in 2009 because they had the resources to do it. They were all working hand in glove and the size of the shipments they were arranging shows just how big they were on the European drugs landscape.

The drug dealer may have seemed to have a close relationship with Freddie, but his ties to Dublin meant that he was all too aware of the threat posed by Thompson and his associates. In a secret recording by surveillance teams attached to the NCA, Mulvey was recorded telling his partner: 'Do you understand how these people work? If they can't get to me, they get to the people you love. They kill the people you love.'

It was similar to the message Thompson shared with two gangland investigators on one occasion, when he was brought back to Kevin Street Garda Station for a drugs search. Freddie was asked about his role within the Kinahan gang:

Deco wants out but he's in way too deep. Too much has happened. If Deco tries to get out, they will kill his family. These aren't the type of people who take no for an answer. They will kill everyone he loves. Deco thought about getting out in the past, but just couldn't. Deco does what he's told – it's as simple as that.

When asked to elaborate, Thompson simply replied: 'No comment.'

Gardaí were of the firm belief, recounted one investigator,

that Thompson was using the name of his dead friend, Declan 'Deco' Gavin, to talk about his own situation:

> He knew he was in too deep and even if he wanted to assist gardaí it was a lost cause because he knew his family would become targets. It was interesting hearing him talk like that and it proved he was a man under serious pressure. On the one hand he seemed to enjoy his life inside a criminal organization, but on the other he was terrified of what could happen to his family because deep down everyone knew they were expendable. When he made those comments, he wasn't his usual mouthy self and was clearly a man under serious pressure. It told gardaí that he knew the people he considered friends and associates could turn on him at the drop of a hat.

Mulvey also knew the cartel gang couldn't be trusted but he continued to mix with Thompson and other cartel members as they were still doing business together. Gardaí suspected many of his shipments reached Irish shores throughout 2011 and into 2012.

The drug dealer carried on working with the cartel until he was finally caught by Lithuanian Special Forces, when they raided his house in Kaunas, on 28 March 2017. At his trial, Judge Mark Wall QC accused Mulvey of 'funding' the sophisticated smuggling operation:

> You were involved in the large-scale importation of these drugs into this country from continental Europe and its onward transportation to Ireland, where doubtless it was to be sold at a great profit. You gave evidence that you yourself have taken cocaine for many years. You would have been acutely aware of the misery and ruined lives that this drug brings in its wake.

The NCA's Birmingham Branch commander, Adam Warnock, issued a statement after the trial, promising: 'We will never stop pursuing serious criminals like Mulvey and we will work with our international partners to ensure we track them down and bring them to justice.'

While he maintained his relationships with 'Bomber' Kavanagh and Mulvey, 'Fat Freddie' had also used his time in the UK and his secret visits to Ireland to meet with another trusted associate of Christy and Daniel Kinahan – Philip Baron.

After leaving Ireland for Spain and Holland around 2001, Christy Kinahan had used his time away from home to build his criminal organization and to establish links with the heads of other crime syndicates. One man on his list of key people to meet was Philip Baron, and it wasn't long before the pair became friends and, more importantly, business contacts. Reports indicated that Kinahan Snr had very little time for young criminals such as Thompson and Gary Hutch, who had been brought into the family business by his elder son, Daniel, but professional criminals such as Baron were warmly welcomed, as one investigator explained:

> People like Christy Kinahan and John Cunningham were old-school criminals and they had built up their organization by cultivating contacts with people like Baron. Baron was seen as a respectable businessman and intelligent, whereas Thompson and Hutch were seen as thugs and often reckless. Kinahan and Cunningham weren't particularly keen on people like Thompson, but they knew he was handy to have around if violence was to be used.

Baron had moved to Ireland in the 1990s and lived in a luxury mansion in Straffan, Co. Kildare, posing as a property tycoon. Known as the 'English gentleman' to his neighbours, Baron kept his secret life, where he worked as a major drugs importer alongside Christy Kinahan, hidden from his friends in rural Ireland. To disguise his illegal activities, he often held functions to raise cash for charities.

Despite having direct access to Christy, Baron was also introduced to Thompson during his trips to the UK and Spain. However, unlike Thompson's relationships with Sines and Mulvey, Baron was not a fan of the Dublin native.

According to gardaí, he'd wasted no time in letting 'Fat Freddie' know what he thought of him when they first met in 2010. Unbeknownst to the two criminals, Baron was being monitored by the former Garda National Drugs Unit after he was linked to a massive €350 million drugs-smuggling racket in the UK. At this stage Thompson was regarded by Spanish police as Daniel Kinahan's 'right-hand man', but, one investigator later said, Baron did not afford 'Fat Freddie' equal status:

> Thompson was still an employee of the Kinahans so there would have been times when he would have had to meet Baron to discuss cartel business. Baron may have helped Thompson when he was in England, with the odd safe house, but they never got along. There was intelligence to suggest that Baron complained directly to Christy Kinahan about Thompson's behaviour. Thompson was also over every paper in Ireland and Baron did not want to be seen in his company, especially in Kildare. Baron believed his own hype and saw himself as a businessman who only dealt with like-minded individuals. He was the mastermind behind millions' worth of drugs being smuggled into the UK and definitely believed someone like Thompson was beneath him. There were times when Freddie acted as his driver, but

this arrangement didn't last for long. This guy owned yachts, designer watches and sports cars, but Thompson didn't have any of this stuff because he was too stupid to realize that he was just being used for violence.

Gardaí knew that Thompson was earning plenty of money from the cartel, and that he had access to large quantities of cash as he moved around so much, but he wasn't in the same league as his colleagues.

On another occasion in 2010, said a security source, gardaí also received intelligence that the pair had been involved in a heated exchange at a hotel in the UK after Baron refused to deal with Thompson:

> They were shouting at each other because Baron wanted to deal with someone of a higher status and someone who knew what they were doing when it came to the money aspect of the criminal organization. Thompson was disappointed at the way he had been treated and his ego had taken a knock, but he knew there was nothing he could do about Baron because he remained close to Christy Kinahan. There were other times in Spain when he would have disguised himself when he was meeting senior Kinahan representatives and Thompson would have known nothing about the meetings. Baron had responsibility for logistics and transport for the Kinahan gang, whereas Thompson was often kept away from these dealings because his job was to concentrate on weapons.

Keeping his distance from Thompson, Baron, who was a member of the prestigious K Club in Co. Kildare, worked closely with Kinahan's associate Matthew Dunne, whose home in west Dublin had been targeted under Operation Shovel.

During a subsequent police property application at Dublin District Court, Dunne attempted to have items seized from his home during the raid returned. They included photographs of friends, mobile phones, watches and documents. Detective Sergeant Greg Sheehan, who had been investigating the Kinahan cartel since the 1990s, told the court: 'Some people in the pictures are suspects. The items were seized during an investigation into organized crime.' The material was kept by the State and never returned.

It turned out to be lucky for Thompson that Baron didn't want him around, as the 'English gentleman' had no idea that he was the focus of a major investigation by gardaí and the NCA. He'd been identified as a target back in 2009 when a fellow gang member, Paul Yearsley, was arrested and shouted at officers: 'What are you doing about Philip Baron? He's ten times bigger than me.'

Following the completion of the joint Irish and British investigation, Baron was arrested at his luxury home in May 2011 and charged with involvement in a major UK-wide drugs-smuggling operation. He would spend the next two years fighting his extradition before finally losing the battle. Following the end of his trial in June 2013, Baron received an eighteen-year sentence, after pleading guilty to masterminding the supply of fifty-two tonnes of cannabis and cocaine into the UK, from Costa Rica and North Africa, between 2005 and 2009.

At Baron's sentencing, Judge David Aubrey told Liverpool Crown Court how Baron sold drugs on a 'commercial scale so he could lead the life that he did', and addressing him said:

It was driven by avarice and greed. It was a trade and an empire and you cared not for the lives of others. You have destroyed lives. It may have led people to commit crime. It may have led to despair and desperation. None of that concerned you. You were only concerned with yourself and leading a lavish lifestyle.

The Kinahan cartel had lost one of their key associates following Baron's arrest in 2011, but Thompson had wasted no time finding new contacts to add to his growing list of underworld sources. While he was in Birmingham, 'Bomber' Kavanagh had also introduced Freddie to Lee Cullen, a businessman and Dublin socialite who was desperate to win the approval of the Kinahan cartel.

Cullen, a close friend of the model Katy French, who died from a suspected cocaine overdose on 6 December 2007, was a well-known figure on the Irish social scene in the 'Celtic Tiger' years and was a close associate of the property tycoon James Mansfield Snr. Amassing a huge property portfolio while he was also importing luxury cars into Ireland, Cullen and his company, Exclusive Cars, became a target for the CAB over outstanding tax bills. It launched 'Operation Tie' to investigate Cullen and his company after the recession hit in 2009. Although he has settled one tax bill for €2.5 million with Revenue, Cullen still owes €700,000 to the Irish State.

At the time of the economic crash, Cullen had thirty properties registered in his name. However, the homes were repossessed in 2009 when he was unable to repay the loans after his car company went out of business. Struggling to fund the lifestyle he had enjoyed during the period of the 'Celtic Tiger', Cullen had turned to the Kinahan cartel and his friend Freddie Thompson for help. Using cash that he had kept hidden from the CAB, Cullen offered to contribute towards the funding of drugs shipments into Dublin, in return for a percentage of the profits from the deals. His expertise in the transport industry was also put to good use when the cartel tasked him with supplying cars from his contacts in the UK. Investigators also believed that Cullen's business associates in the UK helped the Kinahan cartel to launder cash. An investigator from the NCA explained how:

> Cullen had strong links to Birmingham and the motor trade, and he wasted no time in making people like Freddie Thompson aware of his connections. Thompson spent a lot of time in the UK and, from what we can gather, he used his time to work with Cullen in obtaining vehicles that were to be used by his associates in Ireland. Cullen got involved with Thompson and his associates because he had no other way of making cash following the collapse of his business in Ireland. He still posed as a legitimate car buyer when he was in the UK, but this was just a front to mask his real activities of involvement in drugs importation, providing logistics to organized-crime gangs and VAT fraud. Some of his contacts were also used to launder cash for Thompson's associates but he wasn't making anywhere near the same profits. Like others in this field, Cullen saw himself as a businessman, but he had no idea of the people he was getting into bed with. Whenever people like Thompson made demands from him, he responded in a heartbeat. He was out of his depth and did what he was told.

In his first venture into the narcotics trade in 2009, Cullen and a cartel associate, Christopher 'Git' Russell, had agreed to help fund a €2 million consignment of cannabis. Its destination was Dublin and the deal had been organized by the Kinahans from their base in southern Spain. Hidden in tractor tyres, the drugs were sent to Northern Ireland, where they would be stored for a short time before being brought over the border. However, the deal ended in disaster for Cullen when the haul was discovered and seized by the Police Service of Northern Ireland (PSNI). Even though the drugs were gone and the investors had suffered a huge loss, Cullen was left in no doubt of the threats posed by his new business partners when he was warned by Thompson, Gerard 'Hatchet' Kavanagh and the enforcer Paul Rice to pay his share of the consignment. By one investigator's later account:

> Cullen was left with no choice but to pay because he knew he would be killed if he didn't. He knew the risks of working with people like Thompson and if things went wrong and drugs were seized, the cash still had to be paid. Thompson had nothing in common with Cullen and was clearly using him for his own ends. When Cullen got involved with Thompson and other cartel figures he was running around like a big-time gangster. When he started making money again, he would often loan cartel figures cash because he was terrified of what they would do to him.

Despite suffering a financial loss over the 2009 shipment, Cullen had maintained his links with Thompson and other leading associates of the cartel. He featured in the NCA's investigations into James Mulvey, in which officers suspected Cullen of providing vans for the transportation of guns. On other occasions in 2009 and 2010, UK and garda investigators suspected Cullen of providing vans for the transportation of drugs and of sourcing a rocket launcher. The stash and the weapon were later recovered by gardaí at an industrial unit previously linked to Cullen. During their long-term investigations into Lee Cullen, detectives from the CAB said that the former socialite 'supplied cars to criminals and played a part in the laundering of the proceeds of crime for a number of these senior crime figures'.

By September 2011, Cullen was living permanently in the UK, and continuing to provide vehicles to Thompson and his associates in the cartel, including Liam Byrne and Sean McGovern. When Freddie was setting up his base in Dublin again, he was stopped by gardaí on a number of occasions as he drove around his turf. When questioned about their cars, the gangsters would say the vehicles had been loaned to them by a UK-based company, thereby preventing gardaí from seizing them. However, the former socialite's decision to join forces with the Kinahan cartel and to become a key figure in organized crime would ultimately cost him twenty-one years of his life, after he was convicted in 2018 for importing weapons into the UK. Cullen was just another one on the growing list of Thompson's associates who would find themselves ending up in prison.

As Thompson settled back into Dublin, he had no intention of giving gardaí the opportunity to arrest him, but the fallout after Kelly's murder was something he'd have to deal with.

8. Taking Care of Business

Frederick Thompson has had no meaningful
employment since his teenage years and has
remained in receipt of social welfare allowances.
During his rise through the ranks of the Kinahan
organization he was able to fund trips to Spain,
Holland and the UK.

Kevin Street Garda Station report

The northside drug dealer Michael 'The Panda' Kelly had many enemies, but suspicion for his murder soon fell on Ryan and the Real IRA. Taking stock after the killing, Thompson was all too aware of the threat posed by Ryan, his associates and also the INLA. They remained active, despite 'Whacker' Duffy's return to prison in the UK on 22 July 2010, after he admitted killing Sergeant Michael Newman in Derby in 1992. Freddie was even more paranoid and security-conscious than usual, as he knew the dissident Republicans would have his name on their hit lists.

A week after the funeral, Thompson was stopped in a car registered to Kelly Quinn, the girlfriend of Freddie's cousin and cartel associate David Byrne. Sitting in the back with his 'hood pulled up and wearing a bulletproof vest', Thompson was clearly trying to travel incognito. In a typical effort to show off, he urged gardaí to complete their search quickly as he was 'expecting a call from John Gilligan from prison'.

Gilligan, a veteran criminal whose gang were behind the murder of the journalist Veronica Guerin, was serving a sixteen-year sentence for drug dealing. Detectives knew that Thompson had dealings with him through a gang of young drug dealers from the Clondalkin area who were being supplied with drugs and guns by Freddie's gang.

On 4 October 2011, Thompson was stopped by three members of the gardaí who were on patrol close to the entrance of St Teresa's Gardens in Dublin's south inner city. According to the officers, Thompson began 'to put his hands in his pockets in a nervous manner and was wearing a bulletproof vest'. He was brought to Kevin Street Station for a drugs search, where his erratic behaviour did not stop. When the three-man garda team searched him at the station, seizing his mobile phone, Thompson roared loudly that 'he had no phone or property' on him, as the surprised officers looked on. The phone was later sent to the garda technical experts for analysis, but it did not contain any evidence. Released from the station, Thompson returned to his family home, where gardaí continued their overt surveillance operation.

A number of weeks after Kelly's funeral, gardaí received intelligence that Thompson had been approached by Alan Ryan and warned he would be murdered if he didn't pay tax on his drug deals. Thompson ignored the demand, however, and instead threatened to place a €350,000 bounty on Ryan and on innocent members of the Ryan family. 'Fat Freddie' had more than the gardaí and dissident Republicans to worry about. He'd heard that investigators in Spain had put the finishing touches to their European Arrest Warrant for Thompson's detention in connection with Operation Shovel.

Finally completed by mid-October, the warrant made its

way to Dublin on 13 October 2011. In their introduction on Thompson, Spanish authorities asserted that he was part of an 'illicit organization' involved in 'drugs importation, weapons smuggling and money laundering'. They detailed how the Kinahan cartel had established companies for the purpose of 'laundering money to legally introduce it into the market to conceal its illicit origin'. In order to achieve their aims, investigators stated, the cartel had 'set up a complex financial and business network' using lawyers who 'specialized in this area of law'. The 'Shovel' team remarked: 'These lawyers have used their knowledge of the law to set up companies so that the organization's business dealings appear legal.'

Elaborating on Thompson's involvement in organized crime, Spanish detectives said he was using another man's identity:

> He is the holder of a Spanish foreigner's ID number and has a police record in his country of origin (Ireland) for crimes of damages, theft by force, public disorder, forgery of public documents, reckless driving and others. Furthermore, as a result of investigations carried out in Spain and in collaboration between Ireland and the United Kingdom, it is known that Freddie has been under investigation in both countries for narcotics related offences.

On his role within the Kinahan cartel, they believed that:

> Thompson together with Gary Hutch are the men who are closest to Daniel Joseph Kinahan, as can be inferred from telephone tapping and surveillance operations. They are his trusted right-hand men and carry out jobs directly related to the organization's criminal activities. Freddie and Gary are just one step below Daniel, are very close and share equal

status. They sometimes give orders to each other without being able to determine who is higher up in the organization. They are equals, good friends and share a flat. Freddie and Daniel have a strong personal and professional relationship. This is evident in the large number of telephone conversations they hold, such as the one held on 4 February 2010, between Freddie and Daniel. In this conversation, Daniel says to Freddie, 'I need you at the roundabout in two minutes, I'm leaving.' Freddie replies by saying, 'okay'.

According to the Spanish police, Thompson was also tasked with running the weapons importation section of the cartel's business. The 'Shovel' investigators added: 'One of Freddie's jobs is to obtain weapons for the rest of the organization, as is evident from the conversations he held with Gary Hutch. Like Gary, Freddie's duties also include acting as a bodyguard and chauffer.'

The warrant also provided details of Thompson's business trips for the cartel:

Telephone-tapping operations and surveillance operations have revealed that Freddie travelled to Amsterdam, to where Daniel had also travelled on various occasions, to weigh up the possibility of preparing and supervising a large shipment of drugs which was to be picked up in Ireland.

Authorities in Holland also suspected one of the Kinahan cartel's main suppliers was a Moroccan-based mafia organization run by a Dutch-Moroccan criminal, Naoufal Fassih, who would later emerge as a target for gardaí investigating Thompson's activities. As part of the surveillance on Thompson's trip to Holland, investigators discovered that another of Freddie's friends, Gary Finnegan, had 'travelled to Málaga to personally meet with Daniel to discuss the shipment'. Investigators in both the Dutch and the Spanish teams believed:

> Daniel was going to supposedly finance part of the shipment. A surveillance operation was launched at Málaga Airport and officers saw Ross Browning, another one of the persons under investigation, arriving at the airport to collect him. He was driving the car usually driven by Gary Hutch, which is owned by a company under investigation for drugs and arms trafficking.

Other associates identified on the warrant included Gavin Abbot, who, although he was from the north inner-city area of Dublin, had worked closely with Thompson in Spain. Investigators identified Abbot as an associate who travelled there regularly and who they said had 'a strong relationship with the gang'. During their investigation to finalize the warrant, officers in Spain also examined Thompson's employment situation on the Costa del Sol:

> Results showed that Freddie does not have any movable or immovable property registered in his name. He has made no statement as to his job and therefore does not have legally declared funds to support himself in Spain. Everything indicates that, like in previous cases, he supports himself with money obtained from illegal activities, including drugs trafficking for this organization.

Gardaí in Kevin Street Station in Dublin supported their counterparts in Spain by investigating Thompson's financial situation from the Irish perspective:

> Frederick Thompson has had no meaningful employment since his teenage years and has remained in receipt of social

welfare allowances. During his rise through the ranks of the Kinahan organization he was able to fund trips to Spain, Holland and the UK.

Although he was usually conducting cartel business on overseas trips, gardaí noted that Freddie also had the money to treat his wife and son to summer breaks in southern Spain and to Christmas visits to Amsterdam, where, on one occasion, he posed for the camera in his partner's scarf and hat as they visited an ice rink. Gardaí suspected that on his trips abroad Thompson used younger members of the gang to smuggle cash, usually hidden in their underwear. On one occasion Spanish police stopped him travelling with a younger boy and it was discovered the boy was carrying a large sum of money in his bag.

The Operation Shovel extradition warrant concluded:

Based on the information, there are grounds to believe Frederick James Thompson has committed the crimes of unlawful association punishable under Articles 515 and 517 of the Spanish Criminal Code, possession and trafficking of arms punishable under Article 563 and crimes against public health. The offences also include participation in a criminal organization, illicit trafficking in narcotic drugs and psychotropic substances and illicit trafficking in weapons, munitions and explosives.

When the warrant to arrest Thompson arrived in Ireland, officers from Kevin Street Garda Station prepared themselves to execute it the following day. They arrived at Thompson's family home early on the morning of 14 October, but there was no sign of him. Gardaí were concerned they had missed their opportunity to arrest him. However, they returned around 2.25 p.m. to find Thompson sitting in the living room enjoying a cup of tea. Placed in handcuffs and escorted to a waiting garda car, Thompson shouted: 'I don't have any money – I'm done now', as neighbours looked on.

Once in custody, Thompson, wearing a hooded top over a baseball cap, was brought to the High Court in Dublin by members of the Garda National Bureau of Criminal Investigation's Extradition Unit. As he walked the short distance to the court, flanked by gardaí, Freddie mentioned the film *The Blues Brothers*, saying: 'Everybody needs someone to love, someone to hold.'

Thompson's brother Richie and partner, Vicky, sat in the public gallery throughout the brief hearing. Garda Sergeant Sean Fallon told the court that when Thompson was handed a copy of the arrest warrant and extradition document he had commented: 'No, I can't read. I'm not taking that.' The garda team knew this was a lie as they still had the letters he'd written to Vicky Dempsey when he was in prison. When Freddie was then asked about the offences on the warrant, the court heard he'd replied: 'No comment.'

Judge Michael Peart told the court he was satisfied the person named in the warrant was in court and remanded Thompson in custody. Thompson's lawyers failed to have legal aid granted, despite Freddie instructing them that he was 'broke', and had been living off handouts from his mother.

Thompson was transferred to Cloverhill Prison in west Dublin and did not appear at the High Court again until the following week. His legal team informed the court that Thompson had instructed them that he wanted to be extradited to Spain 'straight away'. By that stage, all of those arrested under Operation Shovel had been released, and one investigator explained how Thompson was confident that his chances of walking free would be better on Spanish soil:

> It suited him to go to Spain because many of his associates were convinced there would be no charges arising out of the 'Shovel' investigation. He could go to Spain, get bail and then live under the protection of the cartel. He would have been a lot safer in Spain than he would have in Ireland. It was a no-brainer for him to deal with the extradition request as quickly as possible.

Thompson's wish to return to Spain was granted on 28 October. He was brought to Dublin Airport from Cloverhill Prison under an armed escort from the Emergency Response Unit. Driven in a prison van, flanked by four bulletproof vehicles, Thompson, classed by the Spanish as a 'Category A' prisoner due to his involvement in organized crime, was met by two police officers from the 'Shovel' team. At the same time, extra gardaí arrived at the departure gate to ensure there was no trouble. Emerging from the prison van around 5 p.m., after a two-hour wait, Thompson then boarded the 5.20 p.m. flight to Madrid, accompanied by the two Spanish investigators. Armed with two plastic bags and €73.14 in prison money, the criminal was on his way back to Spain.

After being brought from Madrid to Málaga, Thompson was placed in the Alhaurín de la Torre jail in Andalusia. Just three days after arriving in Spain, however, Freddie's decision not to oppose extradition paid off. Appearing at a court in Estepona, Thompson was charged with drug dealing, weapons smuggling and unlawful assembly before being released on bail. As part of his bail conditions, he was forced to hand over his passport and sign on at a court twice a month until his case was heard. The court also ordered him to remain in Spain until the case was finalized.

To celebrate his release from his short stay in prison, Daniel Kinahan organized a party for Thompson at the cartel-funded Auld Dubliner pub on the Costa del Sol. The cartel's godfather, Christy Kinahan, was not there as he had been extradited to Belgium to serve the remainder of his four-year sentence for money laundering. However, under his son Daniel's leadership, it was business as usual for the cartel during Christy Snr's absence.

Over the course of the next few months, Thompson continued to revel in the high life in Spain. Though the Spanish surveillance operation under 'Shovel' had been wound down, Spanish police suspected Thompson had been making secret trips to Holland and the UK, breaking the terms of his bail, but they had been unable to catch him.

As Thompson, living it up in a luxury apartment, celebrated Christmas in Spain, his associates in Dublin's south inner city came under the garda spotlight. Investigators received reports that they were involved in taking hampers from the poor:

Some of the people involved in this were very close to Thompson and people were afraid to say anything because they knew how dangerous he was. He may have been out of the country, but he still had influence, especially in the south inner-city area of Dublin.

In the first few months of 2012, Thompson, still out on bail, went about his normal life in southern Spain – spending his days at the gym, meeting with his legal representatives and working for the cartel. It had been almost two years since the 'Shovel' raids, but the gang remained increasingly paranoid. Business was booming as the cartel were smuggling regular shipments of drugs and weapons into Ireland, with Thompson responsible for the gun-running side of the operation. He was also assigned the new role of 'pool boy' and ordered to clean Christy Kinahan's pool on a weekly basis, while the godfather served his sentence in Belgium. Gardaí believed that Thompson complied as, though he was close to Daniel, Christy was the ultimate boss and when he issued orders people followed them. 'Fat Freddie' still had a lot of clout in Dublin, but when he was in Spain he did what he was told as he wanted the cartel on his side.

Thompson was also a regular fixture at the newly opened Macklin's Gym Marbella (MGM), established by the boxer Matthew Macklin and Daniel Kinahan, who was now presenting himself as a boxing promoter. One insider at the gym described how it was run like a 'cult', adding:

> In 2012, Daniel was presenting himself as MGM general manager and was recruiting fighters to the gym by promising them huge amounts of cash. When some of the boxers asked for money, Daniel would have people like Freddie Thompson hanging around as a blatant form of intimidation. Thompson always said he loved boxing, but he was afraid to get into the ring when any white-collar charity fights were being arranged. Fighters were genuinely terrified because they knew the type of people they were dealing with. Thompson's reputation was well known at this stage and he was loving the notoriety when he was in Spain.

Though living it up in Spain, Thompson found himself in trouble with the local authorities in the summer of 2012 when he was arrested on three occasions for public-order offences. He was reported by tourists who didn't know who he was. According to one investigator:

If Thompson wasn't on cartel business he didn't have much to do and when he had free time he spent it going to the gym in the morning before going to pubs and clubs around Marbella at night time. When he was drunk, he would often abuse tourists for the clothes they were wearing or their appearances. It was a classic example of thuggish behaviour from him directed against completely innocent people. He went to Spain with just over €70 in his pocket but yet he still managed to find the cash to fund a good life for himself.

After Thompson's third arrest, he was told his bail would be revoked if he insisted on abusing tourists to the region while under the influence of alcohol. The Spanish police kept an eye on him but there were no further incidents.

Even though 'Fat Freddie' was stuck in Spain, his fourteen-year feud with Brian 'King Ratt' Rattigan and his gang was far from over. His number one target – Gerard Eglington – was feeling the heat as he had been informed there was a €20,000 price on his head. Thompson had offered the bounty as he was determined to pay Eglington back for his role in the attack on his brother, Richie. The Rattigan gang enforcer, who had been jailed for four years in 2003 after a stolen car he was in caused a horrific crash that killed Garda Anthony Tighe and Garda Michael Padden, had left Dublin when he heard about the price on his head. He moved to a property in Kilnacourt Woods, Portarlington, Co. Laois. Eglington made the mistake of believing he was safe there, outside the kill zones of Crumlin and Drimnagh and far away from the long-running feud. Living openly in Portarlington, Eglington had integrated with the community, joining a local football team. It wasn't long before he was asked to leave, however, when his photograph started appearing in the newspapers as a man who was at war with the notorious criminal 'Fat Freddie' Thompson. Despite this, Eglington remained popular with his neighbours and would often leave his front door open so they could drop in and out. It was a decision that would cost him his life.

Eglington was targeted just a few weeks later, after he ignored advice from the gardaí that his life was under threat. On the morning of 24 September 2012, two gunmen calmly walked into his home, through the unlocked door, and shot him four times in the back. The shooting occurred in the kitchen in front of his two children, who were very lucky to be unharmed in the attack.

Terrified neighbours rushed to Eglington's aid and he was brought to Tullamore General Hospital. The Rattigan enforcer was pronounced dead a short time later. The killers had struck at the same time as gardaí were preparing to issue a warrant for Eglington's arrest. He was accused of violent disorder, assault causing harm and possession of a knife at a pub in Portarlington the previous year. At the time of his murder, he was also awaiting trial on a violent-disorder charge over the attack on Richie Thompson.

Gardaí received intelligence a few days later that Thompson had celebrated the killing with a meal at a top restaurant in Marbella. It would not be the last time Thompson would enjoy a meal following a murder. One investigator confirmed that:

This is what Thompson did after most murders. He went to a fancy restaurant with members of his gang for a debrief and a celebration that another life had been lost. It was his way of celebrating closing a deal. Life meant absolutely nothing to him. Killing was an integral part of his business.

As Thompson celebrated the latest execution linked to his gang, gardaí suspect his associates in the south inner city were also given clearance to murder a 32-year-old drug addict called Declan O'Reilly. Just hours after the Eglington killing, O'Reilly was on his way to buy fireworks with his twelve-year-old son when he was shot multiple times in the chest and neck. The gunman had emerged from a BMW car on Dublin's South Circular Road. O'Reilly, who was on the phone with a drugs counsellor at the time of the shooting, was heard telling his son to 'get an ambulance'. The drug addict, who had been acquitted of murdering a fellow inmate, Derek Glennon, at Mountjoy Prison, seemed unaware he was under threat from Thompson's gang and was planning to go to college. Gardaí determined O'Reilly's murder, which remains unsolved, was not feud-related, and it has been linked to associates of Thompson over an unpaid drug debt. According to one officer:

> Thompson and his gang sold drugs to a lot of people in the south inner city and the suspects in this case are associates of his gang. Nothing happened in the south inner city without their say-so and they would have known after a short time who was behind this callous murder in front of an innocent child.

The father, also called Derek, of the Mountjoy Prison murder victim offered his sympathies to the O'Reilly family after the killing: 'His family were terrified of something like this happening and I feel sorry for them . . . This cycle of death has to stop.'

A former Justice Minister, Alan Shatter, described the two murders as 'barbaric', and went on: 'The callousness of their actions shows that the perpetrators lack even a shred of humanity or decency.' Enda Kenny, previously Taoiseach (Irish prime minister), also condemned the killings, stating:

'This is brutal treatment by people who have ordered the destruction, assassination and the murder of people in public in front of children on the street. Life has become very cheap indeed.'

While Thompson did not seem particularly interested in O'Reilly's murder, the death of Eglington was a major coup in the enduring feud. The enforcer was the most senior member of Rattigan's gang to be taken out since the killing of Anthony Cannon in 2009. The only long-term associate left who had remained loyal to Rattigan was Neil 'The Highlander' Fitzgerald, and he was serving a ten-year sentence for pointing a gun at Detectives Gardaí Ken Donnelly, Richie Kelly and Declan Boland during an armed stand-off in July 2008. Despite being in prison, Fitzgerald, originally from Australia, had been telling other inmates that he was determined to kill Thompson. Like many of those before him, Fitzgerald would not fulfil his promise.

Thompson received another boost that month when the Real IRA's chief, Alan Ryan, was murdered by a north-Dublin crime gang. With the INLA's boss, 'Whacker' Duffy, already back behind bars, life was looking a lot brighter for 'Fat Freddie' as he basked on the Costa del Sol.

9. Lack of Respect

I haven't forgotten about the €60,000 you owe me.
Freddie Thompson

The Operation Shovel investigation was still active, but Freddie received an unexpected boost from the Spanish authorities at the end of November 2012. They returned his legitimate passport, permitting him to legally leave Spain. In a disappointing development for the joint police task force, the Spanish 'Shovel' team was satisfied he was unlikely to face any charges over the drugs or weapons importation accusation because they had no evidence linking him to the cartel's operations.

Thompson wasted no time in returning to his home turf. Arriving in Dublin on 17 December 2012, 'Fat Freddie' had his first interaction with gardaí twenty-four hours later, when he was spotted walking with his associate, the former car dealer Michael Frazer, in the Stannaway Road area of Crumlin, south Dublin. Dressed in a black jacket, jeans and baseball cap, Thompson, who had also grown a beard, was searched by two members of the gardaí who were on patrol. During their brief exchange, Thompson, who had spent the vast majority of his time in Spain pumping iron, said: 'Ye can't call me fat any more', obviously proud of his slimmed-down figure.

Gardaí in Crumlin and Kevin Street Stations had been

placed on high alert after receiving information from their Spanish counterparts that one of their major targets was returning home, because, in one investigator's analysis:

> Every time he came back to Ireland there was always the concern that there would be an increase in violence. He just couldn't help himself and it was like a drug to him. The community would also be on edge and gardaí would be more aware of his presence because we all knew his war with Rattigan was still ongoing and it was just a question of waiting. No matter where he went violence always followed him. When he wasn't around the south inner city there was certainly a lot less tension and it gave the community some breathing space to get on with their lives. A rifle with a telescopic sight was also discovered just a week before he returned to Ireland and this was also worrying because it was linked to his gang.

Detective Superintendent Peter O'Boyle from Kevin Street Garda Station, who would later lead a team of investigators into Thompson's activities, assured the people of the south inner city that no criminal was 'untouchable', in what many colleagues believe was a statement directed at Thompson:

> Our team of dedicated officers are actively targeting the small number of individuals involved in crime. The number one priority for us is to safeguard the lives of the people of this area. The excellent work being done within the community by residents' associations and various groups goes unreported, while the actions of a small group of mindless criminals unfortunately makes the headlines. I would also urge the young people of the area to stay away from these gangs because they bring nothing but misery to them and their families.

Despite Detective Superintendent O'Boyle's positive comments on the gardaí's commitment to targeting organized crime, in a worrying development garda headquarters revealed how many of Ireland's organized criminals were working closely with outfits from Eastern Europe, particularly Russian gangs. Martin Callinan, a former Garda Commissioner, added: 'The presence of Russian organized-crime groups operating in Spain is also influencing the activities of Irish criminals there. Gardaí are also working closely with international law enforcement agencies to monitor these groups.'

Thompson too remained under the watchful eye of gardaí over the festive season. Detectives often spotted him socializing in pubs around the south inner-city area of Dublin, obviously enjoying himself, and one of them described how:

> He really loved being back in Ireland at that time and he was going to these pubs because he wanted to show people that he wasn't on the run and that he was still in charge. He wouldn't go to the pubs on his own and always surrounded himself with a group of young thugs for protection. No matter where he went, there would always be some kind of trouble.

Violence was Thompson's trademark and it soon followed his return to Dublin when, just three days after Christmas, another of his childhood friends was murdered in a gun attack. A petty criminal, Christopher 'Git' Warren, whose brother Paul had been murdered by Rattigan's hitman Gary Bryan in 2004, was shot in the stomach at the Royal Canal Bank in the Phibsboro area of north Dublin. He died a few hours after he was brought by an associate to St James's Hospital. Initially suspecting Warren was another victim of the Crumlin–Drimnagh feud, because of his brother's links to Thompson and the murder of Joey Rattigan, gardaí quickly established that he was most likely killed in a punishment shooting gone wrong. Christopher Warren was targeted because he had been accused of hitting a woman in a pub on 26 December, just two days earlier.

The Director of Public Prosecutions later ruled there would be no charge in the murder. The chief suspect was a drug dealer from the south inner city who regularly bought drugs from Thompson's gang. Gardaí had received intelligence that Thompson was 'incensed' by the killing, postponing a return to either Spain or Holland so he could attend Warren's funeral on 7 January 2013. As with many decisions in his life, it would be one that would end in disaster for 'Fat Freddie'.

Christopher Warren hadn't been involved in organized crime, but there was a huge garda presence on the morning of his funeral at St Teresa's Church, Donore Avenue, because he was well known and respected amongst serious criminals in Dublin's south inner city. Keeping a discreet distance, gardaí watched as mourners gathered to pay their respects to the second member of the Warren family who had died in violent circumstances. Detectives were also out in force that day to monitor Thompson and make sure one of his enemies didn't make a move against him – members of the Rattigan faction and of the Real IRA were hoping to avenge the death of Alan Ryan. According to one officer:

> When there was a suggestion that Freddie Thompson might attend the funeral, and because he was still under threat from a variety of sources, gardaí couldn't take any chances. Thompson had only been seen at his family home and at a few pubs that Christmas and this would have been one of the rare occasions when he was out in public. His decision to attend the funeral and postpone his return to the Continent

was definitely his way of showing people in his community where his loyalties lay and how he was still in control. On the other hand, people would also have known that if Warren's killers were customers of Thompson's gang, he would do absolutely nothing because business always came first.

Following the funeral, Thompson joined mourners for Warren's wake at Morrissey's pub in Cork Street, south inner-city Dublin. Along with his first cousin David Byrne and an old friend, Anthony Harte, Thompson, who was wearing glasses, spent the evening drinking with local residents. During one exchange with a nineteen-year-old, Christopher Conlon, who wasn't involved in crime, Thompson slapped the young man in the face. Gardaí believed that shortly after the encounter words were also exchanged between the pair in the toilets of the premises. Twenty minutes later Thompson's propensity for violence surfaced when he armed himself with a beer bottle, hurled it at his victim, and then punched him in the back of the head. During the melee, Thompson punched a woman on the nose and was also suspected of slapping the face of a young woman whose partner is a contract killer for the Kinahan cartel.

Mourners scrambled for cover, as a bar employee pressed a panic alarm and members of the gardaí's South Central Divisional Crime Task Force arrived on the scene. According to an early report on the incident by gardaí: 'Initial inquiries show there was a large row inside the pub and it spilled out onto the street.' Within minutes of arriving, gardaí established who was involved in the fight, and one officer later detailed the implications:

Tensions were already high that day with the funeral but once gardaí knew who was behind the attack in the pub there was serious concern that it could lead to further violence. Freddie Thompson just couldn't help himself. The fact he picked on someone who wasn't involved in anything and used a bottle in this attack shows just how cowardly he was. The fact he started a fight just hours after a funeral showed once again Thompson's lust for violence. Having him involved in this incident was bad enough, but the fact that he had been accused of hitting the partner of a contract killer also caused further problems because there could quite easily have been further violence. Gardaí were dealing with people who were extremely violent.

Once CCTV had been secured from the pub, after gardaí obtained a warrant, investigators had clear evidence: 'Footage shows Frederick Thompson started a fight with Christopher Conlon which escalated into a large row involving fifteen people. CCTV shows Thompson throw a bottle at Christopher Conlon.'

One investigator described how, after identifying Thompson, Byrne and Harte from the footage, and initially hoping to charge the trio with assault, gardaí were left frustrated when Conlon and all the many other witnesses refused to get involved:

There wasn't a single complaint or statement made from anyone who was in the bar that night so it would have been very hard to get an assault charge over the line. It wasn't a surprise to see the victim keep quiet because he must have been terrified of the repercussions. However, all was not lost, because there was the possibility of a violent-disorder charge, which was a serious charge and carried a maximum ten-year sentence. To have people like Thompson and Byrne off the streets for that length of time would have been a fantastic result for gardaí and for the people of Dublin.

On 9 January 2013, gardaí made their move. They swooped on Thompson's family home and the other properties he was associated with, but he was nowhere to be found. During the search of his mother's house, gardaí were told by a female relative that Thompson 'returned to Spain this morning, via the north'. Gardaí also spoke to the victim, who had two black eyes, but he again refused to make any complaint.

One week after the incident, both Byrne and Harte were arrested at their homes in Crumlin, south Dublin. They replied 'No comment' to all of the investigators' questions. The pair were later released without charge. Detective Garda O'Donovan and then Sergeant Paul Murphy from the South Central Divisional Crime Task Force team were able to continue with their investigation, an officer later explained, even though Thompson had not been caught:

> It didn't really matter that Thompson wasn't around because if he had been brought in for questioning he would have said nothing anyway. Gardaí were confident that the evidence gleaned from the CCTV footage clearly showed Thompson being the aggressor in this case. The CCTV tracked his every move and he never made any attempt to cover his movements that night. It was ironic because Thompson always went to bars with extensive CCTV coverage because he felt safer. He would have known that bar would have been covered in cameras, yet he still initiated an unprovoked and violent attack.

Detectives established that Thompson was now back in Spain, but the garda investigation on the case remained active. The completed case file, minus any witness statements but containing the CCTV footage and the garda's hypothesis on the sequence of events in the pub, was finally sent to the Director of Public Prosecutions later that year. Gardaí were determined to arrest Thompson over the bar attacks and pushed to get a conviction in his absence. They could then arrest him if he returned to Ireland.

The investigating team's hopes of capturing Thompson were raised when intelligence suggested Freddie had proposed to his partner, Vicky Dempsey, for a third time. An investigator remembered: 'They were always falling out and getting engaged again. If the rumours were to be believed, there was every chance he might have tried to return to Ireland, but there was still no sign of him.'

The DPP also ruled David Byrne and Anthony Harte should be charged, and, as they had remained in Dublin, the investigators were able to take them back into custody. Both men were granted bail and were released shortly afterwards.

On 20 March 2013, Thompson received some more good news in his prolonged war with Brian Rattigan when his arch-enemy, who had starred as one of the ugly sisters in a performance of *Cinderella* in Portlaoise Prison, received a seventeen-year sentence for running a million-euro heroin supply network from his cell. During his appearance at the Special Criminal Court, the hearing was told how Rattigan, who had been in custody since 2003, had also undertaken an 'Alternative to Violence' course. A detective who investigated both criminals pointed out that Rattigan's attempt at rehabilitation was in marked contrast to Thompson's activities in prison: 'The two men were similar when it came to their propensity for violence, but the only thing Thompson did when he was inside was try and run the prison and get a team of loyal prisoners around him for protection.'

At Rattigan's trial, Detective Sergeant Brian Roberts from the Garda National Drugs Unit, now an inspector, also reminded the Special Criminal Court that many drug users across Ireland were 'living in fear' from crime gangs like Rattigan's because of unpaid debts. Mr Justice Paul Butler welcomed the insight into Ireland's drugs scourge:

This is a very, very serious case. We are grateful to the evidence given by Detective Sergeant Brian Roberts on the effects of drugs and heroin on our society. The evidence will be useful for other cases. The accused has been involved in drugs and violence and this has affected his family.

Brian Rattigan apologized to the senior investigator Detective Sergeant Joe O'Hara for making threats against him, but blamed Thompson's associates for leaving a shotgun cartridge in the detective's car in 2008. Speaking outside the court, retired Detective Superintendent Denis Donegan welcomed the verdict: 'The media previously described this man as a dealer in death and destruction, and indeed that is what he is.'

Thompson, however, remained on the garda's 'Most Wanted' list throughout the summer of 2013. Gardaí continued to receive intelligence of Freddie's secret trips to Ireland and often issued nationwide alerts reminding officers to be aware of his possible return. His trips home were primarily on cartel business and included meetings with senior gang members in a range of locations, from Dublin's top hotels to caravan sites in Co. Wexford. On one occasion, detectives from Kevin Street Station travelled to Wexford to try to catch Freddie but were unable to locate him.

It was business as usual for Thompson's associates, despite his absence, and they did not let up flooding the streets of the capital with drugs. However, the gang suffered another setback on 6 June 2013, when gardaí from Crumlin and the Garda

National Drugs Unit, supported by the Emergency Response Unit, swooped on thirty homes in the Crumlin area of Dublin under 'Operation Trident'. Gardaí arrested twenty-nine people in the crackdown, including Jack Dempsey, the father of Thompson's partner, Vicky. The aim of 'Trident' was to target members of Thompson's gang who were involved in selling heroin and crack cocaine in the south inner city. Undercover officers had spent five months earning the trust of Thompson's associates, buying heroin, cannabis and cocaine from them to build up a relationship. During the operation the undercover garda teams even held meetings with some of Thompson's most trusted associates as they gathered enough evidence to bring charges of possession of drugs with intent to supply against twenty-two members of the gang.

Thompson, whom the gardaí believed to be in Holland at this point, was said to be 'furious' when he heard about the operation. According to one investigator: 'There was intelligence to suggest that Thompson was livid after the arrest because gardaí weren't just targeting his gang's business, they were also targeting people close to him.'

The news didn't get any better for 'Fat Freddie' a few weeks later. In September 2013, the Director of Public Prosecutions concluded there was enough evidence to charge Thompson with violent disorder. Following the DPP's decision, Thompson had to remain in Holland, the UK and Spain if he wanted to evade arrest. He was often in Birmingham during this period, working closely with 'Hatchet' Kavanagh as both men collected cash on behalf of the cartel. Thompson, however, was left in no uncertainty about the gardaí's determination to convict him once and for all when it was reported in the *Irish Sun*, on 19 January 2014, that a European Arrest Warrant had been issued for him. The warrant charged him with violent disorder on 9 January 2013 and declared Frederick Thompson had 'used or threatened to use unlawful violence and such conduct, taken together, was such as would cause a person of reasonable firmness present at said place to fear for his or another person's safety'. Despite facing a charge with a potential ten-year sentence, 'Fat Freddie' continued to sneak back to Ireland for meetings.

Thompson's luck finally ran out on 5 May 2014, seventeen months after he'd gone on the run, when he was arrested by Dutch authorities in an apartment in Overtoom, a village situated between Amsterdam and Utrecht. Travelling on a false passport in the name of an innocent student, and wearing a fake beard, Thompson and two associates were arrested after the car he was travelling in was stopped by five units of Dutch police. His arrest coincided with the funeral of Christy Kinahan's estranged wife, Jean Boylan, and happened just a day after another Rattigan loyalist, Christopher Zambra, who had clashed with Thompson in the past, was shot dead.

As Thompson remained in custody in Amsterdam, senior gangland figures from around Ireland gathered in Dublin to pay their respects to the Kinahan brothers. Closely monitoring the potentially volatile situation, gardaí received an insight into possible internal tensions within the cartel. Graffiti branding Thompson's best friend, Gary Hutch, a 'Rat' had been painted on the walls of the Russian Orthodox Church, situated beside Mount Jerome Cemetery, where the funeral was taking place.

Thompson had his own problems as he was waiting for news of his extradition back to Dublin. He also faced an anxious wait to see if the Dutch authorities would charge him with travelling on a false passport. Following a meeting with gardaí, authorities in Holland decided to hand him over as the charge of violent disorder was more serious. Detective Garda O'Donovan travelled to Amsterdam with a member of the gardaí's Extradition Unit and brought Thompson back to Ireland, arriving in Dublin Airport on 20 May 2014. During the flight, Thompson joked with the arresting officers, often offering them food. A passenger on the same flight told of his surprise when he noticed Thompson: 'He was laughing away and didn't seem too worried about who saw him. A few people recognized him and as soon as we landed he was first off the plane.'

As passengers looked on, Thompson was escorted off the aeroplane by Detective Garda O'Donovan and Sergeant Paul Murphy, before he was brought to Dublin District Court. During the hearing, Detective Garda O'Donovan told the court that Thompson had made no reply when charged with the offence of violent disorder. The investigating officer also objected to bail on the grounds of the 'seriousness of the offence' and a 'possible ten-year prison sentence upon conviction'. He also told the court it was his belief Thompson was not a resident of Ireland and that he had travelled to Spain shortly after the incident.

Thompson's solicitor objected, informing the court that his client did not pose a flight risk and enjoyed a 'presumption of innocence'. However, Judge Michael Walsh remanded Thompson to Cloverhill Prison.

As Thompson once again adapted to prison life, he soon found himself in trouble with the Irish Prison Service. On 17 June 2014, in a random search, prison officers recovered a mobile phone hidden in his bed. It was seized and 'Fat Freddie' later received a €200 fine.

The following month, on 10 July, Thompson's associate Anthony Harte appeared before Judge Mary Ellen Ring for a sentencing hearing after pleading guilty to the violent-disorder charge. During his hearing, Detective Garda O'Donovan told the court how Harte was shown on CCTV punching and kicking the victim. Harte's defence solicitor told the court his client 'fell in with a poor peer group in his late teens and later began taking cocaine', and before the incident had been 'drinking all day'. During the same hearing, the court heard Harte had also admitted handling three stolen motorbikes worth €25,000, along with Thompson and their cartel associates Darren Foster and Richard O'Reilly. Harte, who distanced himself from Thompson after the incident, later received a punishment of 220 hours' community service after entering a guilty plea.

Six days after Harte's appearance in court, Thompson was back before the High Court in another attempt to secure bail. Though Thompson's aunt, Sadie Byrne, the mother of David and Liam Byrne, offered surety of €13,000 and Thompson's brother Richie offered €6,000, Freddie's application was refused.

Just one week later, with the CCTV evidence stacked against him, Thompson pleaded guilty to the violent-disorder charge and was told he would be sentenced in early 2015. Gardaí were delighted Thompson was on remand and off the streets, because every time he was back in Dublin violence and mayhem followed him.

Being back in prison, however, didn't curb Thompson's violent tendencies. On 6 August 2014, detectives received intelligence from the Irish Prison Service that Thompson had threatened a prisoner as he was being brought back to his cell in Cloverhill, ranting: 'I haven't forgotten about the €60,000 you owe me.' Terrified Thompson would place a bounty on his head, the inmate later moved to Turkey after his release. As a security source said: 'The fact Thompson was in prison didn't matter. He still had the associates and the resources to target people.'

On another occasion during Thompson's time on remand, a man who was receiving an official warning from gardaí that his life was under threat told officers that he was sharing a cell with Thompson. Gardaí would later note: 'He seemed very proud of this fact and claimed that within the prison there was talk of him being groomed to take over from Freddie in the future. He is an extremely cocky individual and firmly believes he is too cocky for gardaí.'

'Fat Freddie' was one of the main players on the Irish gangland scene and, as such, was held in high regard, especially among younger prisoners. Everyone knew who he was connected to, and because the Kinahans had a lot of resources at their disposal it was easy to see why Thompson could rely on the backing of many prisoners in the jail.

On 19 August, Thompson's involvement in the violent-disorder incident was mentioned again when the partner of the woman he had been accused of slapping was arrested by gardaí in relation to the unlawful possession of firearms. According to gardaí at the time:

> This individual made reference on a couple of occasions to Freddie Thompson striking the mother of his child during an incident at Morrissey's. This individual was very animated about this and said that Thompson was lucky he made it to Spain and that it was not the end of it.

During the months he spent on remand, Thompson found life on the inside difficult at times as he was often attacked by other inmates. His membership of the cartel gave him protection, but they couldn't be with him 24/7, and as Thompson was always throwing his weight around there were occasions when inmates stood up to him. In early September 2014, gardaí on patrol close to Dublin's Heuston station stopped a suspected drug dealer from the area, who told the officers that Thompson had 'got a hiding in the yard from another prisoner'.

Gardaí also received further intelligence that Sean McDermott, who was serving a seven-year sentence for firing shots into the home of the Kinahan cartel's contract killer Gary Gleeson, had assaulted Thompson. Gardaí declared: 'Information has been received that Sean "Six Pence" McDermott from Ballyfermot assaulted Freddie Thompson in Cloverhill. Thompson has been throwing his weight around, but McDermott got the better of him.'

'Fat Freddie' may have felt he had troubles, but they were nothing compared to the problems his old friend Gary Hutch was about to encounter.

10. Under Pressure

> It was quite a serious fracas. He [Frederick
> Thompson] slapped someone, he threw a bottle and
> he punched someone. It seems he started the dispute.
>
> Judge Martin Nolan

While stuck on remand in Cloverhill Prison, Thompson was not involved in the day-to-day running of the cartel, but by the summer of 2014 he knew that all was not well between his old friends Daniel Kinahan and Gary Hutch.

Back in 2010, the Spanish police team on Operation Shovel had classified Freddie Thompson and Gary Hutch as being 'trusted right-hand men' and just 'one step below' the gang boss, Daniel Kinahan. Surveillance from 2008 onwards had also established that the trio worked closely together on cartel business across Europe. It was no surprise to gardaí when Hutch, suspected of involvement in a €7.6 million tiger-kidnapping raid at the Bank of Ireland in Dublin in February 2009, had turned to Daniel Kinahan for help with laundering his share of the massive payout.

According to underworld sources interviewed by the crime journalist Paul Williams, Daniel Kinahan had agreed to launder €2.5 million of Hutch's share of the crime, through one of the many companies the cartel had established for this sole purpose. However, by the time Thompson was in custody on the violent-disorder charge, Hutch had asked for his money back many times but there was still no sign of any return on his investment. By the summer of 2014 the 'right-hand man' had resorted to threats — warning Daniel that he would reveal how the Kinahan cartel had double-crossed many of their international business partners, including Robert 'Mink' Kok, who had been caught with fifty-three kilos of cocaine in Lebanon in 2011. The graffiti at Jean Boylan's funeral was a clear indication that tensions were mounting. Gardaí suspected it was the work of Thompson and his associates.

As hostilities between the one-time friends increased, Hutch was blamed for a gun attack outside Daniel Kinahan's home in Estepona on 3 August 2014. According to sources, Hutch had recruited a close associate for the murder. The 'right-hand man' planned to steal €2 million in cartel cash to make the assassination look like a robbery. During the incident, the innocent boxer Jamie Moore was shot in both legs but survived. Blamed for the failed attempt on Daniel Kinahan's life, Gary Hutch was left with no other option but to leave Spain and take refuge in Amsterdam.

Tensions within the Kinahan cartel also surfaced when Thompson's long-term associate and the cartel enforcer, Gerard 'Hatchet' Kavanagh, was shot nine times in the back, chest and head. The hitman opened fire in front of horrified onlookers as Kavanagh enjoyed a drink at the Harmons Irish bar in Elviria, southern Spain, on 6 September 2014. Initial suspicion fell on Russian gangsters who Kavanagh had previously threatened, and Spanish police linked the Russian mafia to the attack. However, another major line of inquiry was that he had been targeted because he was suspected of keeping €100,000 of cartel money for himself. Authorities in Spain believe the murder may have been sanctioned by the Kinahan cartel. At the time of writing, no one has been charged with the murder, but another of Thompson's close associates, James Quinn, also from the south inner city and a nephew of Martin 'The Viper' Foley, remains the chief suspect in the case.

Four days after Kavanagh's murder, Javier Arias, the lawyer acting for Kinahan's elder son, lodged an application at a Spanish court requesting police protection. Daniel Kinahan admitted that he was 'in fear of his life' but denied any links to Kavanagh.

A security source outlined how Kavanagh's murder had also caused concern for Thompson:

> Thompson was a bit edgy when he heard the news and he was increasingly paranoid. He was genuinely worried that he could be a target if it emerged that the Kinahan gang were wiping out their associates. He was also worried about the tension between Gary Hutch and Daniel Kinahan. He didn't know what to think at the time and was isolated because the prison service was watching his every move after he had been caught with the phone. Thompson was telling people in the prison that he hoped Hutch and Kinahan could resolve their differences because he had good time for both of them.

Thompson's increasing paranoia may have explained his actions in the final months of 2014, when gardaí believe he was orchestrating attacks on his former friend Michael Frazer. In November, Frazer, whose home had been bombed by Rattigan's gang during the Crumlin/Drimnagh feud, cheated death after a gunman rammed his car in the Inchicore area of south Dublin, before opening fire on him. According to a security source, Thompson signed Frazer's death warrant after the pair were involved in a personal row. The source maintained: 'This was yet another example of Thompson turning on his friends by ordering the hit on Frazer over something trivial.' It would not be the last time Frazer would be targeted by Thompson's associates.

In the early months of 2015, Thompson focused on preparing for his sentence hearing at Dublin Circuit Court on 2 February and on running his drugs business. Despite his incarceration, 'Fat Freddie' made sure his influence was still felt, both in and outside Dublin. On 21 January 2015, gardaí in Athy, Co. Kildare, recorded details of officers stopping a man from the Finglas area of north Dublin. He was wearing a bulletproof vest and claimed: 'Freddie Thompson has a hit out on me.' Gardaí suspected the man, who wasn't regarded as a major criminal, had been targeted over an unpaid debt. A security source explained:

> It wasn't unusual to find people who were on the run from criminals like Freddie Thompson coming to places like Athy. This individual was clearly in fear of his life because he was wearing a bulletproof vest. Thompson's gang had already got to Gerard Eglington in rural Ireland and this man wasn't taking any chances.

Another man who had just been released from prison also informed gardaí in Kilmainham, south Dublin, that 'there was a threat on his life' because he had been involved in a fight with Thompson. The former inmate, who wasn't part of any gang, later told officers of his intention to move to Waterford.

Before Thompson's court date he suffered a setback in his personal life, when the mother of his child and partner of fourteen years, Vicky Dempsey, ended their relationship. One of her friends, who did not want to be named, said:

> Vicky just wanted to lead a normal life and she couldn't do this because of Freddie's continued involvement in crime.

He would continue to bring her nothing but misery and that's why she decided to end their relationship so she could concentrate on their son. They would remain friends, but she just couldn't cope with the pressure of being with someone who was constantly under threat and constantly trying to stay one step ahead of the gardaí.

By the time Thompson appeared in court over his involvement in the violent incident at Morrissey's pub in January 2014, his first cousin David Byrne had been acquitted of the same offence. Freddie's barrister, Michael O'Higgins, apologized on his client's behalf to the other customers who were in the bar that night and to the bar's owners. He explained that the incident was 'sparked by what started out as slagging' to which his client had an 'unacceptable reaction'. While accepting that Thompson had been involved in a number of clashes with fellow inmates during his time on remand, Dublin Circuit Court was told how he had raised cash for the charity GOAL by participating in fun runs in prison and that he was undertaking computing and literacy courses.

Sentencing him to a twenty-month sentence, backdated to the time he was charged with the offence in May 2014, Judge Martin Nolan criticized Thompson's role in the incident:

On the evening in question it seems there was some sort of dispute. What he did was quite serious. It was quite a serious fracas. He slapped someone, he threw a bottle and he punched someone. It seems he started the dispute. The appropriate sentence is twenty months.

For some investigators, Thompson's supposed remorse and rehabilitation were a 'cynical ploy' by him to secure a reduced sentence. One of them said:

1. Freddie Thompson and his partner, Vicky Dempsey, celebrate the birth of their son in 2000. This is when his gang and Brian Rattigan's went to war in the Crumlin–Drimnagh feud.

2. Thompson's family enjoying a trip to Spain in 2007 as he cements his position in the Kinahan cartel.

3. (*left*) Freddie and Vicky dressed up for one of their many nights out in the midst of the Crumlin–Drimnagh feud.

4. Thompson's arch-enemy, Brian Rattigan, after he appeared in court in 2010 charged with five counts of possessing heroin.

5. A senior Kinahan cartel associate, and Thompson's first cousin, Liam Roe.

6. The INLA terror chief, Declan 'Whacker' Duffy, who was also involved in a feud with Thompson.

7. The Birmingham-based drug dealer and Thompson associate James Mulvey.

8. The hitman Paddy Doyle and Thompson enjoying a night out on the Costa del Sol in 2004.

9. Thompson and his first cousin David Byrne, stripped for the camera on a night out in 2002. Byrne was shot dead at the Regency Hotel in 2016.

10. (*left*) Nathan Foley, who acted as a 'spotter' on the day Daithi (David) Douglas was murdered in 2016.

11. (*below left*) A senior Kinahan cartel associate, Sean McGovern. He is now based in Dubai.

12. (*below*) A Kinahan cartel member, Liam Byrne, on a rare visit to Dublin in 2017.

13. A studio photograph of the brothers Christopher (*left*) and Daniel Kinahan in Dubai.

14. Happier times: the veteran criminal Gerry 'The Monk' Hutch (*second from left*) enjoying a night out with James 'Jaws' Byrne (*left*) and Sadie Byrne, parents of David and Liam Byrne.

15. (*above*) Taking aim. Thompson having fun during his time in Amsterdam in 2010.

16. (*right*) Thompson and Vicky Dempsey enjoying the sun in southern Spain in 2008.

17. (*below*) Thompson chilling out on a trip to Spain, also in 2008.

18. August 2002: Thompson accompanied to court by gardaí after being charged with assault.

19. Gardaí escort Thompson to a plane ahead of his extradition to Spain under Operation Shovel.

20. A CCTV image of Thompson in Morrissey's pub on Cork Street moments before he attacked an innocent man.

21. Thompson is brought back from Amsterdam to stand trial for violent disorder in May 2014 by Detective Garda Seamus O'Donovan and then Sergeant Paul Murphy. Both officers would later play a role in the Daithi (David) Douglas investigation.

22. A slimmed-down Thompson with family members after his release from prison in 2015 for the attack in Morrissey's pub. They are (*left to right*) his brother Richie and sister Lisa Jane.

23. (*far left*) Now wearing designer threads to go with his sleeker figure, Thompson in Dublin in April 2016.

24. (*left above*) The fake driving licence Thompson was using during the Kinahan and Hutch feud in 2016.

25. (*left below*) The bogus passport Thompson was using when he was caught by police in Holland in 2014.

26. A CCTV image of a gunman at the Regency Hotel seconds after the murder of David Byrne. Byrne's body is obscured by the counter but his feet can be seen protruding.

27–30. A sequence of CCTV images showing David Byrne running scared at the Regency. The last two images show him looking towards the lobby area of the hotel. In changing direction, he ended up running towards his death.

31. Boxing fans at the Regency run for their lives as shots ring out.

32. A CCTV image of a gunman inside the Regency hunting the mob boss Daniel Kinahan.

33. A CCTV image of one of the gunmen fleeing the scene at the Regency.

34. Thompson (*green hat*) joins Sean McGovern (*left*) and Liam Byrne (*second from left*) at the Byrne family home following the murder of David Byrne.

35. Thompson with Cartel associates, UK businessman Maurice Sines (*left*) and Thomas 'Bomber' Kavanagh (*right*), at the Byrne funeral.

36. (*right*) Thompson stands alongside Daniel Kinahan at the Byrne funeral.

37. The bloody scene inside the Shoestown shop on Dublin's Bridgefoot Street after the murder of Daithi (David) Douglas in July 2016.

38. Feud victim, Daithi (David) Douglas.

39, 39a. CCTV images of Thompson minutes after the murder of Douglas on nearby Meath Street. The bottom image shows Thompson (*sitting, to the right of the frame*) giving a woman the keys of his car.

40, 40a. CCTV images of Thompson and friends arriving at a Dublin city centre restaurant the night of the Douglas murder. They were celebrating the successful hit.

41. A Moroccan crime boss, Naoufal Fassih, is brought from the High Court by Chief Superintendent Paul Cleary (*behind Fassih*) and Irish Prison Service staff after he was discovered in Dublin.

42. Some of the weapons seized from the Kinahan cartel arms dump recovered at Greenogue in January 2017.

43. A mugshot of Freddie Thompson after his conviction for the murder of Douglas.

44. (*top*) Thompson's ex-partner Vicky Dempsey meets Sabina Higgins and President Michael D. Higgins when they were on the campaign trail in October 2018.

45. (*above*) Vicky Dempsey at her flower stall on Dublin's Grafton Street, October 2018.

46. (*right*) Vicky Dempsey enjoys the high life in Dublin in 2006.

47. Garda Commissioner Drew Harris (*centre, blue tie*) with the team who investigated Thompson's role in the murder of Douglas.

48. Detective Chief Superintendent Pat Clavin, chief bureau officer at the Criminal Assets Bureau.

49. Detective Superintendent Seamus Boland, Drugs and Organised Crime Bureau.

50. Detective Superintendent Peter O'Boyle.

51. Chief Superintendent Brian Sutton.

52. Detective Sergeant Adrian Whitelaw (*left*) and Chief Superintendent Paul Cleary following Thompson's conviction for murder.

53. Superintendent Joe Gannon, who ran the South Divisional Crime Task Force.

54. Assistant Commissioner John O'Driscoll from the gardaí's Special Crime Operations unit.

Thompson knew that he was potentially facing a ten-year prison sentence, but he was cute enough to know that if he did a few things when he was in prison to show that he was trying to improve his education or help others it would increase his chances of securing a reduced sentence. He knew how to play the game – he knew the system because he had been involved in it from no age. This was a man who loved violence and murder and cared for no one but himself. He would have known if his sentence was small, he would be out in no time because of the time he had spent on remand. Turns out he was right. His offence was deemed at the lower end of the scale, but the option was still there to put him away for a longer time. He had received a three-year term for assault in the past so this sentence would have been nothing to him. Even if he had received half of a ten-year sentence things would have been a hell of a lot different for the people across Dublin.

Winking at his mother, Elizabeth, and a small group of friends, Thompson smiled as he was returned to his prison cell.

The following month, he was informed by the Irish Prison Service that his release date would be 1 August. Regarded by the Irish Prison Service as a 'troublesome prisoner', during his time in prison Thompson had to be kept apart from sixty other inmates after they were classified as being associates of Rattigan and other gangs. One senior prison source told how:

He had to be moved around a lot in Cloverhill because he was seen as having a negative influence on other inmates – especially the younger ones. He loved being the centre of attention and loved the notoriety of being in the press, and he used this to ensure he had the loyalty of inmates for his own protection.

According to intelligence passed to gardaí on 18 March 2015, Thompson was in 'good form' in prison as he continued to receive visits from his family every Monday. His mood changed, however, when Paul Kavanagh, the younger brother of 'Hatchet' Kavanagh, was shot dead on 26 March, in Drumcondra, north Dublin. Irish Prison Service sources received intelligence that Thompson had spoken to other inmates about the killing. One source claimed:

> Thompson was telling other inmates that he didn't know what to make of the killing because he was unable to speak to anyone. He seemed concerned about it because he read reports in the media that a major line of inquiry was that Kavanagh was targeted by the Kinahan cartel after he had been accused of keeping their money. Thompson had always been paranoid and was genuinely concerned that if the Kinahan gang was cleaning house then he could quite easily be a target after his release because he knew an awful lot.

Concerned about growing threats of violence, Thompson was transferred to and from a number of prisons as he served out the rest of his sentence. He spent time on a punishment regime in Cork Prison because of his 'disruptive behaviour' and also in the Midlands Prison. He would later serve the remainder of his sentence at Dublin's Mountjoy Prison.

Released from prison on 1 August 2015, Thompson returned to his mother's home in Maryland, south inner-city Dublin. Unlike many of his associates, 'Fat Freddie' had no visible means of wealth and was not listed as a property owner in Ireland. The suspicion, however, was that he had access to a bank account registered in a female associate's name. Though supposedly unemployed, Thompson was still able to travel around Europe, stay in the best hotels and hire his own personal drivers.

Freddie's release caused major security concerns for gardaí, as, worried about the murders of the two Kavanagh brothers and the breakdown in relations between Gary Hutch and Daniel Kinahan, the scared gangster decided to remain in Dublin, avoiding the cartel HQ in Estepona. As his paranoia grew, gardaí believe he was constantly in disguise and staying at different safe houses around the city.

A week later, gardaí received intelligence that he had spent a few days in Tenerife before travelling to Birmingham. Thompson obviously decided he was safer in the UK than in Dublin, as he remained there under the protection of Thomas 'Bomber' Kavanagh and Maurice Sines.

Around the same time, intelligence reports revealed that a meeting had been held in the Spanish capital, Madrid, between Christy Kinahan, his sidekick John Cunningham, Gerry Hutch, his brother Patsy and other Hutch associates. The aim of the meeting was to broker a deal between Daniel Kinahan and Gary Hutch. In return for Gary's safety, the Hutch representatives agreed to pay €200,000 in compensation to Daniel Kinahan for the shooting outside his apartment in Spain the previous year, in which the innocent boxer Jamie Moore had been injured.

Once the deal had been brokered, Gary Hutch, who had remained in Amsterdam under the protection of associates of the Hutch gang, returned to the Costa del Sol. However, unlike in previous years, Hutch did not have the support of his friend and former flatmate Freddie Thompson. In the view of one investigator in Spain:

When Hutch went back to Spain, he was increasingly isolated and no longer had Freddie Thompson by his side. Nobody seems to know why he went back because the distrust between him and Daniel Kinahan would always be there. Gary Hutch must have felt safe because he had his uncle, who was a big player on the underworld scene and went back a long way with Christy Kinahan, negotiating on his behalf.

Staying at an apartment at the Angel de Miraflores complex in Estepona, Hutch's background was unknown to many of his neighbours, with one resident describing him as 'pleasant and quiet'. Hutch spent his days at Daniel's gym, going for runs and smoking cannabis, but his decision to trust the cartel would prove to be fatal.

On 24 September 2015, at around 11.20 a.m., Gary Hutch was ambushed by a gunman, but as he attempted to open fire the contract killer's weapon jammed. Hutch seized the opportunity and fled for his life. CCTV footage caught Hutch's obvious panic as he ran towards the back gate of the complex and realized it was firmly closed and locked. As he turned to run in another direction the shooter opened fire, hitting Hutch in the back. Lying on the ground, Gary Hutch yelled: 'No, no' before the killer fired the final bullet into his body.

In the days after the murder, Hutch's good friend Freddie Thompson kept a low profile in the UK as the finger of suspicion pointed in one direction only – towards the Kinahan cartel.

The gang's involvement in the killing would later be proven when a long-term Thompson associate, James Quinn, was identified as a member of the hit team after his DNA was found in the gunman's getaway car. A former boxer, Quinn had once shared a cell with his victim's brother, Derek 'Del Boy' Hutch. He'd also acted as an enforcer for Thompson's gang before relocating to Spain around 2009. Making frequent trips back to Dublin at Thompson's behest, Quinn had built up a reputation as someone not to be crossed. It was no surprise to gardaí that he had been summoned to work for the Kinahans at their base on the Costa del Sol or that he'd assassinated a former friend. One garda source said:

> Thompson and Quinn go way back. They worked together in the south inner city and then they also worked together when they were in Spain. Thompson, Hutch and Quinn did a lot together and would have spent a lot of time socializing. Quinn may have been very close at one stage to Gary and his brother, but when he was given orders to target Gary, he duly obeyed them. Friendship and loyalty didn't exist when Daniel Kinahan gave the order for someone to be targeted – you did what you were told.

Under Operation Shovel, Thompson, Quinn and Hutch were often recorded making calls to each other, arranging nights out. Quinn subsequently claimed that he wasn't friendly with his victim, but a transcript from a secretly recorded call on 23 January of that year reads: 'Gary says he's going to buy a bottle of wine and a hooker from the other side of the street. James Quinn says he'll be around shortly, and Gary says he'll get two hookers to bring back.'

On another occasion, when Thompson and Hutch were socializing, Hutch rang Quinn to come to a pub to 'sort out two guys looking for trouble'.

Despite stating that he was with a prostitute on the morning of Hutch's killing, Quinn, who owned a yacht, drove a Bentley and had a number of luxury homes in southern

Spain, was later jailed for twenty-two years. A jury had ruled that Quinn was the getaway driver during the hit. He lost his appeal against the sentence in February 2019.

Quinn's conviction was seen as a blow to the cartel, particularly to Thompson. According to one source:

> James Quinn was one of Thompson's and Daniel Kinahan's top enforcers and he would have been very hard to replace. Quinn was recruited as a teenager to Thompson's gang because they all knew him from the south inner city. Thompson also kept on the right side of him over the years because he knew just how dangerous he was. Though Thompson's associates were suspected of targeting his uncle, Martin Foley, Quinn's loyalties still lay with the cartel – family came second.

Two weeks after Hutch's murder, gardaí received intelligence that Thompson had become increasingly paranoid. One investigator explained:

> He was under serious pressure at that moment and lost a lot of weight because he was worried that he could be next. Thompson was hoping that his family ties to major players within the cartel such as Liam Byrne would keep him alive. He also knew that there was no way associates of Hutch would let the murder go. Though he didn't trust Daniel Kinahan, his aim was to prove that he was still a vital cog in the Kinahan organization. Just like in the Crumlin and Drimnagh feud, he sided with the strongest faction. His previous relationship with Gary Hutch and other members of the Hutch family now meant nothing.

Thompson distanced himself from Gary's younger brother, Derek 'Del Boy' Hutch, after the killing. Gerry 'The Monk'

Hutch was also close to Thompson's uncle, James 'Jaws' Byrne, and had supplied the limos for Freddie's brother Richie's wedding, but the relationship didn't stop the paranoid gangster from siding with the cartel.

The Hutch and Kinahan factions braced themselves for further attacks after the murder. The cartel were preparing for war and the Kinahans ordered Thompson back to Dublin in October 2015 so he could strike back in the event of any outbreak. They also wanted to use his experience from surviving a feud. In a show of loyalty Freddie returned to Dublin immediately.

Just weeks after he got back, Thompson's feud-related experience was called upon, following the death of an innocent 21-year-old student, Lorcan O'Reilly, at a Hallowe'en bonfire in the Oliver Bond flats, in Dublin's south inner city, the childhood home of the Kinahan brothers. Lorcan, along with twenty-two other youths, was making his way to Block L of the flats complex at 2.30 a.m. on 1 November when he was confronted by a fourteen-year-old who was swinging a hurley, getting involved in a row between two other teenagers. Lorcan tried to break up the fight and managed to grab the hurley.

The teenager then shouted: 'You don't know who I am. You wanna watch who you're talking to!'

Lorcan replied: 'I don't care who you are.'

Yelling 'you watch' as he rushed off, the teenager returned minutes later armed with a knife. Approaching Lorcan, he plunged the knife into the 21-year-old's chest. As his attacker retreated, Lorcan approached him and was stabbed a second time, just below the right eye.

The teenager fled and Lorcan was brought to St James's Hospital by a local man, Mark Harris. Lorcan was pronounced dead a short time later.

At 3.55 a.m., gardaí were made aware of the incident when they were contacted by the hospital. Just ten minutes earlier, the gardaí's Command and Control section had also been contacted by a woman who claimed she had information about a stabbing at the Oliver Bond flats complex.

Within days of the killing, gardaí in Kevin Street Garda Station had identified the chief suspect as a young associate of Thompson. However, almost immediately, they encountered a wall of silence from many of the people who had witnessed the stabbing. It later emerged that when he learned about the killing Thompson sent his associates to the area to warn many of those present to remain silent. In another incident, a member of Thompson's gang was suspected of driving to the area and pointing a gun at a group of young people to frighten them. In the opinion of one source:

> It was classic Freddie Thompson. His young associate was a suspect in the killing of an innocent young man and all he cared about was his associate escaping justice. He sent his gang to Oliver Bond to warn people not to talk to the gardaí. It was the most extreme form of intimidation and people in the area were very concerned because they were aware of the suspect's links to Thompson. Thompson had terrified the people of the south inner city for years and this was just another example of it.

Despite the threats and intimidation, the investigation team, led by Detective Inspector Paul Cleary and Detective Superintendent Peter O'Boyle, who would go on to lead major investigations into Thompson, had secured CCTV footage which would form a key part of their case. In a later submission to the Director of Public Prosecutions, gardaí concluded: 'The intimidation of witnesses in the case started immediately with messages subtly delivered to residents in Oliver Bond House not to co-operate with gardaí. Potential witnesses knew the calibre of the culprit which was incentive enough to remain silent.'

Detectives, however, received a boost when five witnesses ignored Thompson's threats and made statements. In their statement, one of the witnesses who had been shown CCTV footage outlined their concerns because of the suspect's links to Thompson when they said: 'I named him but I'm afraid now. I am afraid of my life because of who he's connected to.' Another witness would later reveal how she heard the young thug say about Lorcan: 'I'm going to kill him.'

As part of their case, gardaí also asked for the identities of the witnesses to remain anonymous in the event of any trial:

> It is proposed to redact the identities of these people. Their account of what happened on the night in question will be fully disclosed in the Book of Evidence for the defence to examine. There is a duty of care to protect these witnesses and, as this is a fluid situation, gardaí are monitoring for any escalation in intimidation. This aspect will be under constant review and any necessary steps will be taken to protect witnesses and preserve the integrity of the case.

In another submission to the DPP, detectives stated: 'This was a senseless killing by an angry young child. It would appear that both parties slighted each other prior to the calculated but catastrophic action taken by the teenager. He has at no time expressed the slightest remorse.'

When compiling background on Lorcan, gardaí described him as a 'popular young man in the area and everybody spoken to had high praise for him', while his killer, despite his tender years, was regarded as someone who was 'well known to gardaí'. Highlighting the suspect's links to Thompson, detectives subsequently asked the DPP to consider holding any future trial in the non-jury Special Criminal Court:

> There is no suggestion to terrorism or threats to the State, this recommendation is made with a firm eye on the organized-crime element involved in this case. Although only fifteen, the suspect's connection to organized crime is indisputable. He is an associate of Freddie Thompson who was one of the main protagonists in one of the nation's worst gangland feuds over the last fifteen years. He is associated with a notorious international criminal, Christopher Kinahan, who is now in a major gangland feud with the Hutch family. Access to resources, including firearms, personnel and money to maintain a wall of silence, is readily available.

Gardaí outlined further concerns when they stated: 'Due to a possible sentence upon conviction and the fact that most of the eye witnesses are very accessible, there is a huge incentive to either intimidate witnesses or interfere with a jury.'

As Thompson's young associate went to ground following the killing, Lorcan's violent death sparked widespread revulsion in the local community. Hundreds of people turned up for the student's funeral on 11 November. Speaking at the service, Fr Richie Good from the Augustinian Church in south inner-city Dublin hailed Lorcan as a 'peacemaker': 'All we can do is cry, and ask the question why did this happen? The reason it happened was Lorcan was true to his nature. Lorcan was a peacemaker. It was acting as peacemaker that brought on this tragedy that cost him his life.'

A few days before the funeral, Fr Niall Couglan, from the south inner city, also condemned knife crime when he said:

'To pull a knife on someone is a sneaky and cowardly act. It is not manly – it is weak. It is dangerous and it is savagery on a scale that is hard to comprehend.'

The local community's reaction didn't affect 'Fat Freddie'. In the weeks after the violent stabbing, according to one investigator, gardaí received intelligence that Thompson had been 'schooling' the young teenager in the event of an arrest:

> There was a suggestion that the teenager wanted to come clean, but when Thompson got his claws into him he was told to reply 'no comment' to every question if he was arrested. Thompson was clearly passing on his own experience and it didn't matter that an innocent young man was dead.

Thompson continued to shield his young apprentice, awaiting developments in the case, but he soon had other serious problems to contend with.

11. War Games

Those involved in serious organized crime, people like Freddie Thompson, could be friends one minute and sworn enemies the next. There is a lot of paranoia out there – they're under pressure all the time, from the gardaí and from each other.

Former Assistant Garda Commissioner
Michael O'Sullivan

Liam 'Bop' Roe had once told gardaí he was 'done' with Thompson, but, in reality, he remained loyal to his first cousin after Freddie's release from prison in August 2015. He was regarded by gardaí as a 'trusted lieutenant' of the Kinahan cartel, because of his family connections to Thompson and the Byrne family, and detectives were not surprised when a gunman, suspected of being a member of the Hutch gang, attempted to kill Roe on 6 November 2015. Roe was smoking a cigarette outside the Red Cow Moran Hotel in Clondalkin, Dublin, as the hitman approached and pulled the trigger. The weapon jammed and Roe, along with other senior cartel figures standing nearby, ran for their lives.

Gardaí were in no doubt the failed assassination bid was the revenge attack they had been expecting for the murder of Gary Hutch. It would not be the last attempt at payback – and 'Fat Freddie' knew he was a prime target. Reporting on the incident in the *Herald*, on 9 November 2015, the crime journalist Ken Foy wrote how detectives had received intelligence that associates of Gary Hutch had planned to murder 'anyone' with links to the Kinahan faction. A security source confirmed:

> Thompson would have been at the top of any hit list drafted by the Hutch gang because of his close ties to Gary and other members of the Hutch family over the years. Many on the Hutch side believed Thompson would have known about the plan to kill Gary but did nothing about it. They would always regard him as a traitor and he would always be a target for them.

As Thompson and his allies prepared for war after the attack on Roe, an associate of Gerry Hutch and former IRA member, Daithi Douglas, was left seriously injured after he was shot three times close to his home in Killala Road in Cabra, north Dublin, on 8 November. Suspicion immediately centred on the Kinahan cartel because of Douglas's previous links to Gerry Hutch.

Remaining preoccupied with the predicament of his young apprentice, however, Thompson booked two tickets on a flight to Heathrow Airport, London, on 22 December. From there, gardaí believed Thompson and Lorcan's killer travelled on to Gran Canaria and spent Christmas at the Servatur Casablanca hotel in Puerto Rico.

The garda inquiry into the attempt on Roe's life was ongoing and the cartel were running a parallel investigation. The gang had received information that a convicted drug dealer, Darren Kearns, was one of two gunmen involved in the attack. A few days after Christmas, Kearns became a target for a hit team recruited by the cartel.

On the evening of 30 December, while Thompson and

his young associate were enjoying the festivities in Gran Canaria, Kearns, thirty-three years old, was shot dead in front of his wife as they left a restaurant in Blackhorse Avenue, north Dublin. Though Kearns was blamed by the cartel for the attempt to kill Roe, gardaí would later establish that he was at another Dublin location at the time of the shooting, but, in gangland, rumours and the word of an associate were enough to get someone killed.

Tensions continued to rise following the murder of Kearns. A failed attempt by Eamonn Cumberton – a member of INLA and Kinahan contract killer – to target Gerry 'The Monk' Hutch as he drank in a bar in Lanzarote over the festive season did nothing to ease the situation. Hostilities flared again after a knife attack on Gary Hutch's brother Derek in prison.

Thompson's focus, however, remained fixed on protecting his young associate and they returned to Dublin on New Year's Eve. A few days later, on 3 January 2016, Thompson, along with Lorcan O'Reilly's killer, was a passenger in a black Range Rover being driven by his brother Richie, when they were stopped by gardaí. Thompson immediately engaged with officers saying: 'Jesus, guard, don't be sneaking up on me. I thought I was gonna get one in the back of the head.'

In their exchange with Thompson, the officers recorded how the criminal had 'lost a lot of weight, had a full beard but was in good form'. His young associate, who had two black eyes, a swollen nose and cuts to his face, informed the patrol team that he had 'fallen from his bike'. Gardaí later established, however, that the teenage killer had been attacked in a pub by friends of Lorcan O'Reilly.

The following day Thompson and his young associate boarded a flight to Düsseldorf, Germany. From there, the pair made their way to Amsterdam. In the words of a security source:

> Thompson was obsessed with protecting this young fella because he didn't want him going to prison. He knew there was still a lot of anger in the community over the O'Reilly killing and he was determined to keep the lad out of Dublin until things calmed down. He also knew there was a war brewing and that he too could have been targeted by the Hutch gang or even his own associates, who saw him as a liability. He'd only been out of prison a number of months, but he had chaos, death and carnage follow him everywhere he went. He was a man who claimed to be unemployed and he was travelling around Europe. His young associate should have been in school yet here he was travelling all over the place with one of Europe's most dangerous criminals.

After spending a month in the Dutch capital, Thompson and his young associate returned to Ireland on the day that would change the gangland landscape in Ireland for ever.

By the time Thompson, who carried a bulletproof vest in his luggage, and Lorcan O'Reilly's killer landed in Dublin Airport at 8.10 p.m. on 5 February 2016, his first cousin and key member of his inner circle, David Byrne, was dead. Byrne, the cartel's boss, Daniel Kinahan, and other senior gang figures had gathered at the Regency Hotel in north Dublin for a weigh-in ahead of the 'Clash of the Clans' event at Dublin's National Boxing Stadium on 6 February 2016. As the event got under way, a dissident Republican, Kevin Murray, along with his accomplice, who was dressed as a woman, fired shots into the air, causing panic among the spectators, including children. As cartel figures ran for their lives, three gang members, armed with AK47 assault rifles and dressed up as officers from the

Emergency Response Unit, swept through the hotel hunting their prey – Daniel Kinahan. As Christy Kinahan's heir was brought to safety by his bodyguards, David Byrne was cornered in the hotel lobby and shot six times. A senior cartel associate, Sean McGovern, and his friend Aaron Bolger were both shot in the legs, but survived.

Lasting a mere two minutes, the most daring attack in Irish gangland history made headlines around the world. It led to gardaí, backed by the real Emergency Response Unit, flooding the capital with officers.

Reeling from the loss of one of their most senior Irish members, 'Fat Freddie' Thompson and other key cartel figures were summoned to a pub in Dublin's south inner city the following day. In attendance were Daniel Kinahan, the enforcer Paul Rice and Byrne's devastated older brother, Liam. Rice was one of the cartel's closest associates and had been working as an enforcer for them for years, collecting debts from their customers.

Still unsure of his position within the cartel, Thompson received the assurance he so desperately craved when he was appointed to lead the war against Gerry Hutch. The targets included associates of 'The Monk', as well as anyone even remotely connected to the veteran criminal. In the analysis of one investigator:

> The Regency Hotel attack probably saved Freddie Thompson's life. Before David Byrne's killing, Freddie was on thin ice because he was seen as a liability by senior cartel figures and he was someone who was expendable. The only thing that was keeping him alive was the fact of his family ties to the Byrnes and because he did what he was told. When the Regency happened, having Freddie Thompson out of prison

was a major boost to Daniel Kinahan because the cartel now had an asset who was both loyal and thrived on this type of mayhem. They knew Thompson was someone who loved violence, but, more importantly for them, someone who had the experience of organizing murders, participating in murders and arranging the logistics for attacks. Freddie Thompson was also someone who had survived the Crumlin and Drimnagh feud, and his expertise in this field would be necessary as the Kinahan side went to war against the Hutch Organized Crime Group and anyone connected to the Hutch side.

Daniel Kinahan returned to the sanctuary of his headquarters in southern Spain following his council of war. He didn't have long to wait before the cartel's killing machine swung into action. Just three days after Byrne's murder, and despite a huge garda presence in the capital, Eddie Hutch, a taxi driver and Gerry's older brother, was shot dead at his home in Ballybough, north inner-city Dublin. He was regarded by many as a soft target, and his assassination was the beginning of a killing spree organized by Thompson and his associates.

Following a car chase just minutes after Hutch's murder, Thompson and his first cousin Liam 'Bop' Roe were arrested by gardaí. A team from the Burglary Response Unit had activated their siren, after noticing that the front-seat passenger in a red Audi A5 was wearing a hat and scarf over his face. They had signalled the Audi to stop, but the car sped off. It was later stopped by officers at the junction of Cork Street and St Luke's Avenue in Dublin's south inner city. Thompson fled from the stationary vehicle, but he was arrested a few minutes later close to the Coombe Hospital. Accused of resisting arrest, both Roe and Thompson were brought to Kevin Street Garda Station for a drugs search. 'Fat Freddie' told gardaí that he had given 'instructions to Liam Roe not to stop'. Thompson's clothes were seized during the search, as small spatters of blood were identified on his tracksuit bottoms. The clothes were sent to the detectives investigating the murder of Eddie Hutch, but the blood was later identified as Thompson's, ruling him out as a potential suspect.

A few days later, Thompson and his cousins Liam and James Byrne were watched every step of the way by the Emergency Response Unit as David Byrne's remains were returned to his family at their home in Raleigh Square, Crumlin, south Dublin. Due to the heightened tensions, the Byrne family in conjunction with the gardaí had decided to hold his body at a secret location outside Dublin. Gardaí feared that the Hutch gang, who according to intelligence reports had access to grenades and were being supported by dissident Republicans from Northern Ireland, were planning to target members of the Byrne family. Waiting outside while his cousin's remains were brought into the heavily fortified house, Thompson was then driven to the residential area of Rathfarnham in south Dublin. Once there, the criminal, who was wearing a bulletproof vest, green baseball cap, jeans and a hi-vis jacket was stopped by gardaí. Detectives had received intelligence that Thompson and his gang had access to a safe house in the leafy suburb. In the car they identified Thompson, a cartel associate, Gareth Chubb, who was carrying €900 in cash, the killer of Lorcan O'Reilly and another young man from the south inner city who would go on to kill for Thompson and his paymasters. Gardaí recorded that all four were 'acting nervy and were uncooperative'.

With gardaí on high alert ahead of the Byrne funeral, Thompson's position in the cartel's inner circle was evident when he headed to Dublin Airport to collect Daniel Kinahan and his younger brother, Christopher Jnr, as they flew in from Faro, Portugal. On their way to the airport, Thompson and his older brother Richie, who has no criminal convictions, were stopped in the Islandbridge area of south Dublin, under 'Operation Hybrid'. The 'Hybrid' initiative had been launched by gardaí across the city and involved armed officers setting up checkpoints close to the homes of those linked to the two feuding factions. Gardaí discovered that both men were wearing bulletproof vests and they found two jackets and another three bulletproof vests in the boot, along with three baseball caps under the driver's seat. One officer on the team commented: 'It was not unusual for someone like Freddie Thompson to have different items of clothing in a car. He was constantly changing his appearance then because he knew he was a major target.' Earlier that day, he had also been stopped entering the Byrne family home, and the officers had found three mobile phones in his possession.

Arriving at Dublin Airport at 4.30 p.m., looking agitated, Thompson sneered menacingly at a group of reporters who had turned up to question his boss. Watched closely by armed detectives, Thompson attempted to take pictures of the reporters on his phone, before he was warned by a member of the gardaí that he would be arrested if he didn't stop.

Walking into arrivals at 5 p.m., Daniel and Christopher Kinahan were met by Thompson and brought to the waiting car, under the watchful eye of the gardaí. Before entering the vehicle, Daniel Kinahan was asked by an *Irish Sun* journalist if he had any knowledge about the murder of Eddie Hutch.

He replied: 'Please stop chasing us. Thank you.'

'Fat Freddie' kept uncharacteristically silent throughout, as he was busy constantly looking around, clearly expecting an attack. They quickly drove off, refusing to answer any questions.

On the same day as the cartel's boss, Daniel Kinahan, arrived back in Ireland, the Hutch family issued a statement via the *Sunday Times*, claiming:

> Gary had a falling out with the Kinahan organization. This matter was resolved. Gary was then murdered for no reason. You cannot trust these people. The Kinahan organization have attempted to kill Gerard on several occasions in recent months. We are being terrorized by the cartel. We believe the Kinahan drugs cartel murdered Eddie at his home in Dublin having approached him days before with demands for money.

If gardaí were unsure of Thompson's current status within the cartel, they received an affirmation of his standing when he stood alongside Daniel Kinahan and other senior associates, including Thomas 'Bomber' Kavanagh and Maurice Sines, for David Byrne's funeral service. It was held at the St Nicholas of Myra church, Francis Street, in Dublin's south inner city. In a navy suit and blue tie, Thompson was dressed similarly to other Kinahan cartel members – in an obvious show of strength.

Speaking at the funeral, Fr Martin Dolan called for an end to the violence: 'Hatred has no place in the plan of God. It is so anti-Christ it belongs in the realm of evil. And the greatest evil is the wanton destruction of human life. Hatred destroys not just the hated but the hater.'

Following the service, which was attended by over 1,000 mourners, close family members, including Thompson and his associates, were brought in a fleet of eleven limousines to a reception in west Dublin. Commenting on Thompson's role at the funeral, one officer said: 'If anyone thought that he had been frozen out, then his appearance at the funeral proved he was still very much centre stage. This was extremely worrying for gardaí because a feud was his area of expertise – this is what he lived for.'

A few hours after the funeral, Thompson returned to the Byrne family home in Crumlin, south Dublin, and was again stopped by gardaí manning a checkpoint outside it. Wearing a camouflage-coloured bulletproof vest, he engaged the officers in conversation by asking a series of questions about their weapons and boasting about his own firearms training in Spain. Recording the encounter, gardaí noted that Thompson was in 'buoyant form, despite attending his friend's funeral'.

Two days later, Thompson and a young accomplice, who was being groomed to become a killer for his gang, were stopped in the Parnell Road area of south Dublin. 'Fat Freddie' admitted that neither he nor the driver were wearing seatbelts, but said this was to allow them a 'quick getaway' if they came under attack by the Hutch gang.

With an increased garda presence around Dublin and with key figures being targeted on both sides, Thompson was given the go-ahead by Daniel to take the teenager who had stabbed Lorcan O'Reilly on a trip to London. Thompson was taking no chances and wore his bulletproof vest to the airport, but passed it to an accomplice before boarding the flight. According to one detective:

In the days after the Byrne and Hutch killings, Thompson was wearing a bulletproof vest everywhere he went. It was as if he was reliving the Crumlin and Drimnagh feud, only this time it was more intense. He had ballistic vests in cars and in safe houses and he knew it was an essential part of his kit to stay alive.

Gardaí believed Thompson travelled to London before making the journey to Birmingham, where he provided an update on the feud to associates of the cartel, Thomas 'Bomber' Kavanagh and Maurice Sines. Around the same time, gardaí were also busy compiling intelligence on the main players connected to both warring factions. In their assessments of Thompson's capability to wage war against the Hutch faction, investigators believed his gang had access to over 100 weapons, including sub-machine guns, AK47 assault rifles, .38 revolvers, Glock handguns and silencers, and that he had key lieutenants tasked with importing and storing the weapons. Gardaí also established that Thompson had ten close associates and an additional twelve 'lower tier' cartel members working for him. These included young criminals, such as Nathan Foley from the south inner city, who were trying to join the gang.

In files compiled in Spain after the David Byrne murder, Spanish police collected data on the danger posed by Thompson and his associates. They claimed:

This criminal group is involved in the importation and distribution of controlled drugs, murder, firearms and serious assault. The gang are believed to have significant connections throughout Europe and especially around the city of Birmingham in England. It is estimated Freddie Thompson, the Kinahan gang and their associates have access to over 100 weapons, and they have been distributed between Thompson for murders and also to their associates. The Kinahan Organized Crime Group is offering huge sums of money to have the Hutch Organized Crime Group wiped out.

Part of Thompson's role, gardaí believed, was to attract new killers to the cartel's ranks by offering €5,000 'sweeteners' to young men desperate to make a name for themselves with the gang. For €5,000 these youngsters were prepared to murder anyone associated with the Hutch family. As part of their efforts to target senior Hutch associates, gardaí also believed that a million euros had been set aside by the cartel, with €500,000 offered for the murder of Gerry Hutch and another €500,000 for shooting a loyal Hutch associate, James 'Mago' Gately.

While Thompson and Lorcan O'Reilly's killer remained in the UK, gardaí received intelligence that Freddie had travelled to Liverpool. As one investigator described, they suspected it was part of a plan to secure support among drugs gangs in the city for the cartel's war with the Hutch faction:

Freddie Thompson was a very busy man in the early days of the feud and was most likely sent to the UK by Daniel Kinahan to drum up support among their associates in some of England's biggest cities. During his time in Birmingham, he also made regular trips to Liverpool with the Byrnes. The Byrnes were massive Liverpool supporters and would regularly attend games when they were meeting associates to arrange drugs shipments. Thompson and the Byrnes knew Liverpool well and had built up connections to major gangs there over the years. Freddie was instructed to throw money at the feud in return for support and he was simply following orders. Thompson would also have known that Gerry Hutch had connections to Liverpool, so they were simply getting in first.

As gardaí continued to flood the streets of both the north and south inner-city areas of Dublin, sixty-one people on both sides of the feud were officially warned by officers that their lives were in danger and given Garda Information Message (GIM) forms. Among those officially warned was Freddie Thompson, when he and Lorcan O'Reilly's killer returned to Ireland from the UK on 1 March 2016. Gardaí noted that for Thompson receiving a GIM was a common occurrence:

> He knew the drill and often laughed when the forms were delivered to him. Gardaí were simply following protocol, but it didn't seem to bother him because he had been living under threat from one gang or another since his teenage years. He had somehow managed to survive his feud with Rattigan and also with Declan Duffy and must have received dozens of GIM forms over the years. To people like him they were often seen as a badge of honour.

With armed officers a feature of everyday life in the north and south inner-city areas of Dublin at that time, investigators from the gardaí's Drugs and Organised Crime Bureau, established in March 2015, were working tirelessly with local detective and uniformed units to prevent further loss of life.

Former Assistant Garda Commissioner Michael O'Sullivan investigated the activities of Christy Kinahan in the 1980s. O'Sullivan is now running the international anti-drugs-trafficking agency Maritime Analysis and Operation Centre in Lisbon, Portugal. On 1 February 2019, the EU-funded centre recovered cocaine worth €800 million, the largest maritime drugs bust ever made. Former Assistant Garda Commissioner O'Sullivan outlined how Thompson was one of the gardaí's main targets in the early days of the feud:

Freddie Thompson would certainly have been high up the food chain at that time but none of these criminals were invincible or indestructible. People need to be reminded that there are no untouchables out there. Some of them believe their own hype and propaganda. Those involved in serious organized crime, people like Freddie Thompson, could be friends one minute and sworn enemies the next. There is a lot of paranoia out there – they're under pressure all the time, from the gardaí and from each other. If serious players are locked up this can cause serious disruption to their group. If someone who plays a key role within a gang is arrested this can lead to them imploding. Gardaí have shown they have the capacity to disrupt and dismantle the gangs.

Thompson was well aware that he was a key target for the gardaí, and he flew back to London again the day after receiving the GIM. With his return ticket booked for 10 March, he would arrive back home ready and willing to cause more murder and mayhem.

12. Marshalling the Troops

> While the feud continues, all garda members, from
> the uniformed community officers to the specialist
> and tactical responders, will maintain a local,
> national and international relentless pursuit of
> those involved at all levels.
>
> Assistant Garda Commissioner Pat Leahy

In the weeks following David Byrne's funeral Thompson was regularly stopped by gardaí wearing elaborate disguises and often a bulletproof vest. It was a way of life he seemed to have become accustomed to in his almost two decades of involvement in organized crime, both at home and abroad. Despite telling gardaí that he would 'sort that out myself' when warned his life was in danger and often laughing in the faces of officers delivering official garda warnings of a death threat, Thompson was clearly taking the threat to his life seriously. Constantly looking over his shoulder, Freddie Thompson, Gary Hutch's former best friend, knew he was one of the main targets for the Hutch gang and he took measures to keep his family safe.

On one occasion, gardaí on patrol in the south inner city had stopped a woman who was standing outside Thompson's family home in Loreto Road, Maryland. When questioned, she informed the officers that she was at the property to meet a builder. Gardaí then established Thompson's plans to install steel reinforced bars behind a hall door in his mother's house, which had been the target of bomb and gun attacks during the Crumlin–Drimnagh feud. Though rarely staying there, Thompson was taking no chances. Ironically, Freddie's female associate required the help of the two cops after getting her key stuck in the front door. Taking stock of the new security measures, the detectives later recorded the details on the garda Pulse system, which records details on incidents and information, including photographs, on anyone who has been charged by gardaí. The new security measures would be useful information in the likely event of future searches at the property.

While Thompson dealt with security issues, he refused to allow these distractions to disrupt him from his main job – identifying targets for assassination so that Daniel Kinahan, Liam Byrne and the rest of the KOCG would get their revenge.

It came as no surprise to gardaí when Thompson's gang struck again on 23 March 2016. Like Eddie Hutch, Noel 'Kingsize' Duggan was an easy target. A long-term associate of Gerry 'The Monk' Hutch, Duggan, a convicted cigarette smuggler, was shot dead as he sat in his Mercedes outside his home in Ratoath, Co. Meath. The murder clearly showed that Thompson and his associates saw anyone connected to the Hutches, not just the main players, as legitimate targets. The following day – Holy Thursday – Archbishop Diarmuid Martin condemned the violence: 'When will these people learn that violence and revenge only lead to further violence and revenge? They feel that violence is their strength; yet violence will be their downfall.'

Stopped by gardaí on Good Friday, Thompson showed an attitude to the murder that was a far cry from the senior cleric's and epitomized the value he placed on human life. As officers searched the vehicle, Thompson, wearing as ever a bulletproof vest, mentioned the Duggan killing.

'What about Kingsize? I hear there won't be too many cigarettes being sold on the northside now. Ha, pushing daisies now,' Thompson laughed.

During the brief conversation he also spoke to officers about the enduring feud and mentioned a firearms seizure by gardaí.

Four days later, Thompson, again wearing a bulletproof vest, was stopped close to his home, along with his long-term associate Gareth Chubb and a young driver gardaí believed was being groomed to become a hitman. Claiming that he had been to Dublin Zoo, Thompson again referred to the Duggan murder, asking: 'What's the story with Kingsize? What's going on?', before telling gardaí he had men patrolling the Phoenix Park 'for his protection'.

Following a search of the vehicle, gardaí believed he had taken time out from the gang war to make a visit to Tayto Park, an amusement park, in Ashbourne, Co. Meath. As one source explained:

> Thompson knew he was under serious threat but yet that didn't seem to stop him visiting popular tourist attractions. He knew they were very public and it would have been very hard for someone to target him there. He was also using Dundrum Shopping Centre in south Dublin for meetings at this time because it was very open and his gang could watch any potential killer coming in.

In the weeks that followed, Thompson usually only moved around Dublin when he was surrounded by other members of the gang. Gardaí gained another insight into his paranoid and erratic behaviour on 30 March, when he was spotted by uniformed officers entering a number of shops in the Grafton Street area of central Dublin. Surprised that he seemed to be alone, officers would later report that they became 'aware' of other members of the Kinahan cartel being in the area as Thompson enjoyed his city centre stroll.

As gardaí continued to monitor the movements of Thompson and his gang, investigators from Kevin Street Garda Station received a boost when they were told by the Director of Public Prosecutions there was enough evidence to charge the gangster's young associate with killing Lorcan O'Reilly. Arrested at Kilmainham Garda Station on 31 March, the teenager was formally charged by Detective Sergeant Adrian Whitelaw. He was held in custody at the station, ahead of his appearance at Dublin District Court the following day. During his detention, Thompson repeatedly rang Kevin Street Garda Station enquiring about his apprentice's status. On a previous occasion the gangster had called to the station and had been warned over his behaviour, as he sneered at gardaí and made pig noises at officers as they went about their duties.

The pressure and tension were clearly getting to Thompson. Later that same day, gardaí were called to the Thompson family home after they received reports of a man acting suspiciously outside the property. Arriving at the scene, officers spoke to a man who claimed he was waiting for his child to come out from a nearby crèche. During the dad's conversation with gardaí, Thompson emerged from the sanctuary of his home and roared at the officers that the man had been outside his home for half an hour. They accepted the dad's story, and he later went about his business as 'Fat Freddie' went back inside his family home.

Following Thompson's young associate's court appearance on 1 April, he received bail on 8 April, as the DPP considered whether his case would be held at the Central Criminal Court, rather than the Children's Court, the following November. After the court appearance, Thompson, in his bulletproof vest and standing with two bodyguards outside the court, boasted to detectives that he was 'back home for good'.

'I know there's a threat on me but I'm staying around. I'm getting a lot of garda attention but sure won't that keep me safe?' the gangster laughed.

In sharp contrast to his paranoia of the previous day, Thompson revealed he 'felt safe' walking the streets of Dublin when he was asked about the threat to his life by a former *Irish Sun* reporter, Niall O'Connor, now crime editor with the *Irish Daily Mirror*. Pointing towards the uniformed and plain-clothes gardaí present outside the court, Thompson said: 'Looks that way, doesn't it? You'll have to ask the police that one. They're doing their job. That is what they do. They are doing their job.'

In further conversations with gardaí, the criminal then went on to talk about fishing and golf.

As Thompson remained in Dublin, he was constantly on the move. Gardaí noted that a local youth, Nathan Foley, still regarded as a 'wannabe gangster' in the south inner city, was with Thompson on many occasions when he was stopped. Another constant presence was the trainee hitman, who was acting as Freddie's permanent driver. On one occasion when the car was stopped in Dublin city centre, on 13 April, Thompson, who was wearing glasses with no lenses, claimed the trio were simply 'out for a drive'.

Later that evening, Thompson, Gareth Chubb, Foley and his personal driver were spotted by Operation Hybrid patrol officers driving in Lissadel Avenue, Drimnagh, south Dublin. When the patrol car forced the vehicle to stop, the officers discovered that Thompson had once again changed his appearance. This time he was dressed as a woman, wearing pink-framed glasses and a hat. Gardaí later recorded the drug dealer had 'appeared anxious and nervous' when questioned. Bizarrely, 'Fat Freddie' was also wearing 'black garden-style' gloves when officers talked to him, and they noted none of the other people in the car were wearing a disguise. Fearing firearms or drugs had been left in the area, gardaí later searched a number of gardens but without success.

Despite Thompson's sleeping in different places most nights, gardaí also believed he was fulfilling his Kinahan-assigned mission to identify targets for execution. His ability to do this improved when the cartel recruited members of the INLA, based in the north inner city, to help wage their war against Gerry Hutch, his associates and his family. Although Thompson had previously been targeted by the former INLA chief, Declan 'Whacker' Duffy, his differences with the group were swiftly swept aside when a leading member of the dissident Republican terror group, Jonathan Keogh, offered his services.

Gardaí believed that Eamonn Cumberton, another INLA member, and a former cage fighter, had been in the pay of the cartel for much longer, thanks to his close relationship with Thompson's friend Ross Browning, a senior gang member. According to one investigator, the cartel's arrangement with the INLA was 'simply down to money':

Even before David Byrne was killed, Eamonn Cumberton had already been recruited. But once the Regency happened it wasn't long before people like Keogh came along and offered to target members of the Hutch family. Freddie would have known about this arrangement because he was the one who was tasked with leading the war and it wouldn't have mattered to him who was doing the killing – so long as it was getting done. He was regarded by many in the cartel as a psycho who thrived on murder and because of his reputation there was a certain fear factor around him. He simply loved being involved in murder and being the big man again with Daniel Kinahan, and was out to prove a point.

In intelligence gathered by Spanish police after the Regency Hotel incident, detectives established that Keogh and Cumberton had been paid huge amounts of cash by Thompson's associates to lead the onslaught against the Hutch faction. Investigators believed:

> Keogh and Cumberton were working on a list of targets and they were given €100,000 for these. Cumberton and Keogh are very careful and surveillance-conscious. They have been to Spain and used car parks for meetings and often had bulletproof vests. They get paid different amounts depending on their roles in killings. Keogh has also been given a large amount of money by the Kinahans, who have left Ireland, and this is money for someone to be shot.

While Keogh maintained surveillance on a select group of possible targets, the investigators gleaned more valuable intelligence. They discovered that Thompson's old nemesis, Declan 'Whacker' Duffy, who was continuing to move between Dublin and his native Co. Armagh, had been approached by Cumberton to work for the gang, but he had declined the offer.

After the cartel's contracts with Keogh and Cumberton had been signed, a fellow hitman, Glen Clarke, from Co. Kildare, also offered his services to Thompson and his associates. Clarke is the chief suspect in the murder of an innocent man,

Dean Johnson, who was shot dead at Harelawn Green, Clondalkin, west Dublin, on 24 August 2013. The shooter's offer was accepted, and it wasn't long before he received his orders.

On 14 April 2016, Glen Clarke was tasked with killing a long-term associate of the Hutch gang, who the Kinahan cartel, despite having no evidence, maintained was a 'spotter' on the day of the Regency Hotel hit. Travelling by bicycle to Sheriff Street, in Dublin's north inner city, the hitman opened fire at around 12.30 p.m., as his target stood outside Noctor's pub. Standing beside the intended target was an innocent father of three and homeless man, Martin O'Rourke. As Clarke's target managed to dive between two parked cars, O'Rourke was fatally hit above the left eye. He became the first innocent victim of the feud.

Fleeing from the scene, the gunman escaped on his bike down the street, before throwing his gun into a wheelie bin.

There was widespread condemnation following the murder in broad daylight. Father Peter McVerry, a campaigner for the homeless, told RTÉ radio's *Today* show:

> He was a harmless, lovable young fellow with three children. It's a total tragedy for him, his family and friends. He did have a drug problem, but he had been trying to address it. This particular gang feud is particularly dangerous because it has become extremely personal. It's not about money. It's not about gang territory. There doesn't seem a way of stopping it. Normally you could solve one of these things with some sort of mediation – this has gone beyond that. It's a very worrying development. The only way to stop these gangs is for people to give evidence against them.

As details of the shocking murder dominated the news agenda for the day, Thompson also shared his views on the

24-year-old's killing when he was stopped by detectives in the south inner city later that evening: 'It's terrible what's happened in Sheriff Street.'

However, his concern soon ended as he provided details of the shooting: 'That young fellow got six in the back and two in the face with a 9mm.' When asked how he knew this information, he told the officers: 'Ah I just heard it.'

Gardaí were in no doubt, as one officer explained, that Thompson would have met the contract killer in the weeks before the murder so that they could discuss potential targets:

> Freddie was running the show, so he would have known what killers he had at his disposal. There were constant intelligence updates of him at that time being seen in the company of unknown individuals, and Clarke could have been one of them. They were all working in tandem, and it was no surprise for Thompson to talk about the weapon used in the murder.

Clarke's DNA was later found on the discarded murder weapon and he quickly emerged as the chief suspect. As gardaí worked on building a case against the hitman, Martin O'Rourke's father-in-law, Larry Power, expressed his family's grief:

> We can't go through life bearing grudges because the hatred will just consume you. We have to think of a future for the children. Martin's death was 100 per cent mistaken identity and although it's awful to think his children will grow up without their daddy, we have to do the best we can. My daughter Angeline, Martin's partner, lost a baby two weeks after Martin died – through a miscarriage – another life lost because of the trauma she's been through.

Despite the widespread condemnation of the O'Rourke murder, the war being waged by Thompson and his gang was relentless. On 25 April 2016, eleven days after O'Rourke's killing, the contract killer Eamonn Cumberton led a two-man hit team to the now closed Sunset House pub in the Hutch stronghold of Ballybough, in north inner-city Dublin. As one gunman stood guard outside at 9.30 p.m., another walked in and shot the barman, Michael Barr, seven times, including five times in the head.

Originally from Co. Tyrone, Barr was a member of the so-called new IRA, the largest dissident group in Northern Ireland, and a close associate of the Regency Hotel gunman, Kevin Murray. The cartel suspected Barr of supplying the guns used in the attack, but gardaí also believed he was targeted by Thompson and his gang because they suspected him of being one of the shooters that day. 'Fat Freddie' and his gang had been conducting their own investigation and they made their move when they received intelligence that Barr was involved, even though the barman had never been questioned by gardaí and there was no evidence linking Barr to the killing.

Local Independent councillor Nial Ring, later Lord Mayor of Dublin, said a man with special needs who was in the pub had to be carried away from the scene after he went into shock.

The murder had taken less than a minute. Cumberton and his colleagues escaped in a grey Audi, which they abandoned in Walsh Road, Drumcondra, north Dublin. The hitmen set fire to the getaway vehicle as they fled, but Detective Garda Michael Harkin discovered the vehicle and extinguished the blaze, preserving vital evidence in the process. In a later examination of the car, gardaí struck gold — recovering a

'Freddy Krueger' mask, a baseball cap, a Makarov handgun, a mobile phone and a bullet.

The following day, the former cage fighter booked an €800 ticket to Thailand but was forced to postpone his journey, as he had to obtain an emergency passport because his original was due to expire three months later.

Flying to Thailand on 27 April, Cumberton spent a month in the Far East as gardaí received intelligence naming him as one of the two men involved in the hit. When he returned to Ireland on 25 May, Cumberton was arrested by the garda team led by Detective Inspector John Bates from the Bridewell Garda Station.

Constantly responding 'No comment' during his interrogation, the former fitness fanatic made the mistake of asking for a cigarette. Once it was discarded, investigators kept the cigarette end to obtain a sample of the prisoner's DNA. The results showed a match between the DNA on the cigarette and the DNA found on the 'Freddy Krueger' mask and baseball cap recovered from the car. Cumberton's fate was sealed.

The INLA hitman was immediately charged with Barr's murder. He was held on remand until his conviction for the killing at the Special Criminal Court in Dublin on 29 January 2018. The investigation is still open as Cumberton's accomplice remains at large, even though he has been identified as a suspect by gardaí.

Cumberton's swift arrest was a blow to Thompson's killing machine as it deprived him of a committed gun for hire. The Kinahans' feud leader also suffered another setback when investigators probing the Barr assassination identified a man suspected of providing logistical support to Thompson's band of killers. By examining CCTV footage from the central Dublin area, detectives established that the phone recovered from the Audi used in the Barr murder had been bought at the Ilac Shopping Centre by Martin Aylmer, from Marino, north Dublin. Like many young men over the years, the 31-year-old Aylmer owed money to Thompson's gang because of an unpaid debt. When he couldn't pay in cash, as one source explained, he was told there were other ways to cancel his debt:

> Aylmer was from the north inner city, but he was also close to younger members of Thompson's gang in the south inner city. When he couldn't repay his debts he simply offered his services to gangs of killers roaming the streets. He was a main logistics man for Freddie Thompson and others during the early months of the feud. He was easily manipulated and was clearly expendable.

During their investigations into the Eddie Hutch murder, codenamed 'Operation Raglan', detectives had identified Martin Aylmer as a suspect. On that occasion, he was suspected of allowing the killers to store weapons at a lock-up he had in Dorset Street, north inner-city Dublin. Gardaí also believed the same lock-up was used by Cumberton in the Barr killing.

Aylmer was later charged over the Barr murder and admitted to participating in, or contributing to, activity intending to facilitate the commission by a criminal organization or any of its members of a serious offence. It was the first time someone had been convicted of the offence. He received a sentence of two years and nine months for facilitating a criminal organization. The DPP later appealed the leniency of the sentence and a decision is pending.

Reflecting on the case, Assistant Garda Commissioner Leahy reminded young men of the risks attached to organized crime:

This case shows what happens when young men get involved in this feud. This man is right in the middle of the feud and now he has a serious conviction that will be with him for the rest of his life. He will be seen as a liability to one side and an arch-enemy to the other side. I also welcome the fact gangland legislation has been used in this case and it won't be the last time it will be used as our investigations continue.

Chief Superintendent Sean Ward, from the gardaí's North Central Division, also welcomed Aylmer's conviction: 'This demonstrates individuals who participate in activities that facilitate the commission of a serious crime by a criminal organization will be fully investigated.'

Following Cumberton's conviction, Michael Barr's sister, Noleen, provided a stark reminder of the trauma experienced by families caught up in the feud. She told Joe Duffy on RTÉ radio's *Liveline* programme: 'This has torn our family apart. It's left a huge hole behind and we'll never get him back. This death has destroyed us all and has left us devastated and distraught.' She also said: 'I sat and watched Eamonn Cumberton on the day of the verdict. I have no hatred towards him.'

Speaking after Cumberton received his life sentence, Assistant Garda Commissioner Leahy warned that the feud was still affecting families across Dublin:

The feud hasn't gone away, it's not over. We would be silly to say that it was. There is every effort to bring them to justice and we expect in the long run that will happen. We talked about dismantling this organization and we will dismantle this organization. We take no satisfaction from the verdict in this case. Unfortunately, there are no winners in this case as it represents a race to the bottom for those who get involved in such activities. While the feud continues, all garda members, from the uniformed community officers to the specialist and tactical responders, will maintain a local, national and international relentless pursuit of those involved at all levels.

Referring to key figures in the feud, such as 'Fat Freddie' Thompson, the senior officer added:

Some of the people we are looking at are not mere foot soldiers, they are key people in this organization. We are sorry that it has been visited on communities. We have seen the level of violence in the north inner city over many years. It was the frequency of violence that caught everybody. We have a lot of live investigations ongoing at the moment in relation to several incidents before the courts. This is not finished, it has not gone away, and we have to stay well focused on this — we will stay well focused.

It was a promise that would haunt Thompson in the months ahead.

13. Contract Killers

You have taken away my will to live, you have broken
my spirit. Not only did you take my son, you have
taken away a brother, uncle, friend and most of
all a daddy.

Vera Hutch

The Kinahan–Hutch feud is widely regarded as one of the
most intense gangland feuds in Irish history because of the
volume of people killed within a short period of time. It was
no surprise to surveillance teams that by the end of April 2016
Thompson decided he needed a break from his daily routine
of trying to stay alive and his continued interaction with
gardaí. On 30 April, just five days after the murder of Michael
Barr, 'Fat Freddie' left Dublin on a quick visit to Benalmádena,
southern Spain.

During his two-day visit to the region, Thompson spent
his days socializing in bars before returning to Ireland on
2 May. Unlike his previous visits to Spain, there would be no
long-term stay, as Thompson's area of expertise was needed
in Dublin. He met up with the Byrnes and Liam Roe shortly
after he got back to discuss tactics.

On 6 May 2016, Thompson was stopped by detectives
from Kilmainham Garda Station, as he walked down
Rosary Road, Maryland, south inner-city Dublin. Wearing
a black flat cap, dark jeans, a bulletproof vest and black,

thick-rimmed glasses, Thompson co-operated with gardaí as he was searched. He provided an insight into life inside the middle of a gangland feud, telling cops it was 'tough trying to stay alive'. During the brief exchange with gardaí, Thompson's need to boast soon surfaced when he asked if the garda 'Tetra' radio system was linked to other areas of Dublin and if gardaí would know whether there was a shooting in another part of the city.

'This was yet another example of Thompson's bravado,' insisted one investigator. 'He was simply taunting gardaí by insinuating there would be further violence.'

Thompson's interest in the garda radio system, however, also came at a time when investigators suspected his associates were making bogus 999 emergency calls. It was a tactic often used by feuding gangs, as a way of testing garda response times. One such incident occurred on 9 May 2016, when gardaí responded to two separate telephone calls claiming shots had been fired in the Maryland area of the south inner city. Arriving at Our Lady's Road, officers were greeted by a smiling Thompson, minus his bulletproof vest, standing in the doorway of his sister Lisa Jane's home.

The bogus 999 calls were yet another example of his reckless behaviour. Gardaí had a duty to respond to these calls, but it was also a waste of resources and taxpayers' money and meant people in real emergencies could have been deprived of a frontline service. The calls were nothing new and were just an example of the steps Thompson was taking to arrange further hits on his enemies.

As tensions continued to grow, gardaí received intelligence that the gangster and his associates had been barred from a number of pubs in the area. Those told to stay away included Liam Roe, Liam Byrne and his father, James, along with younger members of the gang. As one local resident, who did not want to be named, recounted:

> His associates were asked nicely if they would keep away because people were genuinely concerned about someone coming into a bar and spraying the place with a machine gun. Freddie Thompson and his associates liked a drink, but even he knew he would have been a target if he was sitting in a pub all night. It was very often the case that when Thompson or his associates walked into a pub, people walked out. It was a very tense time in the south inner city. He used to come into bars wearing bulletproof vests and it was as if he was telling people he was a target. How could anyone enjoy a drink in that atmosphere?

Thompson would make his feelings on the pub bans known on 14 May 2016. No sooner had he arrived at a bar in the Rialto area, with his associate Gareth Chubb, driver Nathan Foley and north Dublin associate Graham Gardiner, than the group was asked to leave. Gardiner remains on the run after he was charged with possessing two MP9 machine guns, two silencers, two loaded Smith & Wesson firearms, two silencers and four loaded magazine clips. Calmly leaving the bar and walking to the other side of the road, Thompson waited as two junior members of the gang poured lighter fluid over a car bonnet outside the pub. The gangster was then seen laughing as he was collected in another car before leaving the area. No complaint was made by anyone in the bar. Gardaí launched a criminal-damage investigation, but they did not have enough evidence to press charges.

The garda focus at the time was on preventing further attacks from Thompson, his associates and the Hutch faction, but detectives were also made aware of a threat to

Thompson from a close associate of his old nemesis, Brian 'King Ratt' Rattigan. While being transported to Mountjoy Prison, Dublin, on 15 May 2016, the inmate, who cannot be named for legal reasons, started talking about the recent spate of killings. He then informed prison officers that both he and his cousin had almost been killed on Cashel Road, Crumlin, by members of the Kinahan cartel. When asked who had tried to kill him, he refused to divulge their identities, adding: 'Don't worry, it will be sorted out between ourselves.'

Continuing with his rant, the prisoner also spoke openly about his hatred for Thompson and said: 'Everyone is looking forward to the party that will be coming shortly when the fat fuck Thompson is put into a box. Thompson does not have long left. People would need to be careful aligning themselves with his group.' It was a timely example of the hatred that several criminals in Dublin had for Thompson because of the many rows he had been involved in over the years.

Ten days later, the threat posed by Thompson stretched to Finglas, when a petty criminal stopped by gardaí under Operation Hybrid claimed he had been forced to move to the north Dublin suburb as there was a threat on his life from Thompson.

The people of Dublin were also reminded of 'Fat Freddie' and his gang when a frontline garda, Alan Cummins, based at Kilmainham Garda Station, warned of further attacks. Speaking at the Garda Representatives Association's 38th Annual Conference in Killarney, Co. Kerry, after the Barr killing, Garda Cummins stated:

> Gardaí are overworked and underpaid – but we are more than willing to step up to the plate, provided adequate resources are provided by the Government. We are dealing with extremely

dangerous people who have no regard for human life and will stop at nothing to carry out further murders and attacks.

The Hutch family didn't have long to wait before Garda Cummins's warning of further bloodshed became a reality. On 24 May 2016, Gerry 'The Monk' Hutch's 35-year-old nephew, Gareth, was shot dead outside the Avondale House complex, in north inner-city Dublin. Just like his Uncle Eddie, Gareth was an easy target and he was not considered by gardaí to be a member of any organized-crime gang.

Aware that his relationship to Gerry Hutch made him a marked man, the father of one had expressed concerns for his safety just two days before the shooting, in a conversation with his local representative, Nial Ring. Councillor Ring remembered:

He told me he had been threatened and he wanted to come in and see me, to see if I could help. He was meant to come in yesterday but there was no sign of him. I will offer any advice to anyone who feels under threat. The Hutch family have lots of relatives in this area and they're all very concerned for their safety. Gareth's main concern was that he didn't want to be targeted in front of his son and, unfortunately, he never got the chance to move from his flat.

While aware he was under threat from the Kinahan cartel, Hutch had no idea his former neighbour and INLA member, Jonathan Keogh, had been paid a fortune to wage war against the Hutch family. The night before the murder, Keogh's sister Regina had encouraged her friend Mary McDonnell, who lived just yards from the target, to allow her brother, and his getaway driver, Thomas Fox, to use her property as a base. From McDonnell's home they were able to monitor the movements of their target and also to clean the Makarov pistols to be used in the murder. After Regina wrongly claimed that her brother Jonathan had been threatened by Gareth Hutch, Mary allowed the kill team to take up position in her flat. Watching as Hutch walked to his car, Keogh and a second gunman ran behind their target and opened fire, hitting Gareth twice in the neck, once in the lower back and also in the upper chest. The entire incident was captured on CCTV and the killers could be seen running from the scene.

Speaking at Gareth Hutch's funeral, Fr Paddy Madden told mourners how the Hutch family had, once again, been 'numbed by grief and sadness':

> Fear, pain, grief, anguish, bewilderment are experienced by the family. Every tragedy has a human face. Beyond analysis, comment and speculation we have pain and tears. Breaking the cycle of violence is not easy. It needs courage, restraint, goodwill and the right reason – and a desire for peace.

Ending the cycle of violence was not on the cartel's agenda. Instead, it was ramping up its campaign against the Hutch family with the gang's foot soldiers in Dublin's north inner city often issuing verbal threats in the street. This would soon be followed by graffiti on gable walls across the neighbourhood, branding the Hutch side 'Rats'.

Within hours of the killing, rumours swept through the local community naming Jonathan Keogh as one of the gunmen and Thomas Fox as the getaway driver. Gardaí also had their own intelligence suggesting who was involved. Struggling to cope with his involvement in the murder, Fox handed himself into gardaí. Jonathan Keogh, however, had headed to the UK. The second gunman, an INLA member from north Dublin, was also on the move, making his way to Turkey.

In the weeks before the killing, gardaí believed Freddie Thompson was working closely with Keogh – identifying targets. The list of people the Kinahan gang wanted dead included Gareth Hutch, a friend of Gerry Hutch's previously targeted by the Criminal Assets Bureau, an associate of Noel 'Kingsize' Duggan, the barman Michael Barr and a criminal based in Co. Meath. While Keogh's close associate and fellow INLA member Eamonn Cumberton had successfully assassinated Barr, Keogh had turned his attention to his neighbour. Investigators suspected that Keogh had received €30,000 after the murder, before being dispatched by Thompson to Co. Tyrone, to start surveillance on another target, the Regency Hotel shooter Kevin Murray. According to one investigator:

> Keogh was on a wage and there was some intelligence before the Gareth Hutch murder that he was making trips to County Tyrone to watch Murray's movements. It looks like he only pulled out of that murder because the PSNI [Police Service of Northern Ireland] were also keeping close tabs on Murray. Keogh would never get the chance to target Murray as the Regency shooter later died from motor neurone disease.

Gardaí also suspected Keogh was one of six main killers recruited by Thompson and his associates in the aftermath of the Regency Hotel hit, with one senior investigator asserting:

> Keogh was the head of a murder team contracted by the Kinahan cartel for one purpose only – to carry out murder. His team of killers were aligned to the INLA and were on a wage to kill as many people as possible. Before the Gareth Hutch killing, he would have met with people like Freddie Thompson to plan further attacks. Keogh joined a Republican organization in the middle of a peace process and had

no interest in targeting security forces in the North. It was all about money for him. It wouldn't have mattered to him that someone like Freddie Thompson was involved in drugs. It was very ironic for a so-called dissident Republican to run to the sanctuary of the UK after the murder of Gareth Hutch. Keogh personifies the disease that destroyed his own community and that is the feud – he's the true cancer. He came from that community and yet he targeted his neighbours all on behalf of people like Freddie Thompson and those who live far away in luxury. He also destroyed his own family – and this has all been done at the behest of Daniel Kinahan as he lives in his ivory tower in Dubai.

Following Keogh's departure to Co. Tyrone, gardaí received intelligence that Thompson's associates in the south inner city had been offering cash to drug addicts across the capital to commit murders. As one officer explained: 'Thompson was dealt a huge blow with Cumberton and Keogh no longer on the scene and that's why they were turning to people with drug problems to do their dirty work because they could be easily manipulated.'

Fox was charged with murder in the weeks after the killing, but it would be a further year before Regina Keogh was charged. As she appeared at Dublin District Court on 10 June 2017, the UK's National Crime Agency was monitoring her brother's movements and he was arrested when armed police swooped in London.

The trio would later go on trial and each received a life sentence in November 2018, after they were convicted of the murder. Regina Keogh's friend Mary McDonnell was granted immunity from prosecution after co-operating with gardaí. In his judgment at the Special Criminal Court, Mr Justice

Tony Hunt said that a 'considerable amount of planning and co-ordination went into this killing. All those involved in planning are guilty of the crime of murder.'

Following the conviction, the murder victim's mother, Vera, reminded everyone of the suffering her family had endured thanks to the actions of Thompson and his associates:

> I had the privilege and honour of being Gareth's mother before he was senselessly and cruelly taken from us. It still haunts me every day. It hurts emotionally and mentally just to get out of bed in the morning. I can't sleep most nights without having a nightmare of the horrific morning of 24 May 2016. We struggle every day as a family and I can't comprehend why this happened. There are many times I have even wished that I died that moment with Gareth. You have taken away my will to live, you have broken my spirit. Not only did you take my son, you have taken away a brother, uncle, friend and most of all a daddy. I feel an enormous amount of sadness that his son loses out on having a daddy at the most critical time in his life. Gareth was denied the opportunity of watching his son grow up, he will never get to bring him to his first football game.

During the garda probe into the killing, run by investigators from the gardaí's 'U' District detective unit and North Central Division under the command of Detective Inspector Francis Sweeney, Assistant Garda Commissioner Pat Leahy and Chief Superintendent Sean Ward, officers followed 850 lines of inquiry, took 650 statements, conducted sixty-four interviews, launched nineteen searches and seized a number of firearms. Detectives also examined 40,000 hours of CCTV during the investigation.

Despite the widespread condemnation of the murder of

Gareth Hutch, Thompson remained unaffected. He was in his element running the cartel's retaliation and reliving his days in the Crumlin–Drimnagh feud. Residents of Dublin's southside were once again reminded of that feud when a key ally of Brian Rattigan, the Australian Neil 'The Highlander' Fitzgerald, was murdered. He was shot six times in the chest and head before his body was dumped in Hills Lane, Crooksling, Tallaght, west Dublin, on 5 June 2016. Locals told of their shock at the murder in the quiet country laneway. In an interview with the *Irish Sun*, one said:

> We heard rapid gunfire and assumed it was hunters in the area. You don't expect this type of thing on your doorstep. It's dreadful. That's someone's son. Whoever brought him up there knew exactly where they were going, they knew that lane. It's a very quiet area and people are shocked that this could have happened there.

Following the murder of a key Rattigan associate, Anthony Cannon, in July 2009, the 36-year-old Fitzgerald was the last remaining member of Brian Rattigan's inner circle. He had amassed seventy-seven convictions during a lengthy criminal career that included theft, armed robbery and assault. Jailed for ten years in May 2009 for possession of a firearm and production of a weapon to resist arrest, the gangland enforcer had received the sentence for pointing a Luger pistol at Kevin Street detectives Ken Donnelly, Declan Boland and Richie Kelly. The three officers later received bravery medals for their role in arresting the dangerous criminal in south inner-city Dublin on 23 July 2008.

During his time in prison, the Rattigan enforcer had repeatedly issued threats to 'wipe out' Thompson following his release. In one incident, in November 2009, he had been moved from Mountjoy Prison in Dublin to the Midlands Prison, Co. Laois, after he was attacked by associates of Thompson and warned he would be killed if he continued to make threats against his arch-enemy. However, despite the threats hanging over him, the defiant gangland enforcer had continued to tell fellow inmates that he was coming for Thompson once he was released. In the view of one senior prison source:

> Fitzgerald was obsessed about Thompson and it looked as if his plan for revenge was the only thing keeping him going in prison. He was a psycho in prison and people were afraid to challenge him because he was 6 feet 4 inches and knew how to handle himself. He remained devoted to Rattigan, despite knowing that his power had been diminished with the murders of Anthony Cannon and Gerard Eglington. Fitzgerald never forgave Thompson for the damage he caused to his friends during the feud and would have been mad enough to target Thompson, despite his close links to the Kinahan cartel and the weapons he had at his disposal.

Fitzgerald had continued to openly obsess about his gangland nemesis, but gardaí believed Thompson was also hell-bent on revenge because it had emerged that Fitzgerald's Luger pistol had been used to fire shots at Freddie's family home in 2008. Forensic tests had also established that it was the same weapon that Fitzgerald had in his possession when he was on his way to kill a key Thompson ally, Graham 'The Wig' Whelan. According to one security source:

> Freddie Thompson has a long memory and he has always vowed to kill those he suspected of targeting his family home during the feud. Thompson was up to his eyes in the

Kinahan and Hutch feud, but there's no doubt Fitzgerald would have been on his radar.

Following his release from prison, Fitzgerald had settled in Baltinglass, Co. Wicklow, as he sought to re-establish himself in the criminal underworld. Gardaí believed he was lured back to Dublin for a meeting with a former associate before being shot dead. The investigation into his murder remains open – but Thompson's associates are firmly in the frame. According to a security source:

> This murder isn't connected to the Kinahan and Hutch feud, but due to Thompson's involvement in the Crumlin and Drimnagh feud, and his determination to wipe out the remaining members of Rattigan's gang, he remains a person of interest in this case. There's a strong possibility that Thompson had a role in setting Fitzgerald up to be killed before he got to him.

While he was suspected by detectives of involvement in yet another gangland murder, Thompson was also blamed by associates of Fitzgerald, who believed he was the man who had set up the enforcer. Gardaí were made aware of the rumours in criminal circles after they received a phone call one week after the murder. In a frantic call to officers at Kilmainham Garda Station, a low-level criminal claimed he had been bombarded with calls from the few remaining friends Fitzgerald had left, accusing the caller, Thompson and a former associate of Rattigan, who later joined the Kinahan cartel, of orchestrating the murder. Terrified of being killed, the criminal told gardaí he had left his home in the south inner city and he was wearing a bulletproof vest because he was under threat.

As rumours of Thompson's involvement in the Fitzgerald murder continued to gather momentum, gardaí in Kevin Street also faced a major security headache. They had received information that Jonathan Hutch, still traumatized by the murder of his brother Gareth, was due to attend a confirmation ceremony at a church in the heart of Thompson's stronghold. Despite his family being terrorized by the cartel, Hutch, who was being targeted purely because of his name, told gardaí of his intention to attend the religious service. Mobilizing a team of armed detectives from Kevin Street Garda Station, Hutch, who has no involvement in organized crime, was collected in a garda van by detectives and brought to the church. Once there, heavily armed officers kept guard at the rear and front of the chapel during the ceremony. The incident was a reminder of the life-and-death threat the members of the Hutch family were experiencing on a daily basis, as an investigator made clear:

If members of the Hutch family wanted to attend a christening or family event, it was important gardaí knew about it so a policing plan could be put in place to protect them because the threat at that time from people like Freddie Thompson and his killers was so severe.

While the open warfare of the previous five months demanded a huge garda response on the streets, this was not the only weapon the Irish State had in its arsenal to combat the feuding gangs – as 'Fat Freddie' and his associates soon found out.

14. Operation Lamp

> We don't require people to give evidence and they are
> not required to go to court, so we would urge them
> to tell us what they know. None of these criminals
> are untouchable.
>
> Detective Chief Superintendent Pat Clavin,
> Criminal Assets Bureau

The main focus for the Irish State after the David Byrne and
Gary Hutch killings was the prevention of further loss of life
in the Kinahan–Hutch feud. Attacking on every possible
level was an essential part of the State's approach, and the
Criminal Assets Bureau was brought on board to build a
watertight case to target the gang's assets.

On 9 March 2016, investigators from the Criminal Assets
Bureau, operating under 'Operation Lamp', had raided seventeen properties linked to Thompson's gang. 'Lamp' was first
launched by former Assistant Garda Commissioner Eugene
Corcoran in 2015, before he was succeeded by Detective Chief
Superintendent Pat Clavin. It was run by a garda sergeant and
included three to four detectives, and investigators from Revenue, Social Welfare and Customs who are permanently
attached to the CAB. The Bureau's multi-agency approach,
with the team all working under the one roof in Harcourt
Square, central Dublin, ensured they had easy access to all
strands of intelligence. The operation's remit was to target the

ill-gotten gains of the criminals in the gang, including 'Fat Freddie' Thompson. The investigation team focused their attention in particular on Freddie's first cousins Liam Byrne and Liam Roe, and on their close associates. Politicians and gardaí welcomed the response, especially after the opulent displays of wealth the gang had shown at David Byrne's funeral a few weeks earlier.

Returning to Dublin from London on 10 March, Freddie Thompson was not a happy man, as at the same time his family home was being searched for evidence linking him to the gang's assets, officers were also searching Liam Byrne's company, LS Active Car Sales in the Bluebell Business Park, Old Naas Road, south Dublin. Established in June 2013 by Byrne and Sean McGovern, and registered as a car sales enterprise, the company was believed by gardaí to be a front for laundering cash and for allowing members of the gang, including Thompson, to have access to cars imported from England. The CAB team believed they were the proceeds of crime, and during the raid on the industrial unit officers seized twenty-nine high-end vehicles, worth an estimated €544,115. CAB investigators also seized six designer watches worth €83,750 and two rings worth €29,970, and froze two bank accounts containing €36,760 and €34,840 respectively – all assets were deemed to be the proceeds of crime. Other items impounded during the crackdown included a €12,000 dune buggy, bought in Marbella and previously used by Thompson on his holidays in Spain, and three electric bicycles, each worth €4,200.

In a further blow to Thompson's associates, the CAB investigators subsequently maintained four homes belonging to Liam Byrne, his sister Maria, their late brother David and Sean McGovern were also the proceeds of crime. In their submission to the High Court the CAB team maintained that the combined valuation of the assets seized during the raids was over €2 million.

As part of the thirteen affidavits the CAB team submitted to the High Court on the operation, investigators concluded: 'Freddie Thompson is a leading figure in the Liam Byrne Organized Crime Gang.' In a later High Court ruling on the case, the Honourable Ms Justice Carmel Stewart accepted the assertion by the CAB that Thompson was a key associate of the Kinahan cartel:

> It would appear that members of this organized-crime group have unlimited access to these vehicles on a continuous basis without ever actually purchasing and/or acquiring ownership of them . . . They engaged in commercial activities for the purposes of laundering the proceeds of the gang's activity, transferring wealth between the members of various organized-crime groups, providing a fleet of high-end luxury cars to members of the gang and hiding the beneficial ownership of the vehicles in question.

In further submissions to the High Court, the CAB's Operation Lamp team claimed Thompson's associates were at the 'top tier' of organized crime in Ireland:

> They are part of the wider international Kinahan Organized Crime Group which is involved in the importation and distribution of controlled firearms into this jurisdiction, the UK and mainland Europe. It has associations that facilitate international criminal activity in Europe, Asia, the Middle East and South America. The Kinahan Organized Crime Group is currently involved in a feud with the Hutch Organized Crime Group, which has resulted in the murder of a

number of people. Daniel Kinahan plays an integral part in organizing the supply of illegal drugs into Ireland. Daniel Kinahan controls a significant worldwide assets portfolio and was one of the intended targets of the Regency Hotel. This group originated in Dublin but now has interests in Spain, the Netherlands, South America and Dubai.

Accepting the CAB team's assessment of the gang, the senior judge also acknowledged the cousins' close relationship with the Kinahan cartel when she concluded:

It would appear Christopher Kinahan Snr is now resident in Dubai and that the day-to-day operations of his drug trafficking are managed and controlled by his sons. The court is satisfied, based on the evidence put before it, that Liam Byrne is a close and trusted associate of Daniel Kinahan. They have been observed together at family events, including the christening of Mr Byrne's child in June 2015.

A former CAB detective, Henry Ainsworth, who was part of the raid and search on Byrne's garage, stated: 'The investigation was aimed at Byrne because of the wealth he had amassed, but Freddie Thompson was a key member of the gang.' Referring to Thompson's uncle, James Byrne, and his wife, Sadie, the investigators contended:

The Byrne family are synonymous with organized crime in Dublin. James Byrne Snr was a previous target of the CAB and his wife, Sadie Byrne, is originally a Roe, a family with strong links to the most senior organized-crime groups in Dublin. Their children continued their legacy and their sons, David and Liam, became two senior drug traffickers in the organized-crime scene in Dublin. They [James and

Sadie] are now reliant on their child's criminality for income. Liam Byrne is a career criminal and has climbed the criminal ladder to a very senior position.

Unlike with Liam Byrne, the CAB officers were unable to establish any 'immovable or movable' property in Freddie Thompson's name. They were convinced, however, that since his teenage years, he had used others to hide the proceeds of his involvement in organized crime. According to one senior CAB source:

> Freddie was cute enough not to have any properties or assets in his name, but this didn't stop him flying around Europe or eating in the best restaurants in Dublin. Whenever he needed cash, it was readily available to him. His favourite choice of clothing used to be tracksuits but when he got out of prison in 2015 he became more fashionable and started dressing in designer clothes and even wearing a 'man bag'. There was definitely cash available to him and the investigation would also focus on trying to identify these accounts and those individuals who might have set up accounts on his behalf. Thompson didn't have the fancy homes that other members of the gang had, but that's because he was constantly on the move.

As part of her ruling on the CAB's evidence against Thompson and his fellow gang members, Ms Justice Stewart accepted there had also been an 'elaborate pattern of international travel undertaken by various members of the organization':

> A relative of an organized-crime gang member was employed in a travel company and assisted in booking flights and

accommodation for the gang members. Once arranged, a man identified as 'Lee' would arrive at the travel shop on a moped and pay in cash for the organization of said travel arrangements.

Another aspect of the Operation Lamp team's investigation was identifying previously unknown associates of the gang, including 'Lee'. From south inner-city Dublin, Lee Gibson was identified as a young associate of Thompson, one of many young men from the area recruited to the gang, and his role was to assist senior members, as summarized by the CAB team in their High Court submission:

> Lee Gibson is a foot soldier. He is involved in the day-to-day business of the organized-crime group and through the investigation into the car business it has been established that he has been involved in the importation and registration of several vehicles. Lee Gibson travels to the UK and Spain at the behest of the organized-crime group and has been stopped in the company of senior members of the organized-crime group on a regular basis.

Investigators also believed that funds from LS Active Car Sales had been used to pay for Thompson's trip to the Canary Islands in the winter of 2015. In a further submission to the High Court, the Operation Lamp team asserted:

> Investigations have shown an established pattern of international travel undertaken by various members of the group which is not consistent with their declared occupation or means. The analysis of the business account of LS Active identified the payment of €39,325 on travel expenditure for flights at a time when the business only imported one vehicle from the UK.

The CAB team's intensive investigation and surveillance operation had discovered that another man working at LS Active Car Sales was involved in arranging travel for Thompson and other gang members. He was a man with no previous convictions, but who investigators maintained was 'assisting in the activities of this organized-crime group':

> This man is listed as an employee. He comes from a good background and is a perfect frontman for this alleged business as he has been involved in car sales for a number of years and is pleasant and plausible to deal with. He was acting under the direction of Liam Byrne and the investigation has established that he was acting as a personal assistant for Liam Byrne and the wider organized-crime gang by organizing their vehicles – including insuring, taxing, cleaning – and booking flights for various members of the group on the laptop on LS Active premises.

This was a familiar tactic. Throughout his criminal career Freddie Thompson liked to make use of people who were under the radar, to store drugs and weapons and to take care of business for the gang.

In the High Court hearing, examples of the gang members' frequent travels were detailed. The team identified how Thompson's cousin, Liam 'Bop' Roe, had travelled to the UK, Málaga, Dubai and the United States on six different occasions between 9 July 2015 and 13 June 2016. Supposedly unemployed and in receipt of social welfare benefit, Roe flew on one occasion to see the UFC star Conor McGregor and Chad Mendes fight in Las Vegas in July 2015.

Just over a month after the Operation Lamp raids, Roe was stopped at Dublin Airport on 16 April 2016 by gardaí and when searched was discovered to have €60,000 in cash.

Insisting that his life was funded by his father, a taxi driver, Liam 'Bop' Roe was classed as a 'trusted lieutenant' of Liam Byrne and Freddie Thompson. He had been involved in organized crime 'for most of his adult life'. Gardaí established he had withdrawn the money from a bank account containing €294,000, but he wasn't arrested and was permitted to travel.

During the raid on Roe's home a few weeks earlier, gardaí had recovered a Kawasaki motorbike and an Audi A5, used to drive Thompson around Dublin during the feud, with an estimated value totalling €38,000. Rejecting his application for legal aid as part of his attempt to have the vehicles returned to him, the High Court ruled:

> He is asking the court to accept that he is a man that has no income whatsoever from any source and that he is supported by his father. He maintains that he has no income and yet he purports to be in a position to buy an expensive car and motorcycle. The case in relation to Mr Roe is quite straightforward.

Cars and motorcycles weren't the only ongoing expense for the gang. During their investigations, and contained within one of the thirteen affidavits later presented to the High Court, the CAB team established that electronic bikes had become an important resource for Thompson's gang of drug dealers, as they roamed Dublin's south inner city:

> Through LS Active Car Sales they are sourcing 'toys for the boys'. However, this type of bike is a major resource for the organized-crime gang as they can be folded up into the size of a briefcase. The bike and passenger can be brought to a location and dropped off. It is impossible for surveillance

units to follow them on these bikes as they escape through suburbia and flat complexes. It is suspected by local gardaí that they are used to distribute illegal drugs. Having watched CCTV from LS Active premises, it is evident that this method of transport is one used by members of the organized-crime group. No transaction can be found that reflects a purchase of these electronic bikes from the business accounts of LS Active or Liam Byrne's personal bank account.

Acting on behalf of the CAB, barrister Remy Farrell SC told the High Court the LS Active Car Sales site was being used as a 'clubhouse' for the gang and commented: 'LS Active Car Sales was nothing more than a front for the organized-crime group.' Security sources also believed it was used by Thompson and other senior members of the gang for meetings following the murder of Gary Hutch, as the CAB submitted:

> There was little evidence of car sales business and the premises is used for meetings by various members of the organized-crime gang. It has become clear the motor industry is being used by the criminal fraternity as a trading system.

The Operation Lamp team also established further evidence of the UK businessman Maurice Sines's and international drug dealer James Mulvey's links to the gang. When Sines, who had established a close bond with Thompson during his trips to the UK, stood alongside other mourners at David Byrne's funeral, watching gardaí were not clear on the extent of his ties to the cartel. It was only when the CAB 'Lamp' team were investigating the gang that they uncovered that Sines was the director of a company which had paid €280,000 for 6 Raleigh Square, Crumlin, south Dublin, in December 2015, a property just yards from the Byrne family home. The Criminal Assets Bureau placed the property firmly in its sights after detectives from Crumlin noticed that one of Freddie Thompson's associates, Glen Byrne, the gang's personal builder, was working on an extension at the house. The builder is currently serving a three-and-a-half-year prison term after he was caught with €350,000 in cash and it was established the money was from the proceeds of crime.

Since its purchase in 2015, the property has remained vacant as the 'Lamp' investigators are still working to establish if it was purchased through the proceeds of crime. In its submissions to the High Court on the gang's links with their UK associates, the CAB noted that Sines was a 'regular visitor to Dublin, at which time he is in the company of members of the organized-crime gang', and also remarked how Thompson's associates:

> Stayed at the Westbury Hotel, where it has been established that Liam Byrne has paid for some of their stays. They featured prominently at the funeral of Liam's brother David Byrne. Maurice Sines is pictured wearing the same suit as other leading figures in the organized-crime gang. This was believed to be a display of solidarity by the wider Kinahan organized-crime gang and an indication of the level of trust he [Sines] holds within this group.

The CAB team also discovered that James Crickmore's company had transferred funds electronically to LS Active Car Sales' bank account, providing seed capital for the business to start trading. Crickmore, a UK businessman who was linked to a race-fixing scandal in 2009, also attended the David Byrne funeral. In the UK, Crickmore and Sines are under investigation for their involvement in an ongoing VAT and VRT fraud. The two associates have acquired significant wealth, which they clearly enjoy flaunting. Their close ties to the gang have been highlighted by the two men's attendance at gang-related family events in Dublin. Garda surveillance teams have identified Sines's and Crickmore's frequent trips to Ireland, including their return for the one-year anniversary of David Byrne's murder, joining the Byrne family at his graveside. Gardaí also noted that they brought a Rolls-Royce and a Mercedes Jeep from the UK to Ireland, using them to escort Liam Byrne and his family around Dublin. On one occasion, the STG£300,000 Rolls-Royce was used by an associate of Thompson to bring Liam Byrne's son to his school formal.

Following his release from prison in 2015, Thompson was also a frequent visitor to many of Dublin's five-star luxury hotels. An investigator explained:

> Thompson might have been well known but this didn't stop him from wearing a disguise and using bogus identification to stay in places like the Westbury. When Thompson was conducting cartel business in Dublin they would always stay in the best of accommodation. Thompson wasn't in the same league as Daniel Kinahan when it came to running a criminal organization, but he was someone who could offer protection to people like Sines.

In the two months after the attack at the Regency Hotel, it was established that Liam Byrne had paid €13,026 for Thompson and other associates to stay at the Hilton, Radisson and Fitzwilliam hotels in Dublin. A source commented: 'It was his way of showing thanks to people like Thompson who would be out there trying to avenge his brother's death.'

Alongside establishing Sines's and Crickmore's relationship with Thompson's associates, the CAB team also discovered that in June 2015 the UK drug dealer James Mulvey had paid for the home of the cartel member Sean McGovern. The gardaí knew that Mulvey had previously provided safe houses for Thompson to stay in during his trips to the UK, and access to vehicles, but the team uncovered that he'd gone one step further when he electronically transferred €155,000 from a bank in Mauritius to Sean McGovern's bank account in Ireland so he could purchase a house in Kildare Road, Crumlin, south Dublin. Using a personal trust fund, 'Mule State Foundation', it was maintained in the CAB affidavit that Mulvey claimed the payment to McGovern was provided for the 'purpose of acquiring real estate in Ireland' from an account established for the 'education and well-being of his family'.

The UK's National Crime Agency (NCA) has been working closely with the CAB team on examining Mulvey's links to Thompson and other senior cartel figures, and on his involvement in a multimillion-euro drugs-smuggling operation. When the NCA investigated the purchase from their end they established that Mulvey had cleared the debt to the man the CAB described as a 'trusted lieutenant' of Thompson and Liam Byrne. Bizarrely, on searching Mulvey's home, officers also discovered a note stating: 'It's noted that the board of the foundation has taken the decision to write off the loan of €155,000 provided to Sean McGovern due to his recent demise.' Unable to determine why Mulvey referred to McGovern's demise, as the man was clearly not dead, investigators believed it may have been written just after he was shot at the Regency Hotel on 5 February 2016. NCA investigators also suspected the 'Mule State Foundation' fund was established to hide the profits from Mulvey's global drug-dealing network. One security source believed the payment to McGovern was made out of 'fear':

> The fact Mulvey wiped out a debt owed to him by a senior member of the Kinahan gang and a very close associate of Freddie Thompson shows just how much they were working together. It could also be inferred that Mulvey waived the payments because he was extremely paranoid after the murder of 'Hatchet' Kavanagh and was in fear of people like Freddie Thompson because he knew how dangerous he and his associates were. Mulvey would have been introduced to McGovern through Thompson and they had an association going back a number of years. There's no way Mulvey would have put pressure on McGovern to cough up because of who he was connected to.

The 'Lamp' team later uncovered that an extra €247,363 was spent on renovating the Kildare Road property. Proceeding without planning permission, the building work on the semi-detached house involved constructing extra rooms and a gym. While McGovern's home improvements were under way, the unemployed plumber, who was on the dole, departed on nineteen flights out of Dublin between 18 June and 26 December 2016 – visiting various destinations, including Dubai, Majorca, Amsterdam and Birmingham. Gardaí also believe Sean McGovern met with Thompson at a secret location in the capital after the CAB crackdown.

In a subsequent High Court ruling relating to his home, it was stated that McGovern:

> Claims that he is an unemployed man, having last worked in 2014, and that he has worked at various jobs since becoming

an apprentice plumber in 2003. However, he has provided no details whatsoever as to the dates of his employment or the amount of income earned from said employment. A review of his known bank account reveals that, in 2015, no lodgements were made. There is evidence before the court suggesting the property was mortgage-free, but McGovern has remained silent in relation to the origin of the monies used to purchase the property. The affidavit set out by gardaí sets out a lifestyle with respect to Mr McGovern that appears to be well outside the means of a person who is unemployed and not in receipt of any income.

In a victory for the Operation Lamp team, in February 2019 the High Court ruled that Sean McGovern's home in Kildare Road, Crumlin, and Liam Byrne's property in Grange View, Clondalkin, could be seized by the CAB and forfeited to the State as they were deemed to have been bought through the proceeds of crime There were no objections from McGovern or Byrne.

The only two items outstanding were Liam Byrne's family home at 2 Raleigh Square, Crumlin, which his sister Maria owned, and 213 Kildare Road, Crumlin – David Byrne's home. On 27 February 2019, Maria Byrne consented to the house on 2 Raleigh Square being forfeited to the State, after she notified the High Court she would not be contesting the CAB's plan to seize the property as the proceeds of crime. The CAB initially identified David Byrne's home as being purchased through the proceeds of crime but have now consented to allow his partner, Kelly Quinn, to keep the property because they believed it would be harder to prove.

While the CAB investigation was under way, Thompson and his associates were regularly spotted in each other's company and rarely seen alone, especially following David Byrne's killing. Gardaí had established that the top-tier gangsters were being careful about their drugs business as well, operating a 'hands off' policy when it came to transporting drugs and weapons and making sure the risks involved were dealt with by lower-level gang members. However, investigators maintained that there were 'several incidents of seizures of large quantities of illegal drugs where members of the gang were caught in possession of drugs while Liam Byrne and other senior members were in close proximity'.

The CAB's investigation into Liam Byrne, Freddie Thompson and their associates had exposed their lavish lifestyles, the wealth at their disposal and their connections to some of the most senior players in the Irish and UK organized-crime scene. The Operation Lamp team also revealed how Barry Finnegan, a convicted rapist, was wanted by detectives who were investigating the murder of Eddie Hutch a month earlier.

Finnegan had been identified by Spanish authorities as a 'trusted associate' of Thompson, and in their surveillance of the Kinahan cartel the Operation Shovel investigators had noted that he often met with both 'Fat Freddie' and Gary Hutch. Finnegan was originally from the north inner city, but he formed an alliance with the Kinahan faction. A source explained:

> Finnegan knew a lot of the Hutch family members and was close to Gary Hutch, but when Gary was killed, he immediately sided with the Kinahan side. He was also close to Freddie Thompson and the pair had spent a lot of time together. His decision to side with a group that was killing people from his own community was probably down to money.

Finnegan's relationship with Thompson and his associates was outlined in a submission to the High Court by the CAB after investigators established that a Volkswagen Golf GTD, valued at €11,750, seized from the gang was registered to the convicted rapist:

This vehicle is registered to Barry Finnegan of Hardwicke Street, Dublin 1. Barry Finnegan is a person who is familiar to gardaí as being a senior member of the Kinahan Organized Crime Group. He is currently outside the jurisdiction and believed to be in mainland Europe between Spain and Holland. He is a person currently being sought to assist the investigation into the murder of Eddie Hutch. He is being sought to assist in the investigation, which is part of the continuing feud between the opposing groups. The vehicle being left at LS Active while Finnegan has fled the jurisdiction is a further example of the exchange of wealth between criminals. Finnegan has eleven previous convictions for offences including rape, assault, robbery and various offences under the Public Order and Road Traffic Acts.

In further submissions to the High Court, the CAB claimed Finnegan, who had been jailed for five years in 2007 for violating a fourteen-year-old girl, had 'insufficient legitimate income' to import the car from the UK to Ireland: 'The purchase of this vehicle by Barry Finnegan in the first place has been established as being financed with funds from an unknown source.'

At the time of writing, Finnegan, who told a sitting of Dublin District Court during the feud that his life was under threat, continues to remain outside Ireland. His cousin Gary, named by Spanish officers as a member of the Kinahan 'Organización' and a close associate of Thompson, is also on the run after he was linked to the seizure of five firearms. A security source said that 'Gary Finnegan and Thompson were also very close in Spain and were often seen in each other's company. He was another individual who sided with a gang who were terrorizing his community following Gary Hutch's murder.'

Reflecting on the ongoing efforts by the CAB to tackle Liam Byrne, Liam Roe, Freddie Thompson and other members of the Kinahan cartel, the Irish Justice Minister, Charlie Flanagan, stated:

> I am very happy with the work that they do. They have a cross-agency approach and this is the envy of many of my European colleagues. We've seen arrests and the high-profile confiscations of cars at the luxury end which have been flaunted by people who don't have the means to support such a lifestyle.

The minister's views were also shared by Dublin's Lord Mayor, Nial Ring, who represents the people of Dublin's north inner city:

> I would like to welcome the ongoing work of the CAB in targeting the wealth of organized criminals who have brought nothing but misery and pain on our communities ... it's great to see cars, cash and jewellery being seized from those involved in organized crime.

Chief bureau officer at the agency, Detective Chief Superintendent Pat Clavin, welcomed the support of local communities in the fight against organized crime:

> We are appealing to anyone with information on criminals who continue to flaunt their wealth to please contact us or

Crimestoppers. We don't require people to give evidence and they are not required to go to court, so we would urge them to tell us what they know. None of these criminals are untouchable.

As the CAB team continued their forensic dissection of the gang's assets, focusing on members of the 'top tier', investigators from the gardaí's Dublin South Central Division, based in Kevin Street and Kilmainham Garda Stations, were also preparing to strike another blow – and this time Freddie Thompson was the main target.

15. Operation Thistle

> We were very conscious that the 'A' District was the
> heartland of Thompson and the Kinahan Organized
> Crime Group and we were also conscious of the fact
> that the 'A' District was the area where drugs brought
> into the country by this criminal grouping were
> being sold.
> Chief Superintendent Cleary, Operation Thistle

Four days after the murder of Eddie Hutch, the former Justice
Minister Frances Fitzgerald had confirmed the Government's
commitment to tackling the feuding Kinahan and Hutch factions. On 12 February 2016, she stated: 'It seems that some
gangs are intent on waging a feud where human life counts for
nothing. The gardaí will take all necessary steps to try to prevent further bloodshed but we have to recognize the challenges
they face.'

In a subsequent interview she insisted 'no effort would be
spared' in bringing those behind the violence to justice. In a
clear reference to the Kinahan cartel, she added:

> These gangs are bent on revenge and retaliation, but they
> aren't untouchable. Additional funding has been set aside to
> help gardaí target these gangs. We're dealing with big crim-
> inal empires who have certain people operating here while
> they pull the strings from other countries.

To further demonstrate its commitment to tackling the warring factions, the Department of Justice had also confirmed a permanent 'Armed Support Unit' would be established on a full-time basis in Dublin. These units had been used successfully in the fight against the feuding McCarthy/Dundon and Keane/Collopy gangs in Limerick from 2007 to 2009. Warmly welcomed by parties on all sides of the political divide, the measure was seen as an important response to the growing threat of further violence.

However, unknown to the public at the time, this wasn't the State's only response to the escalating violence. At the end of February, Detective Superintendent Peter O'Boyle and Detective Inspector Paul Cleary, now a chief superintendent, met in Kevin Street Garda Station to discuss the killings of David Byrne and Eddie Hutch. The senior detectives were based in the 'A' District of the gardaí's Dublin Metropolitan Region, the area that had been home to some of the most dangerous criminals in Irish history, including the godfather Christy 'Dapper Don' Kinahan, Martin 'The Viper' Foley, the INLA's chief, Declan 'Whacker' Duffy, and 'Fat Freddie' Thompson himself. During the course of the Crumlin–Drimnagh feud, the task of investigating the mayhem associated with the feud, including the litany of murders, gun attacks, pipe bombings, stabbings and threats, had fallen to senior investigators from the 'A' District.

In the aftermath of the two murders, officers from the Garda Drugs and Organised Crime Bureau, North Central Division, the area in which many members of the Hutch family and their associates lived, and the Emergency Response Unit had devised their own plans to address the inevitability of further violence. Aware of these plans, the two senior officers from Kevin Street agreed that, because 'A' District was home to Thompson and was the stronghold of the Kinahan cartel in Ireland, a specific approach was also required in their area. As Detective Superintendent O'Boyle explained:

> Following the Regency and the murder of Eddie Hutch, we felt it was important for us to have our own policing plan in place because some of the main players involved in this feud resided in or originated in the 'A' District. Those involved in the feud could have been planning attacks but there was also the possibility that they themselves could be targets. We identified targets at an early stage and had great co-operation from Detective Superintendent Seamus Boland and his team at the Drugs and Organised Crime Bureau, CAB and uniformed officers. This was about taking a pro-active approach to a very dangerous situation by targeting those who were involved in serious organized crime by disrupting their activities.

Contacting garda HQ at Dublin's Phoenix Park, Detective Superintendent O'Boyle sought permission to obtain the necessary resources to establish Kevin Street's own specialist investigation into the Kinahan gang's activities in the south inner city. With permission granted from former Assistant Garda Commissioner Jack Nolan, and following meetings with the Drugs and Organised Crime Bureau and other national units, 'Operation Thistle' was officially under way by the beginning of March. The operation was named by the gardaí's Crime and Security Section, part of whose role is to provide the codenames of specialist garda operations. It also gathers intelligence on organized-crime gangs and deals with international and domestic forms of terrorism.

The 'Thistle' team had identified viable suspects and placed many of them under surveillance. They were the gang members regarded by gardaí as 'vital cogs' in the Kinahan drugs operation in the south inner city – and Freddie Thompson was, once again, placed at the top of the garda watch-list. Chief Superintendent Cleary described 'Thistle':

> This operation was aimed at the mid- and lower-level members of the Kinahan cartel behind the drug-dealing, facilitating and money aspects of their business but a primary target for us was Freddie Thompson because he was still residing in the area. He was a high-level target for us considering his previous background in organized crime. We were very conscious that the 'A' District was the heartland of Thompson and the Kinahan Organized Crime Group and we were also conscious of the fact that the 'A' District was the area where drugs brought into the country by this criminal grouping were being sold. Some of his associates that we identified were working as his driver and selling drugs for his organization, but they would go on to become involved in more serious crime. Other targets identified included associates of Freddie Thompson who were acting as facilitators for the group and we were determined to aggressively disrupt their criminal activities. We also ensured that the operation didn't interfere with ongoing garda activity into this criminal grouping and that's why we worked closely with our colleagues in the national units. We had a great response from local residents and also from the business community, who were seeing members of this criminal gang flaunting their wealth on a daily basis.

Just a day after CAB swooped on the senior cartel figure Liam Byrne and other gang associates, investigators from Operation Thistle initiated their first strike against Thompson and his associates. In the early hours of the morning gardaí raided nine properties across Dublin's south inner city and also in the Pearse Street area of the city centre. The homes of the gang member Eoin 'Scarface' O'Connor, Thompson's cousin Liam Roe, a man suspected of identifying associates of the Hutch gang for execution, and another man identified as a 'manager and enforcer' for Thompson were just some of the premises extensively searched. During the operation, which included officers from the CAB's Operation Lamp team, the Drugs and Organised Crime Bureau and the Garda Dog Unit, investigators recovered hundreds of documents linked to the cartel's financial dealings, bank documents, mobile phones, laptops and details of travel arrangements. A quantity of controlled substances was also discovered.

Gardaí gained a rare insight into the cartel's business plans when they recovered documents linking the gang to the wedding business. As one detective commented:

> We think this particular type of business was just one of the many ways Thompson's associates were laundering cash. It was something completely different and they were constantly looking at new avenues to launder their cash. This was a business gardaí hadn't come across before and certainly showed how any type of business was fair game when it came to cleaning the proceeds of their drug dealing.

The inroads into the cartel's operations in Ireland and Thompson's activities continued. In a search of another property the Operation Thistle team discovered €50,000 hidden behind a cooker. Other items they seized included Rolex and Breitling watches, along with a range of jewellery with a value in excess of €20,000. The sinister side of the gang's operations was uncovered, however, when investigators discovered four GPS tracking devices. It seemed Thompson and his associates were prepared to put the skills they had learned on their Spanish SWAT-style training course into practice. Gardaí were in no doubt the devices were to be placed on the cars of the Hutch faction. A security source commented:

> The fact that tracking devices were recovered was a major concern. These items were used for one purpose only and that was to place on the cars of their targets so their movements could be monitored. They had already been used in the past by Thompson and his associates and their discovery proved that once again the threat posed by this criminal gang was very real. The items were brought in from the UK and were easily purchased online. There was no doubt that the discovery of these items helped to save lives.

The first wave of searches had also netted the gardaí drugs worth €112,000 and more than €30,000 in cash. A 73-year-old man was questioned, after he alleged he had been forced to hold the drugs and cash by Thompson's associates. One officer related how it was a common tactic used by Thompson's gang over the years:

> There were a lot of people in the community who were perfect candidates for people like Thompson because they were often vulnerable and desperate for cash. There was also the question of coercion, and if someone owed even a small amount for a drug debt it was very often the case their family members would be forced to hide drugs and cash to waive the debt. But once they did this the first time Thompson would have ordered his gang to keep going back and to keep the pressure on them. Thompson's speciality was murder and mayhem and there's no way he would have stored drugs, weapons or money, or have anyone close to him do something similar. Vulnerable

families in the south inner city were simply used as a means to an end for him and his associates.

Following the launch of the first phase of Operation Thistle, Thompson and his gang knew they were in for a fight. Welcomed by garda HQ, the operation would prove even more successful just a month later, when it identified the links between the Kinahan cartel and one of Europe's most barbaric and dangerous drugs gangs – the Dutch-based Moroccan mafia.

Detective Superintendent O'Boyle and his team had seized dozens of documents providing details of the cartel's transactions and business interests during the raids, but arguably one of their best discoveries was details of a cartel hideaway in a luxury apartment on Lower Baggot Street, in Dublin's city centre. The address was found during a search of the home of a close associate of Thompson and Daniel Kinahan. The cartel member, who worked as a public servant, was seen as a 'facilitator' for the mob. The man, previously identified as a cartel associate, had been placed under surveillance before the 'Thistle' team swooped and had been recorded meeting estate agents and arranging utility bills for the Baggot Street property and others. Gardaí had received intelligence Christopher Kinahan Jnr had used the property, which cost around €2,500 per month to rent, during secret visits to Dublin.

Continuing with their investigations into Thompson and his associates, the decision was made to place the property under surveillance, pending a search warrant being issued.

On the morning of 7 April 2016, eighty uniformed officers and detectives from the South Central Division made their move as the second phase of Operation Thistle swung into action. The Baggot Street apartment and seven other properties were the team's targets.

When officers stormed into the upmarket residence in Lower Baggot Street they found a portly man lying in bed. Asked to identify himself, the suspect produced a Belgian ID card and claimed his name was Omar Ghazouani. As gardaí continued to search the property, the man constantly repeated the name on the document. Despite his attempts to convince the officers he was Omar Ghazouani, they did not believe him, as they had discovered a bogus Dutch passport, along with two Rolex watches, worth €35,000 and €8,350, a €40,000 Audemars Piguet Royal Oak Offshore limited edition Michael Schumacher watch, €12,825 in cash and a pair of €800 Valentino trainers.

On the same day, a key to the Baggot Street apartment was also found when gardaí searched the home of the girlfriend of Daniel Kinahan's childhood friend Jeremy Skerrit. Skerrit was known as a trusted associate of senior cartel members, including Thompson. During the search of the apartment on the North Circular Road, Dublin, officers seized €17,000 they had discovered wrapped in tinfoil and hidden under a mattress. It was later deemed by the High Court to be from the 'proceeds of crime' and returned to the Exchequer.

The man claiming to be Omar Ghazouani was brought to Kevin Street Garda Station for questioning, and his photograph circulated to police forces across Europe. At the same time, an international fingerprint trawl was under way. Within a few hours, Dutch police had identified the target. The man who had been staying as a guest of the Kinahan cartel was one of Europe's 'Most Wanted' and the head of the Moroccan mafia in Holland – Naoufal 'The Belly' Fassih.

Formally identified as Naoufal Fassih, and known to be a personal friend of Daniel Kinahan, the mafioso's arrest highlighted the cartel's connections to major players in the

for possessing a loaded gun and travelling on a false passport, and was regularly stopped with 'Fat Freddie' during the feud. It was in Amsterdam, after all, that Thompson had gone to ground when he faced charges over the mass pub brawl in Dublin at the beginning of 2013.

Fassih's arrest during the middle of the Kinahan–Hutch feud in Ireland sparked concern among Dutch investigators, fearful that the feud could ignite in Amsterdam. The senior investigator tasked with probing the activities of Irish criminals, both operating and hiding in Holland, expressed concerns over the conflict between Thompson and his former allies. The investigator, who works closely with the garda liaison officer in Holland, a former detective with the CAB, said:

> There may be a possibility the activities of this feud could lead to an assassination in Amsterdam. It's a concern people connected to this feud could be targeted on Dutch soil, but also innocent people. We will continue to target those organized-crime gangs who are willing to use an AK47 on a public road. It was previously posted online that Gerry Hutch was in Holland. Our question was – if he's here, who's coming to take him out? We are dealing with our own feuds at the moment, but we have been kept informed of the situation in Ireland because it could come over to Amsterdam. The Kinahan Organized Crime Group is like any other organized-crime gang and if you're involved in drugs it's logical to say you need guns to protect it. All of the gangs like the Kinahan Organized Crime Group have links to the UK, Spain, America, Dubai, Turkey and Morocco and they all work together for the transportation of drugs.

The investigator also offered an explanation for Thompson's association with the Dutch capital over the years:

When deals are being made this is where they come together to meet. All of the main organized-crime groups have people working here and it's easy to meet and mingle. Most of the time the gangs make the deals in Amsterdam, but the drugs go mainly outside. We are working on everything to do with firearms and international crime remains a priority for us.

In an interesting twist, and in a trend often witnessed over the years in gangland crime, the Dutch senior detective believes associates of both the Kinahan and Hutch factions could still finance deals together in his country. He added: 'It is possible they could work together because it's all about money. The feud doesn't make any money for them. Equally, if they were working together, they could also start killing each other over here.'

A Dutch police spokesman, Rob van der Veen, warned the Dutch capital would not be a 'safe haven' for people like Thompson:

Amsterdam will not be a safe location for criminals from Ireland who come here to engage in criminal activity. If they are wanted by the Irish police authorities, we only need a tiny piece of information to locate them and we will – if it's people doing major crimes then our SWAT team will make the arrest. If we have information on international criminals here they will be targeted and pursued. We have a 100 per cent success rate on the Irish criminals we have been asked to search for. We have great co-operation with the Irish authorities.

Back in Ireland, the officers attached to Operation Thistle were continuing their offensive against Thompson and his associates. On 17 May 2016, drugs worth €300,000 were seized from a house on York Street, close to Dublin city centre. The following month, heroin to a value of €1.4 million was confiscated when a flat in Kevin Street, in the south inner city, was raided. Gardaí believed the drugs were being stored for Thompson's gang, and one officer said:

> Thompson was in the middle of a brutal gangland war, but business had to go on. It was all about the money. There was no question of these seizures being linked to his gang. It was a major blow for them to lose such a significant amount of drugs.

Coinciding with the seizures in June 2016, Deputy Garda Commissioner John Twomey reaffirmed the force's commitment to targeting Thompson and his associates, both at home and abroad: 'We are determined to bring the perpetrators of organized crime to justice. We are determined that good will win over evil. People have lost their lives, families have been destroyed, and we need to put an end to it.' In a direct message to those facilitating Thompson and his associates in the south inner city, the senior officer said: 'Those people involved on the fringes, those involved in the logistics, the purchasing of phones and of cars, are equally as culpable. People are only involved in the drug trade for greed and personal gain.'

The offensive under Operation Thistle continued over the summer and investigators launched another four raids in Dublin's south inner city. During the crackdown, officers recovered €10,000 in cash, heroin worth €3,000, an Audi A3 car, a designer watch worth €15,000 and documents which appeared to reveal the gang's plan to launder cash through new car sales companies. Its intention was to register the companies in the names of people without criminal convictions and unknown to the gardaí.

Over the next two years, Operation Thistle would continue to disrupt the activities of Thompson and his associates in the south inner city. By the end of the summer of 2018, officers attached to the specialist operation had been involved in ninety-nine searches, seized drugs valued at €1,786,370, including heroin worth €1,182,050 and cocaine worth €514,200. Twenty-seven people – many with a direct line to Thompson – were also arrested. Sixteen of them were charged on a wide range of drugs offences and a number of files were sent to the Director of Public Prosecutions. Other items seized were €132,970 in cash, designer clothes and jewellery valued at €94,000, and an Audi A4 worth €14,000.

Detective Superintendent Peter O'Boyle assured the local community of the operation's continued existence:

> This operation will continue, and it has had great results against a well-organized crime gang operating in the south inner-city area of Dublin. We have had great assistance from our colleagues in the national units and our efforts have caused significant disruption to the gang's business. We are targeting all structures of the gang and their associates.

Undoubtedly frustrated by Operation Thistle's disruption of his gang's drug-dealing operations, 'Fat Freddie' remained in Dublin throughout June 2016. Rarely leaving his heavily fortified family home, on the few occasions he did so he was in the company of his associates Nathan Foley and the trainee hitman.

On 21 June 2016 a garda patrol under Operation Hybrid searched Thompson's two young associates as they waited at the statue of the Virgin Mary monument on Loreto Road, Maryland. During the search, Thompson emerged from his family home and exchanged pleasantries with the officers. It was one of the last times he was seen in public before 1 July as he was busy putting the finishing touches to a murder master plan – a plan that, for a change, would include a hands-on role for the gang leader.

16. Playing God

I know he has some background history, but that's in
the past. Everybody wants to change. I'm from
China and if you try to do good, you will get a
chance to make your life.

Yumei Douglas

By the end of June 2016, Thompson was under attack on
multiple fronts. The combined efforts of the CAB team
behind Operation Lamp and the 'A' District garda investigators in Operation Thistle were making serious inroads into
Thompson's and Liam Byrne's drug-dealing profits and seriously affecting business. However, despite the success of the
two operations, the permanent feud with the Hutch Organized Crime Gang was at the top of Thompson's agenda. His
modus operandi was simple – to strike at any of the people suspected of attacking his associates. The Regency gunmen
were the primary target, but Thompson and his cousins
hadn't forgotten the attempt to shoot Liam Roe in the Red
Cow Moran Hotel back in November 2015.

The gang's chief suspect, the former IRA man Daithi
Douglas, was still recovering from being shot three times in
the chest as he was walking his dog close to his home in
Cabra, north Dublin, eight months earlier. The former zookeeper, who had been released from prison in 2014 after
serving a sentence for being caught in possession of cocaine

worth €2 million on 13 April 2008, was also being treated for anxiety following his brush with death. Gardaí knew he had been attacked after he was accused of being involved in the attempt to murder Liam Roe; however, investigators in Cabra Garda Station were also following a second line of inquiry. Detectives there had received information that Douglas had been targeted following a pub row with another criminal.

In an interview with the *Herald* after the drive-by shooting, Douglas's wife, Yumei, had insisted that he'd turned his life around following his release from prison in 2014:

> I don't care about whatever his history is, but he's on the good way now. Since he is out of prison he didn't do anything wrong. I know he has some background history, but that's in the past. Everybody wants to change. I'm from China and if you try to do good, you will get a chance to make your life.

Following his release from hospital, the 55-year-old Douglas had been officially warned by gardaí that his life was under threat. The former IRA member didn't take any extra precautions after receiving the Garda Information Message form. He continued to live openly at his home in Cabra, north-west Dublin, and didn't implement new security measures. He focused on regaining his health, going out walking most days with his dog, and he spent time in the shop run by his wife. Established in 2008, 'Shoestown' was located in Bridgefoot Street, south inner-city Dublin, in the heart of Thompson's stronghold. The shop was next to Busy Bee, a children's afterschool group, and was used by families throughout the area to buy children's shoes, toys and other household goods. Douglas didn't seem to realize the risk he was running by entering on such a regular basis the territory controlled by 'Fat Freddie'. The former zookeeper and armed robber also told friends that he had a €10,000 price on his head, courtesy of a criminal based in north Dublin.

Despite these serious threats Douglas continued to lead a normal life, often spending his days at his wife's store. According to one local shop owner, who did not want to be named, Douglas was a popular figure in the area:

> Daithi was always very talkative and very pleasant. Everyone knew he had been shot the previous November but he was looking well and seemed to be enjoying life again. He didn't seem to have a care in the world and certainly didn't appear as if he was under any type of threat.

Thompson, however, still thought they had a score to settle. Unbeknownst to Daithi, as he continued his recovery, the cartel's feud leader had placed Douglas at the top of their hit list. Though it didn't come out in court, it was the gardaí's belief that Thompson and his associates would have been watching Daithi's movements for a number of weeks before they made their move.

Douglas's close friend Darren Kearns had been murdered the previous December, as Thompson had believed him to be one of the two gunmen who tried to kill his cousin Liam Roe, eight months earlier, and he thought Daithi was the second man involved in the attempted assassination. Gardaí suspected Thompson had received this intelligence from another criminal – but not a shred of evidence had been produced to support the claim. In fact, gardaí would later establish that, like Kearns, Douglas was in another part of Dublin at the time of the botched hit on Liam Roe. Officers had secured CCTV from a pub in the Phibsboro area of north Dublin, clearly showing Douglas enjoying a drink with friends. For Thompson, however, another damning piece of the puzzle was that Douglas had once been an associate of Gerry 'The Monk' Hutch. Acting on the tenuous information he'd received, in June 2016 Freddie Thompson signed Douglas's death warrant.

Assembling his murder squad, Thompson nominated as his trigger man the young man who had been his driver and minder in the weeks following the killing of David Byrne, and another young man as the getaway driver. A Kinahan cartel 'foot soldier', Nathan Foley, also joined the team to provide logistical support. Part of his role was to secure mobile phones for the hit squad so that they could undertake surveillance of Douglas's movements.

Around the same time, gardaí received intelligence that Thompson was attempting to obtain garda uniforms to mirror the attack on the Regency Hotel and that he had access to a female garda's official ID card which had been stolen. By the time Douglas was targeted by Thompson eight people had already lost their lives in the feud. There was always concern that 'Fat Freddie' was planning something, but gardaí had no specific intelligence about the name of his next victim.

A crucial component of Thompson's murder plan was the cars the team would use – a Mercedes CLA, stolen from the Navan Road, Dublin, on 23 June 2016, and a silver Suzuki Swift, stolen from a home in Greystones, Co. Wicklow, on 11 June 2016. The plan was that the Mercedes would be used to bring the gunman from the scene of the shooting, while the Suzuki would be a second getaway vehicle. It was later established that a Ford Fiesta car, registered to a man from west Dublin who was suspected of owing money to Thompson, would be personally used by 'Fat Freddie' to help organize the killing. The man was ordered to provide his car to the gang leader as a means of clearing his drug debt. A fourth vehicle, a blue Mitsubishi Mirage which had been registered in a false name, would be used by Nathan Foley. He was out on bail after he'd been charged with possessing cocaine to the value of €10,000. The drugs had been found in his bedroom on 17 June 2016 during a raid by the Operation Thistle team.

Foley was also ordered to act as a spotter for garda patrols on the day of the murder, and he was to drive Thompson and the hit team to Little Caesar's restaurant, in Dublin city centre, for a 'debrief', in the event of a successful outcome.

Once his plans were finalized, Thompson, who had been keeping a low profile throughout June 2016, rarely leaving the house, emerged on Friday, 1 July – the day Freddie had decided Daithi's life would end.

Douglas's day started normally, with his spending time at home in the morning and travelling to his wife's shop before lunch, where he was later joined by his teenage daughter. Engaging with customers throughout the day, Daithi was in good form.

As the gangland target remained in the shop over lunch-time, the wheels of Thompson's murder machine were put in motion. It started with Foley buying two Nokia Lumia Rm1132 mobile phones at 1.38 p.m. from the Cell Hub phone shop in Meath Street, south inner-city Dublin. Earlier that day, one of the gang members had already parked the Mercedes on Merton Avenue, also in the south inner city. Meanwhile, the Suzuki Swift had been parked nearby at St Anne's Road, with members of the murder gang regularly topping up parking tickets throughout the course of the afternoon to avoid the car arousing suspicion or getting clamped.

Following a final briefing from Thompson the murder team set off. Foley, driving the blue Mitsubishi Mirage, collected the gunman and his getaway driver before dropping them off at the Mercedes on Merton Avenue at 3.54 p.m. During the drop, Foley was captured on CCTV passing fuel containers to his associates. Fifteen minutes before this, the gunman had driven the Suzuki Swift, which had been parked on St Anne's Road, and moved it to Carman's Hall, Spitalfields.

After the gunman and the driver had been dropped off at Merton Avenue, they then drove to Oliver Bond Street and parked the car. At the same time, Foley, acting as a garda spotter, was doing laps of the area in his car.

At 4.06 p.m. Thompson drove past Yumei Douglas's shop, before parking the Ford Fiesta in Meath Street. Once there, he went to his family's stall and gave the car keys to a woman while, gardaí later maintained, 'continuing to look in the direction of Shoestown'. Thompson also took this opportunity to destroy his mobile phone by disassembling it.

Just five minutes later, at 4.11 p.m., and with Thompson looking on, the gunman, dressed from head to toe in black with his face partially covered, walked around the corner and into the shop. Yumei Douglas wasn't in the shop at the time but Daithi Douglas was standing just inside the doorway. Taking another step inside, the young hitman pulled out his Spanish-made 9mm Star pistol and opened fire. Douglas was hit six times – in the right side of his face, the left side of his chin, his neck, twice in the torso and in his right elbow. The gunman then placed the weapon beside his victim's head before quietly walking from the scene, as

Daithi's daughter, who had been at the rear of the shop, screamed in terror.

In a later statement to gardaí, the teenager said:

> He was just eating the curry that he got. He asked me if I wanted any, I said no. I just then heard the shots. The first two I thought they were bangers – the kids messing with fireworks. The last two shots I heard I knew were too loud to be bangers. I looked up from the desk and I just saw him lying there. There was blood all around. I went to my dad. I was shouting at him. He didn't say anything to me. I knew he had been shot. I heard him breathe once or felt it. That's my dad who has been shot. When I went over to Dad I saw a gun on the ground. I don't know guns. It had a star on it. I had never seen it before. There was [sic] bullets around him as well.

John Shaw, who ran the crèche next door, also rushed to the scene. He dialled 999 calling for the gardaí and an ambulance. Shaw later outlined how the daughter of Thompson's target 'lost it' after seeing her father lying in a pool of blood.

As the brave teenager comforted her dad, the gunman had got back into the Mercedes and been driven the short distance to the Suzuki Swift in Spitalfields by the getaway driver. They pulled up beside the Suzuki, jumped out and the two-man hit team then set fire to the Mercedes. In a bizarre accident, the trouser leg of the gunman caught fire before, according to witnesses, he frantically put it out. The Mercedes continued to burn as the pair then sped off in the silver Suzuki Swift in the direction of Merrion Road, south Dublin.

In the meantime, Douglas was rushed to St James's Hospital, but was pronounced dead at 4.55 p.m. The feud had claimed its ninth victim.

Struggling to come to terms with the loss of her husband

of thirteen years, Yumei Douglas was baffled by the killing. She later said:

> As far as I know he didn't owe anyone money or had fallen out with anybody. He was shot in November 2015. He told me that he was shot in November because he got into a fight with someone. I don't know why he was shot. I don't know why they'd do it again.

Other witnesses that day spoke of their horror and shock at the shooting in broad daylight. One resident would later tell gardaí:

> I thought it was a car backfiring and then I heard more bangs. I turned to look and saw a guy coming out of Busy Bee. His face was covered. It was like he was running out and I assumed he was coming towards me, so I started screaming at the kids to run down the hill.

Another witness claimed:

> I noticed a male walking from Oliver Bond Street towards Shoestown. His body language was unusual. He looked like someone who was going to cause mischief. Once the shots were fired, I heard a female scream really loud. He wasn't covered up or anything and it's like he didn't care who saw him, nearly as if he was proud of what he had just done.

News of the capital's latest gangland killing made the headlines during the evening news bulletins. A major murder investigation, which included officers involved in Operation Thistle and who'd worked on the Lorcan O'Reilly case, was immediately under way at Kevin Street Garda Station. The team was under the command of the senior investigating officer, Detective Inspector Paul Cleary, today a chief superintendent, Superintendent Patrick McMenamin and Detective Superintendent Peter O'Boyle. The officers all met to discuss the murder, holding a case conference a few hours after the killing to formulate a plan of action.

At the same time, Thompson was holding his own meeting at the Little Caesar's restaurant, off Grafton Street, in Dublin city centre. He was driven to the location by Foley, who parked the Mitsubishi Mirage, one of the four cars used in the execution, at St Stephen's Green Shopping Centre, central Dublin. Arriving at the restaurant at 7.38 p.m., Thompson was joined by Foley, the gunman, the teenage killer of Lorcan O'Reilly who was still out on bail, and a senior cartel associate. Freddie led the celebrations in a downstairs room of the restaurant while the gang enjoyed a three-course meal and had what has been described as a 'murder debrief'. According to one investigator:

> It was essentially a debriefing on the killing and there were high fives all around. It didn't matter to Thompson and his associates that a young girl had heard the shots being fired and ran out to find her father lying in a pool of blood. The fact that Thompson brought his associates out just a few hours after a man's life was taken shows just how callous he really was. They enjoyed a good meal, drinks and posed for photographs. It was simply a party to celebrate a murder.

The party continued into the early hours of the morning, and the group went their separate ways the following day. Foley left his vehicle in the busy shopping centre over the weekend. He needed help to restart the car the following Monday, 4 July, because he had left the lights on.

Though the gang had succeeded in murdering their target, they were still faced with the task of eliminating the remaining pieces of evidence. Top of the list was to destroy the Suzuki Swift, which had been abandoned after the murder in a car park beside Sandymount Strand, close to Sandymount village, south Dublin. On the night of 4 July, shortly after 11.30 p.m., the hitman and Foley, who was still driving the Mitsubishi Mirage, despite it being registered in a false name, drove to the car park in Sandymount. Once there, Foley reversed his car into the Swift a number of times, before getting out carrying a petrol can. He was confronted by a witness sitting in a nearby car.

In a later statement to gardaí the witness said: 'There was no one around. It was really quiet. I asked what was going on. He shouted, "Go away." Then he shouted at the guy in the car, "Should I pour it?" The guy shouted, "Yeah, yeah, faster."'

Continuing to pour petrol on the car, Foley then set fire to it and quickly drove off. In the meantime, the witness had taken a note of the Mirage's registration details, dialled 999 and also used his drink to extinguish the small fire which had ignited in the Suzuki. Unbeknownst to him at the time, his actions had helped to preserve vital evidence.

Fleeing from the scene, and unaware their attempts to destroy the vehicle had failed, the pair were later stopped by members of the South Division Crime Task Force as they drove along the canal towards Crumlin, south Dublin. Arrested on suspicion of criminal damage, the suspects were brought in for questioning before being released without charge as a file was prepared for the Director of Public Prosecutions. Gardaí had also received information that a third man, who they suspected was Freddie Thompson, had been in the car before it arrived at the car park, but they could never prove it. One source added: 'There was a witness who saw three men in the car and the belief was that it was Thompson and he'd decided to get out of the vehicle in case he was arrested.' At the same time, the Mitsubishi Mirage and Suzuki Swift were also seized.

The team in Kevin Street were just three days into their investigation and initially they were unaware of the significance of the seizures of the two vehicles. Up to that point, gardaí had been told by a witness that the killers had left their Mercedes before getting into a 'silver-coloured' car, but they had no make or model to go on. It also wasn't until their subsequent examination of Foley's Mitsubishi Mirage that gardaí discovered a parking ticket from the car park at St Stephen's Green Shopping Centre in Dublin city centre, dated the night of the Douglas murder.

As the huge investigation continued at Kevin Street Garda Station, on 11 July the funeral of Daithi (David) Douglas was held at the Church of the Most Precious Blood in Cabra, north Dublin. Speaking at the service, Canon Damian O'Reilly said that the father of one had died 'in the most tragic of circumstances':

> He was surrounded by those who knew him best and loved him most. They are gathered here in support for those who must continue the journey without David. David made his peace with God, and of that we have no doubts. What he wanted most was to walk his beloved dog and walk in peace in the safety of his family. David, like most of us, lived life his way. Some choices he made were very good choices – especially his decision to marry Yumei and having the wonderful gift of his daughter. Other choices he made in his early life were not the best choices for his life. Today, we gather to say farewell to David, to remember the warmth and love he

displayed to those closest to him. His earthly journey has now drawn to a close and, as we come to lay David to rest, we silently smile as we recall his happy moments in his life and we reflect on some of the bad decisions he made which resulted in the torments that life had inflicted on him, resulting in his tragic death.

Requesting mourners to support the victim's family, the priest added: 'Now is the time they need us most. Let today be a new beginning for us all.'

In the days after the killing, a key priority for detectives was to identify the movements of the Mercedes. Working backwards, the computer expert Garda Ciaran Byrne and the team were tasked with gathering and trawling through images from 160 different CCTV systems from Dublin's busy streets, involving more than 1,500 hours of footage. They focused on the hours leading up to the murder and, after days of examining the tapes, discovered that the Mercedes had been travelling in convoy with the Suzuki Swift on the day of the murder. The investigation team then made a significant discovery – they identified the Ford Fiesta and Foley's Mitsubishi Mirage travelling with the Mercedes at different intervals throughout the day. In one clip, Thompson's Fiesta was identified following the Suzuki on Terenure Road West, south Dublin, at 9.51 a.m. on the day of the shooting. Another image showed the Mercedes being parked on Merton Avenue, south inner-city Dublin, at 10.41 a.m. It remained there until a clip showed it being driven at 3.53 p.m. in Donore Avenue, also south inner-city Dublin, by the getaway driver just minutes before the murder.

Gardaí made another major breakthrough in the case just two weeks after the murder, when they examined further

CCTV images of the Ford Fiesta. Freddie Thompson had naturally emerged as a person of interest in the early stages of the investigation, because the murder had happened on his turf and as a result of his leading role in the Kinahan–Hutch feud. Gardaí believed it was Thompson inside the Fiesta, but the team would have to wait another few weeks before a formal identification was made. With a chief suspect now in their sights, the garda team started working on a main line of inquiry and began building their case against Thompson and his accomplices. Throughout the course of the investigation the Ford Fiesta, seized on 15 July, would be identified on camera thirty times.

In the meantime, gardaí had also obtained footage from business premises in the Meath Street and Thomas Street areas, located just metres away from the murder scene. The detectives' case against Thompson was further enhanced after he was identified on CCTV cameras from the Little Flower Old Folks Centre, a charity which provides meals for the homeless community. Detective Sergeant Whitelaw later identified Freddie standing a short distance from Shoestown, close to his family's market stall on Meath Street and appearing to destroy a mobile phone.

For someone who had been involved in gangland murders since his teenage years, being caught so near the scene of the crime was a schoolboy error. Another officer, however, considered it just one more example of Thompson's arrogance:

> The footage was very clear and it showed Thompson breaking up a phone around the same time Douglas was murdered. These were not the actions of an innocent man. Here was someone who had been involved in planning the logistics of murders for many years but didn't seem to take into account

that there would have been cameras in a very busy street. One can only assume that, in his arrogance and ego, he thought CCTV images of him breaking up a phone would not be enough to convict him of murder.

In a further breakthrough in the investigation, Foley's Mitsubishi Mirage was discovered on CCTV in the St Stephen's Green area of Dublin city centre in the hours following the killing. Examining footage from the surrounding area, gardaí then identified Thompson, Foley and the suspected gunman entering Little Caesar's restaurant. Once the CCTV from the restaurant had been obtained, investigators compiled clear images of Thompson and his associates enjoying their celebration. Officers were in no doubt of the reasons behind the gathering. As one source commented:

> The footage from the Fiesta and Meath Street was directly linked to events before and after the murder. However, the event at Little Caesar's gives an insight into Thompson's thinking, but, more crucially, it also provided details of any associates who may have been involved in the Douglas murder.

Alongside the CCTV strand of the investigation, the seized Suzuki Swift, Mitsubishi Mirage and Ford Fiesta vehicles were methodically examined by the Garda Technical Bureau. Investigators had a boost when they identified Thompson's DNA on an air-freshener cap and hand sanitizer in the Ford Fiesta and his left thumbprint on the rear-view mirror. His DNA was also found on an inhaler recovered from the Mitsubishi Mirage and his prints were on a birthday card and on the rear-view mirror of the car.

With all these discoveries, the case against 'Fat Freddie'

Thompson was getting stronger by the day. Unlike in previous years, and on other cases involving gangland executions, gardaí were convinced they now had enough evidence to charge Thompson with murder.

On the morning of 26 July 2016, officers from the investigation team swooped on Thompson's family home in Loreto Road, south inner-city Dublin, and on the home of a female accomplice, but there was no sign of Freddie. The homes of other associates were also searched, but nothing was found. One of the properties searched included a suspected safe house that gardaí believed had been used by Thompson in the early days of the feud. Aware by that stage that three cars used in the murder had been seized, Thompson knew he was in the frame for murder and he had fled to his friends in the UK.

Thompson wasn't the only member of the gang to disappear. The suspected gunman and his getaway driver were also on the run. Foley, still out on bail over the drugs charge, remained in Dublin as the investigation continued. He was sent to Cloverhill Prison on 8 August 2016, for continued breaches of the terms of his bail bond.

As Thompson remained in exile, detectives pressed on with their investigation. At a meeting on 12 August, Detective Sergeant Whitelaw was shown a compilation of images taken from CCTV footage around the south inner city. The experienced gangland investigator identified Freddie Thompson from each of the eight images he was shown of the gangster in the Ford Fiesta, at Little Caesar's restaurant and from Meath Street. When he confirmed that Thompson, a criminal the detective had investigated for many years, was the man in the picture, a nationwide alert was sent out to all garda stations for Frederick 'Fat Freddie' Thompson to be arrested in the event of his return to Ireland.

In his absence, gardaí also received intelligence that Thompson, who had been officially warned six times since the start of 2016 that his life was in danger, remained under threat from five different crime gangs, including the Hutch faction and friends of Neil 'The Highlander' Fitzgerald. Thompson's absence from Dublin was a setback to the Kinahan cartel leadership and their plans for revenge, which, thanks largely to his ability to organize murders, had been going according to plan. However, Daniel Kinahan was determined that the slaughter would continue – with or without the help of 'Fat Freddie'.

Just five days after Detective Sergeant Whitelaw had identified Thompson's complicity in the murder of Daithi Douglas, a Kinahan cartel hitman, Glen Clarke, struck for a second time. On 17 August, he murdered a completely innocent man in front of his family in the Costa de la Calma area of Majorca, Spain. A Dublin City Council worker, Trevor O'Neill, was shot once in the back after Clarke fired at his target – Jonathan Hutch – who was walking near the victim at the time. Obsessed with revenge, it was clear Daniel Kinahan wasn't just relying on Thompson to run his feud.

Just as in the case of the Martin O'Rourke killing four months earlier, Clarke had made another fatal error. There was widespread anger after it emerged another innocent man's life had been taken. Highlighting the trauma experienced by her family and in her only ever interview, Trevor's wife, Suzanne Power, reminded the people of Ireland of the onslaught on them by Thompson and his associates. She said:

> I don't have to explain to my children what happened because they were there – they saw it. That awful night will now live with them for ever and no child should have to endure this.

Any of us could have been killed that night. Our focus is my children, but we'll never forget Trevor. We never imagined in a million years an ordinary family like ours would be caught up in this mayhem. Each and every one of his friends are broken-hearted. Nothing can prepare you for something like this and our lives have been destroyed.

An investigation team was set up, but the hitman would never face justice for the murder of Trevor O'Neill – or of Martin O'Rourke – as his dead body was found four months later. Gardaí believe Glen Clarke may have died after shooting himself in the head by accident. His family and some investigators, however, think that he may have been murdered.

Assistant Garda Commissioner Pat Leahy, who was involved in the investigation into the O'Rourke murder, expressed his disappointment that Clarke would never stand trial:

My sympathies will always be with the family of this innocent young man. The family and the community deserved justice. The team in Store Street who worked on the investigation put a huge effort into solving this crime. Myself and the team would have liked to have someone before the courts to hold them publicly accountable for that killing.

As Trevor O'Neill's family and friends also mourned his loss, gardaí in Kevin Street were plotting their next course of action as the case against Thompson gathered pace.

17. The Death Knell

This is probably the first and last time Freddie
Thompson will let himself get as close to
murder again.
Daithi Douglas murder investigation team

By the middle of September 2016, gardaí had identified all of
the suspects involved in the murder of Daithi Douglas. The
investigation team had logged hundreds of hours going
through a range of CCTV, DNA and fingerprint evidence
while Thompson remained out of the country.

Freddie Thompson had been identified by Detective Sergeant Adrian Whitelaw from three different sets of footage.
However, the team knew it would not be enough to rely on
in the event of any court hearing. As detectives continued to
work on the case, the decision was made to have the images
identified by a member of the gardaí who'd previously had
involvement with Thompson but who, crucially, was not a
member of the investigation team. Though there were
dozens of officers, mainly from Crumlin and Dublin's south
inner city, who had met Thompson over the years, the decision was made to show the images to the garda who'd had
the most recent encounter with the gang leader. The task fell
to Garda Seamus O'Donovan, who, along with Sergeant
Paul Murphy, now an inspector, had brought Thompson

back to Ireland in 2015 to stand trial for the violent-disorder charge from the brawl after Christopher Warren's funeral.

Following a meeting with the investigation team towards the end of September, Garda O'Donovan was brought in and shown the same CCTV images Detective Sergeant Whitelaw had viewed in August. Having scrutinized the pictures, Garda O'Donovan also identified Thompson from the collage.

As the chief suspect in the Douglas murder remained on the run, detectives in Kevin Street received intelligence that the Hutch gang were planning to target innocent members of Thompson's family by bombing his family home in Loreto Road. Details of the plot were revealed in the *Irish Sun*, as it also emerged that 107 people, including sixty-six extended members of the Hutch family and forty-one associates of Thompson and the Kinahan cartel, had been warned their lives were in danger. According to one security source:

> There were certain Hutch associates who had access to explosive devices at that time and there was a concern they might try something at Thompson's family home. The Hutch gang blamed Thompson for orchestrating attacks in the feud and they were desperate to target him.

Thompson, ever fearful he could be arrested for murder, remained safely outside Dublin and the bomb threat came to nothing.

The investigation team continued to build their case throughout October 2016. In Thompson's absence, says a garda source, gardaí received intelligence that he had ordered a senior associate in Dublin to pay €30,000 for a female friend to attend a two-week stint at a rehab clinic after she became addicted to cocaine:

Freddie Thompson was very close to this girl and, because her family were worried about her addiction, he decided to pay for her to attend a rehab clinic. The situation was so ironic because on the one hand you had his associates being the biggest importers of drugs into Ireland and yet, on the other, he's paying to help someone whose life was destroyed by drugs most likely brought into the country by Thompson and his associates.

With Thompson still on the run, the garda investigation team were waiting for the crucial piece of intelligence that would lead them to the location of their chief suspect. Detectives had received reports of sightings of Thompson in Dublin since his disappearance, but they had been unable to catch him. However, the breakthrough they had been waiting for finally came on Tuesday, 1 November 2016, when a source told gardaí that Thompson would be flying into Belfast from the UK, before travelling across the border to attend a short meeting at the CityNorth Hotel in Co. Meath, located just off the M1 motorway.

Determined not to let Thompson slip through their fingers, the senior investigating officer, Detective Inspector Paul Cleary, along with Detective Sergeant Adrian Whitelaw, Detective Garda Linda Williams, now a sergeant, and Detective Garda Stephen Daly, made the half-hour journey to the CityNorth Hotel from Kevin Street Garda Station. In the meantime, officers from the Garda National Surveillance Unit were drafted in to keep Thompson and the unknown associates he'd met at the hotel in their sights.

Arriving at the hotel shortly after 2.40 p.m., the Kevin Street team were told by their colleagues that Thompson was in the foyer meeting with two associates. In an unlucky break, as the investigators entered the hotel Thompson spotted them. As soon as he saw the four gardaí from the south inner city he knew they were there for him, as they had no other reason to be at a hotel in Co. Meath. His well-honed instincts told him to move straight away and he immediately made his way to the gents' toilets.

The murder suspect's bid to avoid arrest, however, ended in failure when Detective Inspector Paul Cleary walked into the toilet and informed Frederick Thompson he was being arrested for the murder of Daithi Douglas, under Section 50 of Ireland's Criminal Justice Act. As his associates looked on, the most senior member of the Kinahan cartel to be arrested since the attack at the Regency Hotel was placed in handcuffs. In a brief search the gang leader was discovered to have €985 in cash, his passport and a Nokia BlackBerry phone in his possession. He was then escorted to a waiting car as stunned hotel residents and Thompson's two associates watched in disbelief. The two men were also searched, and a mobile phone was taken off them.

In an interview with the *Irish Sun* the day after the arrest, one hotel resident, who did not want to be named, recalled the moment one of Ireland's most dangerous gangsters was arrested:

> The whole thing was over in a matter of seconds and the detectives were very professional. People were watching as the man was brought from the toilet in cuffs and walked through the hotel. It was all rather strange, and it was only the following day when news of the arrest appeared in the media that we realized who was arrested. We'd all heard of him but to witness his arrest was surreal.

Following his arrest, Thompson was brought to Kilmainham Garda Station for questioning by expert interviewers from the Garda National Bureau of Criminal Investigation (NBCI), which falls under Special Crime Operations. Gardaí had an interview plan prepared, using a mix of highly trained and experienced interviewers in organized crime from the 'A' District and also from the NBCI.

Gardaí had contacted Thompson's solicitor on the way back to Kilmainham from the hotel so he could attend the interviews. The length of time they could hold 'Fat Freddie' was set under Section 50 – where a garda superintendent can give permission for a suspect to be held for eighteen hours and a garda chief superintendent can then allocate an extension for twenty-four hours. To get a further extension, gardaí would have to go to court. The time is calculated excluding the amount of time the suspect has rest periods, including a night's sleep.

Beginning at 6.30 p.m., after his solicitor had arrived, the first round of the suspect's interviews with garda investigators started with officers asking Thompson if he knew Douglas and if there was 'any reason' why he, or anyone else, would want him killed. As the interview progressed, Thompson was asked about his friendships and how he'd felt when his cousin David Byrne, in whose memory Thompson had just got a tattoo, was shot dead at the Regency Hotel. The veteran criminal made no response. When asked how he was feeling, if his life was under threat and if he had been told to return to Ireland, the gangster placed his head in his right hand and closed his eyes. He went on to reply 'No comment' to every subsequent question.

Throughout the interviews Thompson's behaviour was typically disruptive. He spent time picking his belly button, eating his finger and drinking water from a bottle before spitting it back into the bottle again. He coughed when questions were being asked and concentrated on scratching his groin and spitting in his hands, before rubbing the spit on his legs.

Constantly twitching in his seat, Thompson continued to answer 'No comment' as the barrage of questions moved on to his personal life, with the interviewers asking him if he enjoyed the nickname 'Fat Freddie', if he would consider returning to Spain, about his relationship with the media, and if he had considered giving up the 'rat race' because of the pressure he was under from the gardaí and others. Thompson stared at his left arm and again refused to answer the questions.

Moving on to the Douglas killing, the detectives asked Thompson if he had been the 'manufacturer' of the murder, before telling him: 'Whether you're on the outside or inside – murder is murder.' The veteran criminal again replied: 'No comment.'

Thompson kept his head bowed as he was asked about the Ford Fiesta used in the murder. Trying to get the exhibition-ist killer to respond, the interviewers said: 'We wouldn't have you down as a Ford Fiesta man – no luxury. A Fiesta isn't a Freddie Thompson car.' As the interview continued, Thompson was asked if he only visited Little Caesar's restaurant in Dublin city centre on 'special occasions'.

Thompson maintained his chant of 'No comment' in response to the litany of questions and the first interview session ended at 11.38 p.m.

Just under nine hours later, the second phase of the inter-views started, on 2 November. Thompson was asked, with his solicitor present, to explain his movements on the day of the Douglas murder. The interviewers commented that he wasn't living up to his 'reputation as the supposed Dublin Boy' because of the poor planning behind the murder plot. Thompson's response was to pretend to fall asleep. 'This was Freddie Thompson once again trying to play games and thinking he was funny,' said one source. 'He had been doing this for years when he was stopped by gardaí. This was nothing more than a display of arrogance and utter contempt for the justice system.' Focusing again on the meal at Little Caesar's restaurant, detectives asked if his appearance at the restaurant was a 'murder debrief', and to explain the mood of his gang after the killing. Thompson again replied: 'No comment.'

As the garda interrogators returned to dissecting his actions on the day of the murder, Thompson started twitching in his seat and stroking his beard. When he was asked about his attempts to destroy evidence after the killing, he brazenly replied: 'No comment.' In a series of questions put to Thompson, he was told:

> We're all agreed that the four vehicles were used in the murder of David Douglas. The Mercedes was attempted to be burnt out but the other three weren't. They're all recovered by gardaí. Where was the planning and expertise? You were all sitting down for dinner. Drinking and chatting about the murder but you hadn't got rid of any of the evidence. You didn't plan that very well. You're meant to be leading this, but it didn't go too well. From what we are seeing on CCTV it's obvious you are organizing the murder of David Douglas. You are an experienced guy. You know how this works. Did you not check CCTV? You are seen coming and going from the car that was used to murder David Douglas. Why would you be so obvious? Why would you do that?

Thompson ignored them and continued to engage in the same actions – scratching himself, picking his nose and saying:

'No comment.' The interview continued with the gang leader being asked why he was 'surrounding himself with young lads', if Nathan Foley was his minder and if his young associates were all loyal. A final garda query was: 'Do they want to be the next Freddie Thompson? They'll need to bulk up.'

The interviews finished for the day after Thompson was told that his DNA had been found in the Ford Fiesta, providing 'irrefutable evidence' of his presence in a vehicle that was 'central' to the murder of Daithi Douglas. Freddie's response was: 'No comment.'

On the same day Thompson was confronted with the DNA evidence, his trusted lieutenant, Nathan Foley, was arrested on suspicion of murder at Wheatfield Prison, before being brought to Kevin Street Garda Station for questioning.

As the third interrogation session started the following day at 9.48 a.m., Thompson didn't realize his young minder was facing a similar barrage of questions. 'Fat Freddie' didn't react as he was told by gardaí that they believed he had 'organized, planned and directed' the murder of Daithi Douglas, and that their theory was supported by DNA evidence and CCTV footage that included images of him breaking up a mobile phone. Gardaí told him that they suspected the mobile had been used to 'direct' the murder and that he was trying to 'distance' himself from the killing by destroying his phone. When asked why he had taken 'the boys' to dinner instead of destroying the cars, Thompson asked to see a doctor. 'Fat Freddie' knew that any suspect has a legal right to see a doctor if they claim they're not feeling well. Appearing to struggle with the non-stop questions and again fidgeting in his seat, Thompson was asked how he was feeling and replied: 'I'm okay. I'm brand new.'

The interviews would end that night with Thompson

again showing contempt for the process when he refused to sign the interview notes.

Commencing on 4 November 2016, at 9.24 a.m., Thompson was brought from his cell in Kilmainham for the next round of interviews. Again, the focus of the interrogation was on the murder, with the gangster being asked why Douglas had to die. Refusing to comment, Thompson started to fidget in his seat when he was reminded how Douglas's daughter had watched her father being shot, with one investigator commenting: 'There's no excuse for that – you ruined her. How would your son feel seeing you shot dead eating a bowl of curry?' Thompson kept his head bowed and refused to reply.

Referring to the Kinahan–Hutch feud, the interrogators also asked Thompson if he had enjoyed a 'good night's sleep' during his period of detention because he was being protected by gardaí.

Building their case, the experienced garda team's plan was to associate Thompson with the Kinahan cartel but also to undermine him as someone who was simply following orders. They wanted to make it clear as well that he was being held on suspicion of murder while Daniel Kinahan and other close associates enjoyed the high life in Dubai. 'Fat Freddie' was asked if he had been ordered to murder Douglas because the landscape in gangland had changed in recent years. In a further exchange with the prisoner, Thompson started to pull up his shirt, pick his legs and scratch one of them, when detectives said:

> You're not top dog any more – the Kinahans are. Were you told to murder David? Maybe they wanted him murdered. Did they come to you? Did they ask Freddie Thompson to plan, organize and direct this murder? Is the order coming

from somewhere else? We believe you are part of an organized-crime unit. Is that what it is – you're not the same force as ten years ago? Did you know his wife and fourteen-year-old daughter worked at Shoestown? Did you see them when you were doing reconnaissance? David Douglas was planned by you. You and your friend conspired to have David killed. You are the man who pulled the strings. You were cocky and careless – two things that will get you in trouble.

The interrogators continued trying to get a response from Thompson so they could use it in the subsequent court case. Of his life in organized crime, the detectives said:

Do you think things have changed? We can see two sides. You've done terrible things, but you've seen terrible things and lost friends and family. You've seen a lot more than ninety-nine per cent of the population – death. It's got to play on you, the terrible things. But there have been plenty of good times too – house, money and holidays.

When Thompson was asked if he preferred life during the Crumlin–Drimnagh feud to life in 2016, he kept his head bowed and made no comment. One detective commented:

Back then you were king ding-a-ling, but 2016 is a different story – there are trials, pressure and people coming to kill you. Have you spoken to a counsellor? You've done a lot and had a lot done to you. There was a time when you were cock of the walk but it's not the same as ten years ago – you're way down the pecking order. The Kinahan boys have come on leaps and bounds. The last ten years you have been on the run – the title is slipping. You were the main man ten years ago, like Paddy Doyle, but now you're surrounded by a bunch of apes. You're using the likes of Nathan Foley to carry out a murder in a town where everyone knows him and your fall from grace is bad. Can you play catch-up and keep up with the guys around you who have gotten bigger than you?

Returning to the aftermath of the Douglas murder and the gang's failure to burn the getaway car, gardaí said the plot was like something from a 'Laurel and Hardy' film. Thompson kept his eyes shut, refusing to respond. Gardaí were well used to this type of behaviour from gangland criminals under interrogation. Thompson was a very experienced gangland figure and it was no surprise that he was following the number one rule when responding to questions during interrogation – no comment.

The interviews continued throughout the day, with the last one for the evening starting at 8.09 p.m. This time the interrogation was focusing on Thompson's identification on CCTV. When told that he had been identified on four sets of footage by Detective Sergeant Adrian Whitelaw, Thompson laughed. He then replied: 'No comment' when asked if the experienced gangland investigator had known Thompson since he was a boy. When he was asked about the origin of the murder weapon and if it had been sent to him from Spain, sourced from the Kinahan cartel, he made no reply.

Completing the fourth day of interviews, one interviewer asked Thompson why the killer had left the gun:

Why did he drop the gun? We've spoken about this cocky, careless planning. The more stuff you leave the more help for the guards. You planned this and look where we are now. You have no one to blame but yourself. You picked some prize beauties. Instead of burning the car – your man burned himself.

During the course of Thompson's detention and questioning for the Douglas murder, gardaí also held numerous meetings with the Director of Public Prosecutions. In their submissions to the DPP, gardaí asserted that the motive for the killing was that the Kinahan cartel blamed Daithi Douglas and Darren Kearns for the attempt to shoot Liam Roe in November 2015. However, gardaí also pointed out that a full investigation had established this wasn't true. In their submission they stated: 'It would appear to be a case of mistaken identity and misinformation.' Gardaí had established both Douglas and Kearns were 'in a different location at the time of this attempt on Liam Roe'. They also informed the DPP: 'Liam Roe is a key Kinahan Organized Crime Gang lieutenant and is a first cousin, and very close associate, of Freddie Thompson, who plays an extremely violent role within the Kinahan gang.'

Gardaí also informed the DPP that the murder was linked to the 'ongoing feud between the Kinahan and Hutch organized-crime gangs'. Providing background on Thompson's role within the criminal underworld, gardaí told the DPP that the gangster:

> is a lifelong serious criminal who is a member of the Kinahan gang, who are well known as an international organized-crime gang. There can be little doubt that, with his standing in the criminal world, he is the one who orchestrated the murder of David Douglas. He has the motive and the criminal muscle to put everything into place – cars and guns, etc. While it is all set up by Thompson, he then used his less experienced associates to carry out the murder after he set everything up.

The gardaí continued to press the DPP for a charge of murder against Thompson by outlining the main strands of evidence in the case. In their submission they commented on their surprise at Thompson's active participation in the murder:

> While the murder happened on the say-so of Freddie Thompson, it is quite surprising he took such an active role in its organizing and planning on 1 July. It would appear he thought he was being clever in using a common nondescript type car like the silver Ford Fiesta, which he had no association with and that the said car would not turn up in this murder inquiry. As a result of this slip-up he has left his footprint all over this murder. This is probably the first and last time Freddie Thompson will let himself get as close to murder again. The three others are all lower level street criminals who would appear to want to be part of this gangland culture and climb the ladder in the criminal underworld. This was their opportunity. They are not as experienced as Freddie in organizing, planning and partaking in murders and, as a result, they too have left their footprints all over this murder. The evidence in this case proves they were all working together, of that there can be no doubt.

Commenting on Thompson's links to Nathan Foley, detectives outlined how the pair were 'long-term associates' who had been 'collated by gardaí on numerous occasions' on the garda Pulse system. Gardaí added:

> While Nathan Foley may have a lesser role to play than some of the others in this murder, he nonetheless plays his part to achieve the end goal which is the murder of David

Douglas. Effectively Nathan Foley has brought both the gunman and the driver of the hit car to the Mercedes to start the route of the murder.

Completing their submissions by informing the DPP that 262 statements had been taken and 290 lines of inquiry had been followed during the course of their intensive investigation, gardaí concluded their request for Thompson to be charged with murder by supplying a damning history of his career as a veteran criminal:

Frederick Thompson has been one of the most notorious gangland figures in this country for the past fifteen years. He has been involved in the Crumlin and Drimnagh feud which has resulted in sixteen gangland murders to date. Thompson is also a very senior member of the Kinahan Organized Crime Gang. This OCG is an international player in drugs importation and distribution. They are involved in numerous criminal activities worldwide and have connections to major international criminals around the world. They have unlimited financial resources and access to all types of available firearms, weapons and personnel. The Kinahan OCG is currently responsible for nine of the ten murders to date in the ongoing feud. This feud does not show any signs of relenting. Freddie Thompson would be used as an enforcer for the Kinahan gang. He is also involved in the running of drugs and weapons for them. Freddie Thompson is no stranger to murder. Three of the other suspects are low-level criminals and would be used by Freddie as his so-called 'gillies'. He uses them to do his dirty work.

In a subsequent interview, one investigator outlined the gardaí's concerns during Thompson's period of detention:

It was a very tense time for everyone and the senior investigating officer in the case was back and forward to the DPP answering any questions they might have. Gardaí had no way of knowing if he was going to be charged and if he wasn't then he would have walked out the door and no doubt fled to a country that didn't have an extradition treaty with Ireland. It was the first ever time that gardaí had evidence of Thompson participating in a murder, but the question of whether he would be charged or not wasn't a foregone conclusion. Everyone was just hoping there would be a charge following his detention.

The senior investigating officer in the case was constantly engaging with the DPP as the evidence secured by the gardaí was being considered and analysed. In final exchanges with the DPP the gardaí highlighted the need for any trial against Thompson to be held at the non-jury Special Criminal Court when they maintained:

> Due to the likely sentence upon conviction for the murder of David Douglas, gardaí believe there is a very real possibility that the Kinahan Organized Crime Gang will try to intimidate or interfere with a jury on behalf of suspected offenders in this case. The gang have the resources and the will to carry out this type of action.

With the period of detention almost up, the team's interviews with Thompson drew to a close. Investigators made a series of calls to the DPP, looking for an answer on whether or not 'Fat Freddie' would be charged. After concluding the final phase of their interrogation on Saturday, 5 November 2016, gardaí reported to the DPP on Thompson's close proximity to the Douglas murder scene and around south inner-city

Dublin: 'It is believed that the presence of Frederick Thompson at these locations on 1 July is attributable to his participation in the offence. Frederick Thompson has failed or refused to provide an account when questioned.'

As the team were finishing their questions at around 6.30 p.m. on Saturday, they finally got their answer. Thompson looked puzzled and then smug when he was informed that he was being released from his detention. However, the colour drained from his face just twenty seconds later when he was told that he was now under rearrest and that he would be charged with the murder of Daithi Douglas. According to one investigator:

> He didn't know what was going on and didn't seem to realize that he was being released from his first period of detention. He was sick when he was charged. Following a tense four days, it was a massive relief to everyone involved in the investigation to have a charge against him.

Held at Kilmainham Garda Station over the weekend, on Monday morning, 7 November, Thompson was brought to Dublin District Court by a four-vehicle garda convoy, consisting of a garda van, two patrol cars and an unmarked car carrying armed officers. There was a heavy garda presence because of who they were dealing with, similar to all cases involving someone who's charged with gangland- or terrorist-related offences.

Dressed in a navy anorak, tracksuit bottoms and black runners, Thompson was the first to appear before Judge David Waters. During the five-minute hearing, 'Fat Freddie', who was granted legal aid, sat with his arms folded.

The senior investigating officer, Detective Inspector Paul Cleary, told the court about Thompson's initial reaction to being charged with murder: 'In reply to the charge, after caution, he said: "No comment."'

Leaving the court, Thompson smiled at a woman who had supported him at the hearing. None of the Douglas family or Thompson's Kinahan associates were present.

For the first time in a criminal career spanning almost two decades, the gangster known as 'Fat Freddie' Thompson, one of Ireland's most dangerous killers, had been charged with murder. It was the beginning of the end for him.

18. Falling Down

> The prosecution does not say he carried out the
> physical act of killing. One hand might have been on
> the gun, but many fingers were on the trigger. It is
> our case that one of these fingers belonged to
> Mr Thompson.
>
> Sean Gillane, SC

Just two weeks after his first ever appearance in court on a murder charge, Freddie Thompson suffered another blow when his young associate, who had been charged with killing the student Lorcan O'Reilly the previous April, appeared at the Central Criminal Court in Dublin. The decision had been made to hold the case in the Central Criminal Court and not the Children's Court due to the serious nature of the offence.

During the hearing on 21 November 2016, closed to members of the public other than relatives of the accused and his victim, the teenager replied 'not guilty' to the charge of murder, but 'guilty' to manslaughter. Acting for the Irish State, the prosecution barrister, Brendan Grehan, SC, accepted the guilty plea, before outlining the events which had led to the killing.

Detective Inspector Paul Cleary, today a chief superintendent, then testified to the court about the gardaí's concerns over witness intimidation, detailing the actions of Frederick Thompson and his associates in the aftermath of the killing. The court would also hear how, despite the fact that twenty-three youths had been present at the Hallowe'en party when the 21-year-old student was stabbed to death, gardaí had 'struggled' to gather witness statements. When asked if the gardaí had concerns for the safety of witnesses, the senior investigator replied: 'Serious concerns.'

Thompson's young associate was released on bail, and the date for sentencing set for 6 February 2017. In the meantime, his mentor, Thompson, remained in custody in Mountjoy Prison, trying to secure a date for his bail hearing. His defence team were also working in the background on trying to have the charges against him dropped due to lack of evidence.

For the remainder of 2016 the gangster's associates on the outside continued their offensive against anyone they suspected of supporting the Hutch faction. Just three days before Christmas, another innocent man, Noel 'Duck Egg' Kirwan, was shot six times in front of his partner, Bernadette Roe, as the couple sat in a car outside her home in St Ronan's Drive, Clondalkin, west Dublin. Gardaí, who confirmed that the 62-year-old had no involvement in criminality, believe the father of four was targeted because he had been photographed standing alongside Gerry 'The Monk' Hutch at the funeral of Eddie Hutch. The Kinahan cartel fixer Jason Keating, who provided phones and placed a tracker on the target's car, later received a ten-year sentence after he pleaded guilty to 'participating in or contributing to the activities of a criminal organization'. However, the chief suspect, a close associate of Freddie Thompson, is still in Dubai, holed up with the mob boss Daniel Kinahan.

In a subsequent interview, Kirwan's daughter Donna outlined her family's trauma:

Our dad was all we had. He was our friend, our safety net – he was supposed to walk me down the aisle one day. We have been stripped of everything – we are a shell of the people we once were. It has destroyed us. I don't feel anything towards him [Keating] but I don't hate him. My dad was a completely innocent man, and if he had known Keating, he would have told him to never get involved in something like this.

As Thompson settled back into life in prison and waited for his appearance at the High Court, the youngest member of his gang was brought before the Central Criminal Court to receive his sentence for fatally stabbing Lorcan O'Reilly. After a week's adjournment, Thompson's young associate received a four-and-a-half year jail term for the killing. He was sent to Oberstown Children Detention Campus, a facility in North Co. Dublin where young people under the age of eighteen are sent to complete their sentences. It was likely that Thompson's young associate would only serve a short term there before he was released.

In his Victim Impact Statement, delivered to the court, Lorcan's father described how his family had found themselves in a 'horrific situation':

He was taken from us in the most violent way. We have to speak on his behalf as he can no longer speak for himself. When Lorcan went out that night none of us thought it would turn out to be the worst night of our lives – and his last. When he was stabbed in the heart that night, it was all of our hearts broken. To go to a hospital and be told by a doctor there was nothing we could do. We tried our best, but he's passed away, and to not even get a chance to comfort him or say goodbye is the most heart-wrenching feeling and the lowest night of our lives.

The only time Lorcan visited a graveyard was two weeks before he died, visiting his grandad's grave with his mother and I. He stood on the spot where he himself is buried now. He told us there was no point in crying, 'Just have a laugh, the way I would want it.' I'm afraid I can't do that, Lorcan, the pain is too much. Lorcan is in our minds all the time. This isn't just our loss – it's his grandparents' loss, his uncles', his aunts', cousins', friends' and the community's loss. He touched so many people's lives and he should still be, except his life and future was robbed.

The following month, Thompson's young minder, Nathan Foley, was brought before Dublin District Court and was also charged with the murder of Daithi Douglas. Again, there was a heavy garda presence at the court due to the serious nature of the charge he was facing. During the proceedings, the court was told it was the DPP's decision to have the trial heard before the Special Criminal Court because the ordinary courts were 'inadequate to secure the effective administration of justice'.

As Thompson remained on remand, he received a boost in April 2017, when his young associate was brought from Oberstown to meet him in the medical wing of Mountjoy Prison on three different occasions. However, the meetings were cancelled as a disciplinary measure, after Thompson was classified as a 'troublesome inmate' who had 'influence' over younger inmates in the prison system.

Despite Thompson's absence from the feud, the Kinahan war machine was still in business. On 3 April 2017, an Estonian contract killer and former soldier, Imre Arakas, flew into Ireland with a mission to target Thompson's one-time associate and Hutch loyalist James 'Mago' Gately. 'Fat Freddie' had met Gately through Gary Hutch when they all spent time together in Spain and Dublin. However, unbeknownst to the man known as 'The Butcher' in his homeland, Arakas's every move was being watched by undercover officers from the garda Drugs and Organised Crime Bureau.

The Emergency Response Unit stormed his safe house the following morning and arrested the hitman, along with a Kinahan cartel associate, Eric Fowler. Investigators recovered an encrypted BlackBerry phone and details of 'Mago' Gately's secret hideout in Northern Ireland. Just after the phone was seized, a quick-thinking investigator Detective Garda Sean O'Neill, took a picture of a thread of messages on the device which were suspected to be from Daniel Kinahan. Detective Garda O'Neill managed to get the image before the phone messages were remotely deleted. One of the exchanges read: 'It seems possible to take him down when he comes out of the car then on the way to the front door. A silencer would be good and it would be very good if the dog [gun] be accurate. It could be just one shot to the head from distance.'

Later jailed for six years, after pleading guilty to conspiring to murder Gately, Arakas is also facing extradition to Lithuania on other serious charges, including murder and possession of firearms. Daniel Kinahan's hitman had failed in his bid to target Gately, but the senior Hutch associate was in the crosshairs again just over a month later. On 10 May, he was saved by his bulletproof vest when another contract killer fired five shots at him as he sat in his car at the Topaz garage in Clonshaugh, north Dublin. Living in Northern

Ireland but making frequent visits to Dublin, he was tracked, gardaí believed, by a two-man hit team before the shooting. Gately, who was also a target for Thompson, made a full recovery from the shooting and remains in hiding.

That same month Thompson was waiting for the ruling on his quest to have the charges against him dropped due to lack of evidence. Both sides had presented their cases to the Special Criminal Court on the reasons why the charges should and shouldn't be dropped and they were waiting for it to make a final ruling.

While Thompson was waiting for the court's response, it was the turn of the Hutch gang to retaliate in its deadly feud with 'Fat Freddie' and the rest of the cartel. Striking for the first time since the killing of David Byrne at the Regency Hotel over a year earlier, they targeted a low-level cartel associate, Michael Keogh, whose brother Johnny had murdered Gareth Hutch. Keogh was shot dead as he sat in his car at Sheridan Court, Dorset Street, north inner-city Dublin, on 31 May 2017. Gardaí believed Keogh was killed because he had aligned himself with his brother's INLA faction and he'd been linked to a number of firebomb attacks on the homes of innocent Hutch relatives.

In the weeks and months following the murder, there was a period of relative calm in the feud. The gardaí in the CAB and the Drugs and Organised Crime Bureau continued their investigations into the warring factions, building their cases against the main players, and the summer months passed without any serious incidents.

On 7 August 2017, the relative quiet was broken when two contract killers for the cartel, Gary Gleeson and Stephen Dunne, were dispatched to murder Thompson's old associate Michael Frazer. It would be the sixth attempt on Frazer's life, with Thompson suspected of being the mastermind behind four of the incidents, dating back to 2015. However, unbeknownst to the bungling hit squad, their every move was being watched and their conversations were recorded by the garda Drugs and Organised Crime Bureau. Before their arrest by the Emergency Response Unit at 7.30 p.m. on the Naas Road, west Dublin, Gleeson was heard telling his accomplice: 'Aim for the head yeah? Head shots or we won't get fucking paid.'

Dunne replied: 'Once I get him a bit, I've to walk right up to him, you know what I mean. As soon as we block him, I'm going to let a shot off in the van yeah, and then once I get him a bit I'll keep walking towards him and I'll just keep shooting yeah.'

Gleeson responded curtly: 'Just riddle him.'

At a later date in the Special Criminal Court, the murder plan was branded by Mr Justice Tony Hunt as 'shambolic, confused and ill-prepared'. Described as 'foot soldiers', Gary Gleeson and Stephen Dunne were each jailed for twelve years.

One week after the attempt on Frazer's life, Thompson received the news he had been waiting for when he was informed that a ruling on his application to have the case against him dismissed would be made at the Special Criminal Court on 31 August. Gardaí remained confident the charges would remain and saw it as just another attempt by Thompson to undermine the judicial process because he knew he was facing the most serious charge in his criminal career. When 'Fat Freddie' had been refused bail at the High Court the previous month he'd immediately reapplied, but having the charges dropped was his real focus.

A few days later, there was more mayhem on the streets of Dublin. On 16 August, two gunmen armed with sub-machine guns targeted the family home of Derek 'Bottler' Devoy in

Balbutcher Drive, Ballymun, north Dublin. Two people, Antoinette Corbally and Clinton Shannon, were shot dead outside the house, as 'Bottler' managed to escape the attempt on his life by running through back gardens.

Meanwhile, in the run-up to Thompson's court appearance, senior prison sources revealed that 'Fat Freddie' was boasting to other inmates of his imminent release. 'He was strutting around like a peacock,' said one source:

> and telling everyone that he would soon be going home because the gardaí didn't have much on him. He had been furious over the decision to refuse him bail at an earlier hearing but was extremely confident that this court date would be the one that sent him home.

However, Thompson's ego suffered a severe shock when the Special Criminal Court dismissed his application. In her address to the court, Ms Justice Isobel Kennedy revealed that the court had considered all submissions in the application and ruled there was 'sufficient evidence' for Thompson to stand trial for murder. A stunned Thompson said nothing during the court appearance, while gardaí were delighted that his application had been dismissed and they refocused on his trial.

Though it was clearly a setback, Thompson refused to give up and spent the following weeks plotting his next move. On 3 October 2017, he was transferred from Mountjoy Prison to the High Court in Dublin, under armed escort, as part of another attempt to secure bail ahead of his trial for murder.

During the hearing, Sergeant Brendan Brogan, from Pearse Street Garda Station, told the court that gardaí were objecting to bail because of the 'seriousness' of the charge and because Thompson was a 'flight risk'. Sergeant Brogan explained that fake travel documents containing Thompson's image had been recovered during a search carried out by the Operation Thistle team. In his final submission to the court, the experienced officer, who had been briefed by detectives investigating the Douglas murder, said there was 'real concern further serious offences would be committed if Thompson received bail'.

The court also heard from Chief Superintendent Francis Clerkin, now retired, who stated as part of his submissions to the court that the refusal of bail was 'necessary' to prevent the 'commission of serious offences', and:

Frederick Thompson, as part of the criminal grouping the Kinahan Organized Crime Gang, has been active for a number of years within the State and is operating at the very top level of serious organized crime. He is engaged in a wide variety of serious criminal activity, namely the importation, sale, supply and distribution of drugs and firearms, international money laundering, murder and witness intimidation. The *modus operandi* of this criminal grouping is predominantly the importation and distribution of drugs into the State and smuggling the proceeds of their criminal activities outside the jurisdiction. I say and believe that this criminal grouping, and by extension Frederick Thompson, have amassed significant wealth from their criminal activities.

In a further submission, the senior officer added:

I believe that Frederick Thompson and this criminal grouping are involved in a murderous feud with another criminal grouping – the Hutch Organized Crime Gang. I believe that if granted bail Frederick Thompson would continue his affiliations with the KOCG and in doing so would continue to commit serious offences. My basis for this belief is that Frederick Thompson organized the murder of David Douglas and directed others in the execution of this murder. He has access to significant wealth and associates and properties throughout Europe. His association to the criminal grouping and that grouping's ongoing feud with another high-profile criminal gang would result in further loss of life at the hands of, or at the behest of, Thompson.

In conclusion, the officer stated: 'I further believe should Frederick Thompson be granted bail that he would fail to answer it.' Chief Superintendent Clerkin maintained that Thompson was 'a flight risk'.

Accepting the gardaí's submission, the High Court judge, Mr Justice Paul McDermott, told the court he was refusing bail on several grounds, including that Thompson 'represented a flight risk'.

Immediately following the ruling, the court witnessed at first hand Thompson's rage. The fuming gangster stood up and yelled: 'Fuck off, I'm not listening to this,' before storming off to the holding area for prisoners. As prison officers attempted to bring him back before the judge, Thompson continued his tirade of abuse.

'I'm not fucking going back in. The state of the country. Ye are all the same,' he roared.

Thompson suffered another blow soon afterwards, when one of his few visitors in prison, Niamh Fitzpatrick, the former lover of the slain crime boss Eamon 'The Don' Dunne, was arrested by officers from the gardaí's North Central Division under 'Operation Spire'. During the search of her home in Ringsend, south Dublin, investigators recovered a Smith & Wesson revolver from an air vent. Fitzpatrick, who claimed the gun was for her own protection, was jailed for five years in January 2018, with two years suspended after she admitted possessing the weapon.

Gardaí believed Thompson's continued detention was undoubtedly saving lives on the streets of the capital. However, they were also convinced his young associates were still involved in swamping the south inner city with heroin and cocaine. As one investigator said:

> Freddie might not have been any use to the Kinahans because he was inside, but there were still young men who were loyal to him and who would continue to make money for him. He may have been in prison, but he still had contacts and he would have been ordering his associates to set aside some money. He obviously didn't have the same influence, but he still had connections to criminals from all over the capital.

Three days after his attempt to secure bail was dismissed, Thompson's legal team were back before the Special Criminal Court to learn the date of his trial for the Douglas murder. Thompson was told the trial was scheduled for 30 April 2018. Foley's trial would be on the same day, but they would not be tried together.

The gardaí's investigation into the shooter and the getaway driver was ongoing. Thompson's two young associates were still on the run, with gardaí satisfied they had left Ireland. If the investigation team received intelligence of their location, they would be immediately arrested.

In the meantime, the Kinahan cartel's campaign of terror against the Hutch Organized Crime Gang continued. On 6 November 2017, four men were arrested after officers from the Drugs and Organised Crime Bureau foiled a planned attack on Gary Hanley, a north Dublin man. The cartel saw him as a threat because they regarded him as a key associate of the Hutch gang, but his friends claimed Hanley had nothing to do with them. One of the men arrested, the contract killer Luke Wilson, another associate of Thompson's young gang of dealers, was found with a Beretta pistol, a ski mask and cans of petrol. Before his arrest, he was secretly recorded by investigators. 'He doesn't even know why our people want him gone because he's such a fucking idiot,' Wilson said. 'Hanley goes to the gym every night. We can get him then. We need to get out hopefully and get paid. It's clear we need to do more homework on this.'

In another success for the gardaí's Drugs and Organised Crime Bureau, Wilson would later receive an eleven-year sentence, after pleading guilty to conspiring to murder and possession of a firearm. Three other men, Thompson's cousin Liam Brannigan, Alan Wilson and Joseph Kelly, all from south inner-city Dublin, have been charged with conspiracy to murder and are due to appear in court in 2019.

A few weeks later another of Thompson's close associates from Blanchardstown in west Dublin emerged as a chief suspect in the murder of Caine Kirwan. The 24-year-old father of one's body was found dumped in a field in Clonee, Co. Meath, on 1 December 2017. Kirwan, whose father, Noel, had been murdered almost a year previously after he attended Eddie Hutch's funeral, had been a key target for the cartel. The KOCG was concerned about him because Caine, a volatile and well-connected criminal, had sworn revenge for his father's murder.

Thompson's cartel associates were involved in another murder on 20 January 2018 – just a few weeks into the new year. A 27-year-old drug addict and armed robber, Derek Coakley Hutch, Gary Hutch's cousin, was gunned down as he sat in a car in Bridgeview halting site, located beside Cloverhill Prison, west Dublin. Considering him a soft target, gardaí believed he was executed simply because of his family ties. The investigation is still active. Ten days later, a Kinahan hit team were also blamed for the murder of a loyal Hutch associate, Jason 'Buda' Molyneux, at James Larkin House flats, north inner-city Dublin.

Following the murders, Thompson warned other inmates in Mountjoy that the feud would never end. A senior prison source said: 'He told Irish Prison Service staff and other inmates the feud would keep on going. He was very adamant about it, and said he also told the same thing to gardaí.'

In the aftermath of the two killings the Justice Minister, Charlie Flanagan, warned those involved in the feud there would be 'no hiding place':

> The horrific and brutal murders, many of which have taken place in cold blood, are totally unacceptable. This feud is highly professional, and we are dealing with killers, hired hands, people coming in from abroad. The Government is fully committed to tackle all forms of criminality and I'll ensure the gardaí are properly and adequately resourced to do their job.

As gardaí continued their efforts to prevent further bloodshed in the first months of 2018 and the Criminal Assets Bureau investigators were unrelenting in their examination of the cartel's money-laundering operation, Thompson was preparing for his trial on 30 April. He was on his own as there had been no contact between Freddie and the Kinahans. Like many before him, Thompson was expendable because he was no longer of any use to them.

Unlike his previous court appearances, throughout his

criminal career of over twenty years, Thompson, now thirty-seven years old, knew he faced a life sentence if found guilty. Distancing himself from other inmates in the weeks before the trial, he spent many of his days in the prison gym preparing for his big day in court. One prison source explained: 'He was trying to get in good shape and in the right frame of mind because he was genuinely convinced he could get off because he said the evidence wasn't strong enough.'

Arriving at the three-judge, non-jury Special Criminal Court on the morning of 30 April, Thompson's legal team, led by the defence barrister Michael O'Higgins SC, requested an adjournment because of some 'outstanding' disclosure issues connected to the case. Agreeing to the request, Mr Justice Tony Hunt remanded Thompson in custody until 2 May.

Returning to the Special Criminal Court two days later, the Douglas case was listed for a two-week period, under Mr Justice Tony Hunt, presiding, sitting with Judge Gerard Griffin and Judge Flann Brennan. Thompson sat with his arms folded as the prosecuting barrister, Sean Gillane SC, opened the State's case against him. The senior barrister maintained:

> The prosecution does not say he carried out the physical act of killing. One hand might have been on the gun, but many fingers were on the trigger. It is our case that one of these fingers belonged to Mr Thompson. The accused and others were working closely in a carefully planned execution of another human being.

Continuing with his address to the court, Gillane outlined how it was the prosecution's case that four vehicles and their occupants were 'operating in concert that day', which would be supported by CCTV footage of their movements. Describing the Mercedes used in the killing as the 'ultimate vehicle', the senior barrister also described how the other vehicles used in the murder – the Suzuki Swift, Ford Fiesta and Mitsubishi Mirage – had been forensically examined. As a result of this examination, Mr Gillane went on, it would be the State's case that two finger marks belonging to Thompson had been found on the rear-view mirror of the Mitsubishi Mirage, and that two fingerprints had been discovered on a birthday card in the glove box. Another finger mark had been revealed on the Ford Fiesta's rear-view mirror. Mr Gillane spoke about the other evidence against Thompson related to DNA, stating: 'DNA matching his was found on an inhaler in the blue Mitsubishi and his DNA was also found on an air-freshener and hand sanitizer in the Fiesta.'

The prosecutor added that it was the State's belief Thompson was the 'bearded man' captured on CCTV driving the Ford Fiesta and also the same man seen dismantling his phone on Meath Street.

During the first day of proceedings, an eyewitness, Shane Egan, recalled the murder of Daithi Douglas:

I noticed a man walking kind of funny, a bit all over the place. I just thought he didn't look right. Then I saw him shoot and he put the gun down beside the man's head. He smirked as he walked away and then he broke into a slow jog. Straight after that, about five seconds later, I heard a young lady scream.

John Shaw, who ran the crèche next door to Shoestown, also gave evidence on the opening day:

I thought it was fireworks when I heard the first bang and then I heard another five or six bangs. I went to the door.

As I was going to the door a man dressed from head to toe in black ran past me. I went to the door of Shoestown and saw David lying on the floor. I told my co-workers to lock the door and keep the kids in their room.

On the second day of the trial the Special Criminal Court was shown images of the gun used in the murder, while on the third day it heard from Deivydas Kukanavza and his then girlfriend, Iveta Sutkote, who had seen the Mitsubishi Mirage ram the Suzuki Swift on 4 July in Sandymount, south Dublin. Sutkote stated: 'There were two or three men in the Mitsubishi. One had the canister and he poured petrol on. He tried to light it up and it was on fire. He just ran.'

As the trial continued over the next few days, the court heard evidence from the State Pathologist, Dr Marie Cassidy, on the cause of Douglas's death and from a forensic scientist, Sarah Fleming, on the discovery of Thompson's DNA on the spotter cars. Fleming said: 'I estimate the chance of finding this profile, if the DNA had come from someone unrelated to Frederick Thompson, is considerably less than one in 1,000 million.'

On 10 May, the prosecutor showed the court a CCTV image of the moment Douglas was killed. The image showed the gunman calmly entering the shop before opening fire.

Detective Sergeant Adrian Whitelaw was then called to the stand. Referring to the CCTV footage from Little Caesar's restaurant in Dublin, the senior gangland investigator said: 'The man in the dark top and the black baseball cap is Freddie Thompson.' Asked to identify the man seen on CCTV dismantling a mobile phone, he replied: 'The man in the cap is Frederick Thompson.' In the final piece of CCTV shown to him, footage of the man driving the Ford Fiesta,

Detective Sergeant Whitelaw testified: 'I was able to identify that person and it's Frederick Thompson.'

Under cross-examination by Thompson's barrister, Michael O'Higgins SC, the gangland investigator was asked how he had identified Thompson as the driver of the Fiesta. Detective Sergeant Whitelaw replied: 'I was influenced by the time I saw him previously, in or around April or May, and he looked exactly like that. I'd seen him in many forms. He looks different today. I know him. It's him. I'm sure it's him. I've always been able to recognize him.'

Thompson's barrister then referred to the quality of one of the CCTV images, asking: 'Can I suggest to you, his own mother wouldn't pick him out in that still image?'

The senior investigator replied: 'You can suggest what you like – I'm telling you that's Frederick Thompson and I can identify him in that.'

Detective Garda Seamus O'Donovan also told the court he had identified Thompson in the CCTV footage, based on his knowledge of the gangster after his conviction for a violent-disorder offence in 2013. 'In that investigation,' he said, 'the only tangible piece of evidence I had was in fact CCTV footage.'

On the eighth day of the trial, on 14 May 2018, Thompson's legal team argued all the CCTV images were inadmissible because they had been obtained 'unlawfully', from property owners who had failed to register their CCTV systems. As part of the defence's strategy, they also claimed Thompson's right to privacy had been breached under Data Protection laws.

When the Special Criminal Court returned two days later, however, after considering the application to remove the CCTV footage as evidence, they dismissed Thompson's claims that it breached his privacy as 'absurd'. In his ruling on the application, Mr Justice Tony Hunt said:

> If it should turn out that the CCTV implicates Mr Thompson, he is not entitled to call in aid the provisions he invokes to cover his tracks. We have found no illegality or breach in An Garda Síochána's statutory duty in gathering the CCTV evidence in this case. We reject the notion that any or all of the CCTV evidence should be ruled inadmissible.

The ten-day trial ended on 17 May with the prosecution closing its case by reminding the court of the CCTV evidence. Sean Gillane SC concluded by reading out the statement of a witness who did not appear and whose name was not given to the court. The witness had seen the alleged gunman after the murder and stated:

> I saw a silver car driving very hard behind me. I pulled in to let it pass. I saw that the car was a silver Mercedes. The car parked up and two men got out. The car went up in flames almost immediately. The driver's leg caught fire and he started to put it out. That's when he dropped his face mask. I saw him and he saw me. He tried to cover his face when he saw me.

The defence team did not call any witnesses and, with closing statements from both sides to follow, the trial was adjourned for two weeks.

The court returned on 31 May with Thompson's legal team asking for a 'not guilty' verdict to be delivered. They maintained the State had established 'no forensic connection' between their client and two of the cars 'unquestionably involved in the crime', the Suzuki and the Mercedes.

In summing up, Thompson's barrister, Michael O'Higgins SC, claimed the DNA findings from the Mitsubishi and Fiesta were not 'temporal connections', while the CCTV images of Thompson in the Fiesta were 'a blur' and 'fundamentally flawed'. Mr O'Higgins also maintained that the footage of Thompson dismantling his phone was 'speculation'.

Resuming the following day, Mr Justice Tony Hunt rejected the defence's move to dismiss the DNA evidence, saying: 'The court has already ruled the evidence met the minimum cogency standard of admissibility and sees no reason to revisit the earlier conclusion at this juncture.'

Following this ruling, another barrister in the prosecution legal team, Tony McGillicuddy BL, maintained the movements of the Fiesta formed a 'seamless part' of the murder. He reminded the court that all four vehicles played a 'vital logistical role' in the killing. The barrister concluded: 'On the basis of all the evidence before the court, the prosecution says the court should find Mr Thompson guilty of the murder of Mr Douglas in 2016.'

Both the prosecution and the defence teams – and 'Fat Freddie' Thompson – would have to wait another three months before they got their answer.

19. Judgment Day

> . . . this man was killed, if not in front of his daughter, who was very young, when she was around, and she came upon her dead parent in the immediate aftermath of his execution . . . I hope that she will somehow be able to recover from it. I can't think of a worse thing.
>
> Mr Justice Tony Hunt

Throughout his quest to win the 2018 Irish presidential election for a second time, Michael D. Higgins travelled the length and breadth of Ireland, meeting people from all walks of life. On 2 October 2018, President Higgins and his wife, Sabina, hit the campaign trail in Grafton Street, one of Dublin's most renowned shopping areas. Chatting to well-wishers as they canvassed for votes, they were asked to pose for a photograph with a woman working on one of the street's well-known flower stalls. Agreeing to the request, the Irish presidential hopeful and his wife joined Vicky Dempsey, former girlfriend of 'Fat Freddie' Thompson, as they all smiled for the camera. A spokesman for President Higgins later confirmed neither Thompson nor his case were discussed during the brief exchange. The spokesman said: 'The President simply greeted Ms Dempsey on request and posed for a photograph as he did with scores of well-wishers as he greeted campaign workers in Grafton Street.'

While everyone was all smiles for the presidential hopeful, it had been a different story for her ex-partner when he appeared at the Special Criminal Court on 30 August.

Initially scheduled for 24 July, the verdict in the Thompson case was postponed until 1 October due to the ever-increasing workload of the Special Criminal Court. The three-judge panel had, Mr Justice Tony Hunt explained, undertaken a 'heavy trial' immediately after Thompson's ten-day trial was completed. However, at another hearing on 31 July, and following concerns expressed by Thompson's barrister, Michael O'Higgins SC, over delays in the judgment, the panel, consisting of Mr Justice Tony Hunt, Judge Gerard Griffin and Judge Flann Brennan, confirmed its judgment would be made on 30 August.

Clutching his Bible, Thompson, dressed in a white shirt, with a navy tie, and dark jeans, was in buoyant form as he was brought into the packed courtroom by his prison guards. The many people in the public gallery had gone through metal detectors and given their names to gardaí before being admitted to the court. Daithi Douglas's family, however, were not in attendance.

Smiling as he greeted his mother, Elizabeth, and sister, Lisa Jane, with 'All right?', Thompson joked with prison officers after they handed him a bottle of water, claiming it was 'freezing'. 'Fat Freddie' looked relaxed as he spoke with his legal team and sat with his hands folded, as members of the investigation team, his mother and sister, and the waiting media pack waited for Mr Justice Tony Hunt to address the court.

Beginning with a warning that the sixty-five-page judgment would 'take some time to read', the court also reminded the media of the reporting restrictions in place regarding the identification of Thompson's alleged accomplices – two of whom had yet to be arrested and with Foley's trial yet to take place. The full name of Mr C., the gunman, was given in court, but it could not be reported. Mr Justice Hunt then started his submission by referring to Douglas's murder:

> Although the paramedic personnel treated Mr Douglas promptly at the scene, which was followed by his swift removal to St James's Hospital, the evidence indicates that he was essentially dead on arrival at the hospital where he was formally pronounced dead at 16.55 p.m. The evidence of Dr Cassidy on day four establishes that the deceased received six gunshot wounds. The murder weapon was placed by the gunman beside the body of the deceased on the floor of the shop. The fatal shots were fired by the pistol left at the scene which was in good condition and had the serial number milled away. As is obvious from this brief statement of facts, there was nothing spontaneous in the circumstances of Mr Douglas's death. This was, in effect, an execution and, as in all such cases, it is the prosecution case that this murder involved intricate advanced planning and co-ordination, the involvement of persons other than the gunman and the use of several motor vehicles in support of the plan to carry out the murder. The prosecution case is that Mr Thompson is one of those who participated in and contributed to the execution of the plan to murder Mr Douglas, but was not the person who fired the fatal shots.

Referring to the witness statements detailing the gunman's behaviour and the getaway car's movements following the killing, Mr Justice Hunt stated how the three-judge panel were 'satisfied' the Mercedes used by the gang, also referred to in the judgment as 'CLA', could be 'traced back from the scene of the murder by various CCTV systems'. He confirmed they were 'satisfied' that in driving around the south inner city on 1 July 2016 the Mercedes was 'preceded by a silver Ford Fiesta' in the hours before the murder.

Listening intently to the judge's comments, Thompson started to twitch, often stretching his arms, cracking his fingers and looking at his relatives. Dealing with Thompson's trusted lieutenant Nathan Foley, Mr Justice Hunt confirmed that all three judges were 'satisfied' Foley had delivered 'one driver and one passenger' to the Mercedes, and went on:

> It follows that these two men were the gunman and the getaway driver in this enterprise and that the Mitsubishi was the means of delivering these two men to their car. We have no doubt, based on other evidence, that the third man who returned to the Mirage was Nathan Foley.

Thompson continued to clutch his Bible as he listened to Mr Justice Hunt referring to the movements of the gang's Suzuki Swift and Foley's Mitsubishi: 'We have no doubt that this Mirage is the car visible on CCTV footage from the Dublin 8 area in the immediate aftermath of the murder of Mr Douglas.' Completing that segment of the report, Mr Justice Hunt highlighted the statements from witnesses who had watched as the gang members attempted to destroy the Suzuki in Sandymount on 4 July.

The judge then mentioned the gang's debrief at Little Caesar's restaurant later that evening, commenting that, based on the CCTV footage: 'Mr Thompson appeared to be smiling and happy.'

Returning to the cars, Mr Justice Hunt spoke about the DNA evidence recovered from an air-freshener and hand sanitizer in the Fiesta and concluded with the damning comment:

It is clear from the evidence relating to the movements of the primary and secondary getaway cars that they were deployed on the day of the murder with the assistance of both the blue Mirage and the silver Ford Fiesta. Just as the movements of the Suzuki Swift were brought into focus from the evidence concerning the Mercedes, the movements of the silver Fiesta on the day of the murder are readily apparent from the CCTV evidence. We are satisfied that the silver Fiesta and the occupants thereof on the 1st of July played a significant logistical role in relation to this enterprise.

Still focusing on the silver Ford Fiesta, Mr Justice Hunt also referred to the car's legitimate status and the fact it was legally registered as being owned by a man in west Dublin. He added:

Given the active role of this car in the reconnaissance of the murder scene and the servicing of the stolen getaway cars, we perceive the advantage to the organizers of the murder from use of an apparently legal vehicle for these purposes, as opposed to the attention that might be drawn by the extensive movements of another stolen vehicle. We are satisfied by the evidence set out that this car was deeply involved on the 1st of July 2016 in the deployment of personnel and vehicles required to give effect to the plan to murder Mr Douglas.

For the first time in the hearing, Thompson's nervous twitching was becoming more regular. As Mr Justice Hunt pointed out the defendant's DNA was also recovered from an inhaler found in the Mitsubishi used by Foley, the cracks in Thompson's armour were beginning to appear. Making a final comment on the Fiesta, and that Thompson's left thumbprint had been found on the rear-view mirror, Judge Hunt stated:

> The forensic evidence confirms what is already proved by the CCTV from the Little Flower Centre, which is that Mr Thompson had physical contact with that vehicle. There can be no accident or coincidence involving the driving of support cars in circumstances where such driving was specifically associated with activities integral to the criminal scheme in question.

As the judgment continued, the writing appeared to be on the wall for Thompson. Judge Hunt added:

> There is evidence that links Thompson to both the Fiesta and the Mirage. He undoubtedly drove the Fiesta when it parked on the footpath opposite his family stall on Meath Street at 16.10 p.m., one minute before Mr Douglas was murdered. There is a substantial amount of evidence tending to implicate Mr Thompson in this enterprise, even before the disputed evidence is considered.

He then turned to CCTV evidence dealing with the cars travelling in convoy and being identified driving on the South Circular Road, Dublin, at 15.55 before the murder took place:

> We find that the driver of the car at that time must have been complicit in the impending murder because the Fiesta was clearly involved in marshalling the Mercedes. There is no room in our view for an innocent interpretation of the act of the driving of the Fiesta at that time and place. Whoever it was, was inexplicably [sic] linked to the final implementation of the murder plan.

Finishing his comments on the movements of the Fiesta before the murder, Mr Justice Hunt said it was 'inherently improbable' that someone other than Frederick Thompson had been driving the car that day, and further:

Considering the fact that the Fiesta was operating directly in conjunction with the primary and secondary getaway cars at 15.55 p.m., it would be both an appalling and unlikely coincidence for Mr Thompson to have blundered unwittingly into this activity by becoming the driver of the Fiesta for some unknown reason and at some unknown place between 15.55 p.m. and 16.10 p.m. We consider that this scenario is so remote that it can safely be discounted as a reasonable possibility on the evidence. Although the driver of the Fiesta is not specifically identifiable due to the low quality of the 15.55 p.m. footage from Donore Avenue, the footage is undoubtedly clear enough to show that the driver of the Fiesta was then sporting a dark beard and dark cap which coincides precisely of [sic] the appearance of Mr Thompson in the high-quality footage fifteen minutes later. It is therefore even less likely, and even more unfortunate for Mr Thompson, that the unknown driver at 15.55 p.m. had the same two physical characteristics that Mr Thompson clearly displayed on Meath Street.

To Thompson's defence that the driver in the Fiesta could not be identified at 15.55, Mr Justice Hunt responded:

Even if the defence hypothesis was correct, the fact that Mr Thompson assumed the driving of a car manifestly associated with a murder that was just about to take place, very close to its point of arrival, would raise a further set of significant and uncomfortable issues for Mr Thompson as to how precisely such a transfer could happen on an innocent basis. We are satisfied that the fact the Fiesta passed the murder scene for the second time that day, a mere four minutes before the killing, had a connection with what was about to happen. It would be an appalling coincidence if Mr Thompson was innocently driving the car to Meath Street and took an indirect route past Shoestown at that time for no apparent reason.

Before completing his judgment on Thompson's association with the murder, Mr Justice Hunt also referred to the gang's ongoing purchase of parking tickets in the hours leading up to the shooting. Thompson had ordered his associates to keep the 'murder cars' constantly topped up with parking tickets to avoid arousing suspicion. They also did not want the cars getting clamped, as this could have prevented the murder from taking place. Mr Justice Hunt explained:

> The inference that we draw from this evidence is that the Fiesta and its occupants were engaged in ensuring that both of the stolen getaway vehicles were kept topped up with valid parking tickets so as not to attract unwanted attention until they were required later in the afternoon.

He also dealt with the defence's submission relating to the lack of evidence about Thompson's use of the mobile phone in the minutes before the murder. Judge Hunt told the court that it was their judgment that it didn't 'affect the matter either way':

> Looked at in context, we can infer that a planned execution such as this will inevitably have involved surveillance of the target and his habits and movements, to isolate a time and place likely to be most suitable for the intended purpose. By

16.07 p.m. the wheels of the enterprise had literally been in motion for twelve minutes. In these circumstances, the phone communication from the Fiesta was not essential at all.

Now into the second hour of the sixty-five-page judgment, Thompson continued to shift in his seat, often putting his head in his hands. After the references to the evidence relating to the cars used in the murder, the feeling in the court was that the judgment was heading towards a guilty verdict.

Mr Justice Hunt then referred to the gangster's behaviour in the minutes after Douglas had been shot dead:

> We are satisfied that his general demeanour between 16.10 p.m. and 16.14 p.m. was restless, anxious and furtive. Mr Thompson parked the Fiesta in almost the same position as Mr Foley had parked the Mirage while he went to the phone shop, just three doors away from the stall. This location had been repeatedly passed by the vehicles involved in this event prior to that time. Perhaps these are minor coincidences but they are, nonetheless, not favourable from Mr Thompson's point of view. At 16.00 p.m. the Mitsubishi passed the stall followed at 16.05 p.m. by the Mercedes, having just left the Swift. At 16.07 p.m. the Mirage was seen at this location for a third time that afternoon. The Fiesta and Mr Thompson arrived and parked there minutes later. If Mr Thompson's arrival at the stall was not related to the impending murder of Mr Douglas, these are undoubtedly a further series of unhappy coincidences from his point of view.

During his time on Meath Street and after dismantling his phone, the judge also noted, Thompson had been caught on camera 'looking up and down the street, walking backwards and forwards in an apparently anxious manner'. Mr Justice Hunt added:

> We have no doubt but that Mr Thompson's demeanour and his behaviour in breaking up the phone and organizing the removal of the phone parts and the Fiesta from the scene at Meath Street were highly suspicious and Mr O'Higgins wisely did not suggest otherwise. If Mr Thompson was innocent of involvement in the murder of Mr Douglas the fact that he engaged in such behaviour at the precise time of that murder, a very short distance away, having just arrived in a vehicle that had been closely associated with the preparations for the murder that day, would be a further and very sad coincidence.

The judge also dismissed a suggestion by Thompson's defence that 'a possible explanation' for his phone being destroyed was because he had identified an unmarked garda car approaching him:

> Mr Thompson did not retrieve his phone or put it back together after the garda car that he supposedly saw passed him on the street. We are satisfied that Mr Thompson could not have fully seen the silver saloon in sufficient detail to recognize it as an unmarked Garda vehicle until it was almost upon him.

Continuing with his summary, Mr Justice Hunt again referred to Thompson's appearance at Little Caesar's restaurant in central Dublin after the murder when he said:

> There is no doubt that, viewed in retrospect, this was a disturbing and unpleasant occasion. Applying the presumption that Mr Thompson is innocent of involvement in the murder we are left once more to observe that his presence in the

Mirage and in the restaurant in the company of Mr C. and Foley is yet another doleful coincidence if Mr Thompson was truly an innocent abroad on that evening. In fact, we have no doubt whatsoever that the presence of Mr Thompson, together with Mr Foley and Mr C. in the Mirage, and subsequently in the restaurant, was not explicable by unlikely coincidence but because the three of them were inextricably linked together on that day by their joint participation in the murder of Mr Douglas. If Mr Thompson was not involved in this conspiracy to murder, it must have surely struck Mr C. that his dining companion bore an uncanny resemblance in appearance and apparel to the driver with whom he had travelled in the Fiesta that morning.

With a guilty verdict seeming increasingly likely the investigating gardaí were looking optimistic after this part of the judgment was read out. The packed courtroom remained silent as Mr Justice Hunt then turned his attention to the identification of Thompson on CCTV by Detective Sergeant Adrian Whitelaw and Detective Garda Seamus O'Donovan. In his summary, the senior judge said:

In assessing whether the recognition by these witnesses is correct beyond reasonable doubt we have had regard, as we are entitled and indeed directed to do, to the evidence accepted by us outside this issue. If these witnesses are not correct in recognizing Mr Thompson, it is doubly adverse that the driver who was wrongly identified as Mr Thompson also had a dark beard and a dark cap in separate pieces of footage at 10.42 a.m. and 10.48 a.m. when Mr Thompson arrived at Meath Street with a full black beard and a black cap at 16.10 p.m. It is a triple misfortune that the passenger in the Fiesta that morning, Mr C., was seen getting out of a car at half seven that evening and socializing with him thereafter in Little Caesar's restaurant. It is a fourth regrettable coincidence that if Mr Thompson was not driving the Fiesta that morning, he had by 7.30 p.m. been inadvertently either driving or been a passenger in not one but two vehicles that were intimately involved in marshalling the getaway vehicles for the murder that afternoon.

Just as he had done during his interrogation for the Douglas murder, Thompson smirked when Mr Justice Hunt accepted the testimony of the two gangland investigators. 'Fat Freddie' closed his eyes and shook his head, as he listened to Judge Hunt then say:

> Having considered the recognition evidence carefully, applying caution, and in light of all the circumstances and the other evidence in the case, we are satisfied there is no doubt but that the witnesses are each correct in their identification. Correct recognition fits comfortable [sic] with everything else that is known about Mr Thompson and the persons, cars and places that he did associate with on that day and mistaken recognition involves acceptance of a string of odd and unexplained coincidences. It must be emphasized that the weight of this conclusion arises from the compelling nature of all of the surrounding evidence and circumstances rather than the intrinsic weight of the recognition evidence.

By this stage, Mr Justice Hunt was nearing the end of the comprehensive judgment. He referred to garda testimony on Thompson's failure to answer questions following his arrest: 'We're satisfied that Mr Thompson failed or refused to account for matters properly put to him under each of the statutory provisions.'

During his summary, Mr Justice Tony Hunt outlined how the court was 'satisfied' that Thompson was directing the getaway cars on the day of the murder and how he had no 'innocent explanation' of his behaviour following the killing. The senior judge also pointed out that the questions put to Thompson during his interrogation were 'specific, reasonable and highly relevant questions' for him to answer in an attempt to prove his innocence.

During the trial Thompson's defence had suggested that the veteran gangster never answered questions from the gardaí and that he was afraid an answer from an innocent person could make the case against him worse. Judge Hunt addressed this issue: 'We are not convinced by these arguments. There is evidence in the case that Mr Thompson has had a number of previous engagements with An Garda Síochána as recorded in the Pulse system.' Freddie's many interactions with gardaí over the years had all been recorded and were now being used as evidence against him.

Concluding his remarks on Thompson's failure to answer questions, Mr Justice Hunt said:

> There is no evidence that suggests that it was a matter of settled policy with him to stonewall the guards on every occasion, nor was such a proposition put to any of the garda witnesses who gave evidence and who had such previous dealings with Mr Thompson.

The judge made it clear that the three-judge panel believed innocent people would not be afraid of telling the truth and that Thompson's 'failure or refusal to account for each of these matters was attributable solely to the want of an innocent account on his part'.

Having reached page sixty-three of the sixty-five-page

judgment, the judge paused and Thompson knew his freedom was hanging by a thread. The odds were clearly stacked against him, considering Mr Justice Hunt's previous remarks to the court. The gangster's shuffling and constant twitching in his seat persisted as Judge Hunt told the packed courtroom he would now be reading the conclusion of the panel's judgment.

Thompson's hopes of a positive outcome to the case were shattered when Mr Justice Hunt said:

We are satisfied that the totality of the evidence establishes the necessary proof beyond reasonable doubt of the guilt of the accused. It is evident to us that Mr Thompson had a visible role in the organization and deployment of the getaway vehicles prior to the murder, that he travelled to the Shoestown store that morning, that he performed a final check on the murder scene four minutes before it occurred, that he behaved in a furtive and suspicious manner at the precise time of the shooting, that he directed the removal of the Fiesta and the pieces of his mobile phone three minutes after the killing, that he travelled in a connected car and socialized with connected persons a short number of hours later.

We are fully satisfied that the evidence justifies an irresistible inference that he played a part in the organization of the murder of Mr Douglas. The court has weighed and evaluated the various strands of evidence and has concluded that all strands of evidence relied upon by this court point only in the direction of guilt. The innocent view of Mr Thompson's conduct and associations before, during and after this murder requires excessive reliance on the occurrence of multiple unlucky coincidences to explain the intersection between Mr Thompson and people, places and vehicles associated with this crime. There is no reasonably possible scenario which could explain Mr Thompson's actions and associations except that for which the prosecution contend. We are satisfied that the prosecution case in this trial was consistent and logical and acceptance of it requires no leaps of imagination.

As Mr Justice Hunt prepared to finish reading the final stages of his judgment, Freddie Thompson realized that his twenty-year career in organized crime was at an end. In an act of petulance and total disregard for the justice system, Thompson calmly stood up, muttered something under his breath, and left the court through the door to the holding area. At the same time, his mother and sister also left the proceedings.

Despite the defendant's absence, Mr Justice Hunt concluded his judgment by stating:

What is important is that the combined weight of all of the strands of evidence is sufficient to convince the court that the legal burden has been discharged by the prosecution and it is now proved beyond reasonable doubt to our satisfaction that Frederick Thompson is guilty as charged of the murder of David Douglas at Bridgefoot Street, Dublin, on 1st of July 2016.

Addressing Thompson's self-imposed absence from the courtroom as he prepared to pass sentence, Mr Justice Hunt said: 'If he doesn't want to be present, he doesn't want to be present. Judge Griffin is pointing out that he's left, he left of his own volition. If he wants to go, let him.' However, following consultation with his legal team, Thompson, this time dressed in a T-shirt and shorts, returned to the court.

In his final address to the court, Mr Justice Hunt reminded the gallery of Douglas's brutal murder:

Apart from thanking counsel as usual for the manner of participation in the case, I want to say two things. I don't know about the rights and wrongs of the deceased, I've not been furnished with any evidence. What we do know is that this man was killed, if not in front of his daughter, who was very young, when she was around, and she came upon her dead parent in the immediate aftermath of his execution, because that's what it was. That's a terrible thing to happen to anyone and Mr Gillane, if you would, convey on to her the Court's sympathies on her experience and I hope that she will somehow be able to recover from it. I can't think of a worse thing.

Referring to the garda team who had brought one of Ireland's most dangerous criminals down, Mr Justice Hunt added:

The standard of the investigation in this case was second to none and we want to pay particular tribute to Garda Byrne and the entirety of the CCTV team. It doesn't take a big leap of imagination to think that the two hours that we saw was produced on the back of an awful lot of slog and boring footwork.

By the end of the day's proceedings Thompson had received a life sentence, dated from the time of his arrest on 1 November 2016.

'Fat Freddie' Thompson's career as one of Ireland's most lethal gangsters was at an end. From now on, he would simply be known as Prisoner 8132.

Conclusion: An Analog Criminal

> Drugs become the currency, the local pub the
> boardroom, and violence the only language that is
> understood and respected by all in the 'company'.
> John O'Keefe, criminologist

Freddie Thompson's problem was he was an analog criminal in a digital age of policing. As far back as a decade before he was finally jailed for murder, others were warning him about his conduct, but he refused to listen. Thompson had long revelled in his 'Jack the Lad' approach to crime, but in a world of increasingly all-pervasive CCTV coverage, forensic advances and phone tapping, he was always living on borrowed time. The signs had been there even back in the good old days of 2008, when everyone else realized that discussing business on the phone was a recipe for disaster but 'Fat Freddie' had continued bragging about having secured guns for Gary Hutch, returning from drugs trips from north Africa and drug taking. This arrogant attitude ultimately led to his downfall.

When Thompson became the most senior member of the Kinahan cartel to be caged for murder, on 30 August 2018, Garda Commissioner Drew Harris described the investigation which led to his capture and conviction as 'world class'. Chief Superintendent Paul Cleary, the senior investigating officer in the Douglas probe, praised the 'dedication' of his team in bringing down one of Ireland's most notorious gangland figures:

> Freddie Thompson has lived in the Dublin 8 area all his life and for the past eighteen years he has been a high-priority target for detective units in Kevin Street and Kilmainham due to his criminal activities. As the senior investigating officer in this case, I would also like to acknowledge the dedication and commitment of the investigation team. This was a large and complex investigation that required hundreds of hours of investigative work.

Gardaí also caused major disruption to the gang, with associates Eamonn Cumberton, Johnny Keogh, Regina Keogh and Thomas Fox all being convicted of murder. Other notable successes for gardaí included the arrest of a senior Kinahan cartel figure, Thomas 'Bomber' Kavanagh, by the UK's National Crime Agency in January 2019, the fact that fifty-nine lives had been saved by gardaí, and the seizure of drugs worth €147 million and ninety-one firearms.

Even though no serious charges have yet to arise from Operation Shovel eleven years on, its very existence caused huge damage to the Kinahan cartel's operations. The suspicion, paranoia and seizure of assets, combined with the downturn in the European property market, played a large part in creating the conditions which led to the murder of Gary Hutch in September 2015, and the current bloody and high-profile Kinahan–Hutch feud.

And while we cannot be sure of the internal decisions made by the Spanish officials who ran the expensive surveillance operation, it is not hard to imagine Thompson's occasional remarks nudging them towards keeping it going.

Another miscalculation made by Freddie – though not just by him alone – related to the determination of the Irish State to respond effectively to the aftermath of the Regency Hotel attack.

The importance of the non-jury Special Criminal Court in sending down cartel hitmen should also not be underestimated. At 'the Special', there are no jurors expecting defence counsels to impress them with TV's 'CSI-style' forensic revelations. Barristers cannot appeal, in an emotive summing up, to any citizen's natural fear of convicting an innocent person. Rather, they must argue their case in cold, clinical terms to three judges who once did the job they do themselves, and who know the law inside out. When it came to the overwhelming evidence – including the CCTV and DNA – presented by gardaí in Thompson's murder trial, the Special Criminal Court did not hesitate to convict. Only Thompson will ever know if the jokey attitude he maintained throughout his trial – including on one occasion patting the lead garda investigator on the back outside the court – was a facade or not. The change in his demeanour as the verdict was read out suggests it was a mask to conceal his true feelings.

Whilst the Special Criminal Court was originally created to try paramilitaries, one of its first major criminal convictions was John Gilligan, the man who Thompson once boasted to gardaí he was going to emulate. In a supreme twist of fate, Thompson is likely to face a very similar destiny to that of his fallen idol. 'Fat Freddie' will be fifty-three by the time he gets out of prison and Ireland's gangland scene will be a different place.

The feud which kept him important for the Kinahans will almost certainly have been resolved and on the ground someone else will be running the Dublin drugs trade. It could even be his old foe, Brian 'King Ratt' Rattigan, as he will be a free man in a few years' time, after he received a nine-year sentence when he pleaded guilty to the manslaughter of Declan Gavin and his conviction for Gavin's murder was dismissed in 2017 by the Appeal Court. It is unlikely the KOCG will have much use for a middle-aged criminal has-been like Thompson, with a reputation for being unable to keep his mouth shut. Gilligan has already learned that Ireland's gangland is not a very forgiving place. In 2014, he narrowly avoided a second attempt on his life when he was shot four times by a Kinahan-linked figure looking to settle old scores. 'Fat Freddie' Thompson could face a similar fate.

Though the gang leader often engaged in conversations with gardaí without revealing details of his involvement in organized crime, the only time he elaborated on his constant fight to stay alive was when he spoke to the guards using the name of 'Deco' Gavin: 'Deco's in too deep and he can't get out.' Thompson was often asked by detectives why he chose the life that he led, but he refused to elaborate.

While Thompson is the only person who really knows why he decided to lead a life of crime, a leading criminologist and lecturer in forensic psychology, John O'Keefe, believes the answer to Thompson's behaviour over the years lies somewhere between the 'murky waters of both nature and nurture':

To law-abiding citizens, the behaviours of 'Fat Freddie' Thompson and his ilk are like something from a movie. What could possibly motivate an individual to behave in such a violent manner over an entire lifetime, with clearly only two possible ends in sight – prison and/or death? Career violent criminals, such as Thompson, will often suffer from genetically programmed personality disorders — in other words they find it impossible to live with themselves or others and they consistently make the same mistakes in life, over and over again.

Suggesting that Thompson could suffer from a personality disorder, the criminologist added:

In the case of extremely violent criminals such as Thompson, the more specific possibility of anti-social personality disorder — commonly described in populist culture as psychopathy — cannot be disregarded. This manifests itself in an utter disregard for the rights of others, coupled with an unrivalled lack of remorse or sympathy for every human being who should cross that person's path. One of the abiding features of this personality disorder is that violence almost becomes recreational in nature and is both unpredictable and catastrophic in its consequences. But genetics alone cannot entirely explain the behaviours of Thompson and other violent gang members.

A heady mix of social, environmental and family factors are also critical in how many Freddie Thompsons this country produces. Many law-abiding and decent citizens come from the part of Dublin that Thompson was born into. Equally, however, its deprivation means it remains a fertile breeding ground for criminogenic behaviours. Low or zero educational achievements coupled with little or no professional life expectations mean that youths soon become feral and adopt what is known as their 'master status'. In other words, if you label someone a 'scumbag' for long enough, unsurprisingly, that is exactly the job title they soon employ of themselves – quite simply, it becomes a self-fulfilling prophecy.

In general terms, Mr O'Keefe also explained how:

> Personality-disordered men such as Thompson see no way out and so the lure of the fast buck and a celebrity lifestyle that drug dealing can offer becomes irresistible. Prison not only fails to become a deterrent, but is seen as simply part of this lifestyle – in the same way that the corporate executive may view long hours and extensive travel as the price they have to pay for their comfortable life. Finally, fatalistic attitudes too become a part of the 'group think' of all such gangs. Just as prison is a certainty for Thompson *et al.*, so too is the likelihood of a violent death the higher up the criminogenic chain they climb. However, viewed against the backdrop of utter dysfunctionality as so described, prison and/or a violent death remain insufficient deterrents to a life that *über*-crime can offer. Drugs become the currency, the local pub the boardroom, and violence the only language that is understood and respected by all in the 'company'.

Dr O'Keefe concluded his examination of Thompson's personality by maintaining:

> It is therefore a deadly mix of genetic, social, environmental and familial factors, combining with a 'perfect' life storm, that ensure that Freddie Thompson and his cohorts can continue unchecked. Indeed, in the final analysis, the surprise is not that we as a country have produced a criminal as violent and as recidivist as 'Fat Freddie' Thompson, and others. The real surprise is that we have actually not produced far more.

For Robert Daly, a psychiatrist, senior lecturer in psychiatry at RCSI Medical School and consultant psychiatrist in Beaumont Private Clinic in Dublin, there are many neurological and psychological theories offering reasons for an individual's decision to pursue a life of violence and crime:

Neurological research from animal studies has shown lower levels of the neurotransmitter, or brain chemical messenger, serotonin in the brains of more impulsive and more aggressive monkeys. Studies in humans have shown similar findings. In addition, some research looking at electrical brain activity has shown changes in brain function amongst violent and sociopathic offenders. The part of the brain most commonly affected is the frontal-lobe areas. The frontal lobes do not develop fully in humans until the mid-twenties, and this brain area is involved in planning, abstract thinking and impulse control. Psychological theories of aggression and violence have recently focused on the importance of modelling, also known as observational learning, amongst men who are violent.

When considering organized crime, social theories are often used to explain how young men become involved. Poor socio-economic standing amongst young men in disadvantaged areas can stifle pursuit of social and financial success, and this leads to seeking success through other avenues such as organized crime. Young men learn violent behaviours quickly and may experience a feeling of intense emotion after violence, sometimes described as similar to taking drugs. Young males in particular will rapidly follow strong leaders. There is also a huge capacity for risk taking in this age group. Taken together, these factors explain how young males are attracted to organized crime.

As Thompson completes his life sentence, the fight against the Kinahan cartel continues, with Assistant Garda Commissioner John O'Driscoll, from the gardaí's Special Crime Operations, vowing:

> The message to communities is that we are determined to dismantle these groups. The investigation into Freddie Thompson was excellent and we are now better placed in terms of intelligence gathering and are engaged in proactive policing in dealing with organized crime. The extent to which we have developed contacts with law enforcement agencies around the world will help us achieve further success. Our aim is to dismantle those organized-crime groups that are causing the greatest damage within this jurisdiction through their engagement in threat to life and also in the trading of drugs and firearms.

Given the amount of toes Freddie Thompson has stepped on through the years, nobody would be surprised if an attempt was made on his life before he gets a chance to rejoin the world of organized crime. Chief amongst those whom he should fear – both behind bars and on the street – should be the men for whom he is serving time. The cartel have a habit of tying up loose ends and 'Fat Freddie' Thompson, with his reputation for shooting his mouth off, might just be viewed as one of them.

Update to 2019 Edition

Almost one year after Thompson received his life sentence for the Douglas murder, the convicted killer found himself in the headlines once again. On this occasion, the senior Kinahan cartel gang member's legal team appeared before the High Court in Dublin to complain about the conditions of his incarceration at the high-security Portlaoise Prison.

After his arrest and charge over the Douglas murder in November 2016, Thompson had been refused bail and held on remand in Mountjoy Prison in Dublin. The following March, months before his trail, the Irish Prison Service classed Thompson as a 'troublesome inmate' who had influence over younger prisoners, leading to tension in the prison, and he was transferred to Portlaoise.

Mountjoy held most of the Kinahan cartel members convicted since the murder of David Byrne at the Regency Hotel attack on 5 February 2016. During his time on remand there, Thompson clashed with cartel killers Barry Doyle, who was serving life for the murder of Limerick rugby player Shane Geoghegan, and Eamonn Cumberton, who was jailed for life for the murder of dissident republican Michael Barr on 25 April 2016.

In Portlaoise prison management decided to place prisoner number 8132 in wing A4, the jail's segregation wing, citing his dispute with Brian Rattigan in the Crumlin and Drimnagh feud. Thompson's only visitors to the prison were members of his immediate family, as one senior prison source explained:

> The people who came to see him were his sister, mother, brother and another woman. No security issues were ever raised during his visits because no criminals were coming to see him. He may have been a senior member of the Kinahan gang but in reality he was expendable just like the rest of them. This is a common trend witnessed over the years when a serious gangster is sent to prison for life. Once they go to jail, they're no longer any use to the people at the top. Thompson kept his head down when he was in prison and didn't cause any trouble because he was on his own. He used to run Mountjoy Prison because he had the support of fellow gang members and was idolized by younger inmates trying to make a name for themselves but this wasn't the case in Portlaoise – he was very much alone.

Now held in isolation from the prison population's 238 inmates, Thompson's only interaction was with convicted killer Warren Dumbrell, who is serving life for the murder of father-of-six Christopher Cawley, and Thomas Fox, the ostracized Kinahan cartel getaway driver who received a life sentence for the killing of Gareth Hutch on 24 May 2016.

According to crime journalist Robin Schiller from the *Irish Independent*, Thompson recruited Dumbrell, regarded as one of the most volatile and most dangerous prisoners in the Irish Prison system. One source told Schiller:

> Thompson is certainly feeling under threat from his one-time associates. As a result, it seems he has had no other option but to try and use Warren Dumbrell to protect him – which is a bizarre dynamic given that Dumbrell does not normally

associate with other inmates, or anyone. This will obviously cause a major headache for prison officials given that both men are absolutely reckless.

Struggling to cope with his isolation, the gangland killer, who had also launched an appeal against his conviction at the Court of Criminal Appeal within a month, instructed his legal team to launch judicial review proceedings against the Governor of Portlaoise Prison, the Irish Prison Service and the Minister for Justice Charlie Flanagan. The goal of these proceedings was to end his detention away from the mainstream prison population. He sought an order quashing his ongoing detention in A-Block in Portlaoise Prison and a declaration that the decision to hold him in A-Block amounted to a breach of his constitutional rights and was in breach of various prison rules.

Thompson's legal team appeared before the High Court on 8 August 2019 and on several occasions in the following months. In a statement issued to the court on his behalf, the veteran criminal insisted that he should be removed from the segregation unit by declaring, 'I've no feud with Brian Rattigan', while maintaining his human rights were being infringed because of the 'extremely oppressive' regime at the prison. Thompson's statement to the court was read during the hearing. He said:

> After I was sentenced I agreed to meet Rattigan and this was facilitated by prison authorities. I sat down and talked with Mr Rattigan who I have only ever met once in person on one previous occasion. We spoke at length about the how the media had fuelled the idea of a feud raging between us. I say that we both agreed that there be no animosity between us into the future. Contrary to what is alleged by

the prison, I am not involved in a feud with Mr Rattigan and any attempt by the prison authorities to use this as an excuse to justify the current conditions of my detention is not correct. The prison authorities are aware of the meetings between us and they are aware there is no feud ongoing between us.

Thompson claimed it might 'suit the prison's agenda' to say there was a feud so they could 'keep me in conditions that violate my rights'.

Thompson's account of his 'sit down' with Rattigan to resolve their differences failed to mention his previous encounter with Rattigan in which his nemesis was shot in the stomach during the Crumlin and Drimnagh feud.

Thompson claimed that despite his clear-the-air talks with his arch-enemy he spent most of his time on 'lock up' in his cell and was denied regular exercise, fresh air and 'appropriate education', breaching his human rights and prison rules.

The gangland enforcer also maintained he was initially placed under Rule 62, which allows for the removal of prisoners from structured activities, without reasons other than to 'ensure good order and security in the prison'. However, in his affidavit, he claimed that though he was taken off Rule 62 during the early part of his time in prison there was no improvement to his conditions. He said he had always previously been housed within the general prison population and that he was being 'treated differently' to other prisoners serving life sentences. Thompson's legal team argued that their client's situation was 'unbearable', with their client's mental health being affected as he suffered from depression.

In correspondence to Thompson's solicitors, the Governor of the jail and the Irish Prison Service denied that Thompson's prison regime was oppressive, insisting the regime met all the statutory requirements. As part of their defence, they also maintained Thompson had been provided with access to facilities including the school, gym, recreation, open-air exercise and other services, while pointing out he could not mix with certain other prisoners due to 'security issues'.

Thompson responded to the Irish Prison Service's claims by insisting he had been 'informally told' he had been kept away from the general prison population because of his 'perceived feud' with Brian Rattigan.

On 5 November, after Thompson had been moved from the isolation block and placed with the mainstream prison population in the preceding twenty-four hours, his legal team withdrew the case. The prison authorities did not admit that the move was related to the High Court proceedings.

On 13 January 2019, at the time Thompson was preparing for his case to appear before the High Court, his gang suffered another blow when Thomas 'Bomber' Kavanagh, the man classed by the Criminal Assets Bureau as having 'equal status' to Daniel Kinahan and of being 'one step above Liam Byrne' in the Kinahan cartel, was arrested in Birmingham.

Kavanagh, who provided advice to Thompson in the early years of his criminal career, was arrested as he arrived at Birmingham International Airport by officers from the UK's National Crime Agency (NCA). They were working closely with the Garda National Drugs and Organised Crime Bureau investigating the Kinahan cartel's global arms smuggling and money laundering network. As Kavanagh was being arrested police officers were searching his home in Tamworth, just outside Birmingham, a heavily fortified €850,000 mansion that included bulletproof glass. As the thirteen-hour search of the house concluded, Kavanagh was charged with possessing an illegal 10,000-volt stun gun disguised as a torch.

Kavanagh remained on bail before appearing at Stoke-on-Trent Crown Court on 2 September where he received a three-year sentence for possessing the weapon. His conviction marked another serious blow to Thompson's former associates. Though Thompson was the most senior member of the cartel to be convicted of murder, Kavanagh was the most senior member of the gang to receive a jail sentence. One senior security source said:

> When Kavanagh sat across a table from Daniel Kinahan he wasn't looking up to him he was looking directly at him. They were equals in a vast criminal organization. Kavanagh has been at the forefront of organized crime in Ireland and the UK for the last 20 years. He's the man who brought his brother-in-law Liam [Byrne] and others into organized crime, he's the man who provided counsel to Freddie Thompson and other younger criminals as they cemented their position in the cartel.

Following his sentence, NCA lead investigator Peter Bellis welcomed the conviction of one of Europe's most notorious crime bosses, saying: 'These types of weapons are extremely dangerous and can cause serious injury or death. This is why they are prohibited in the UK. Our wider investigation into money laundering, drugs and firearms supply continues.'

Assistant Commissioner John O'Driscoll, head of the gardaí's Special Crime Operations, also welcomed the conviction. He said: 'This confirms that cooperation with the National Crime Agency is ongoing. An Garda Siochána anticipates it will lead to further success in tackling organized groups operating at an international level into the future.'

As Thompson languished in prison and as the international investigations into his former associates continued, his gang suffered further setbacks when various members of the cartel appeared before the Special Criminal Court in Dublin on a day of reckoning for the mob on 15 July 2019. Standing before the court that day was another of Thompson's associates from the days of the Crumlin and Drimnagh feud, Declan 'Mr Nobody' Brady, brothers Gary and Glen Thompson (no relation to Freddie Thompson), along with former British soldier Robert Browne.

Brady, who was also a former associate of 'Bomber' Kavanagh, received a ten-and-a-half year sentence after he was convicted of storing weapons for the cartel at the Greenogue Industrial Estate in Rathcoole, west Dublin, on 24 January 2017. The haul, which gardaí suspected were to be used for the cartel's onslaught against the Hutch organized crime group, included nine revolvers, four semi-automatic pistols, a sub-machine gun, an assault rifle and 1,355 rounds of ammunition. Regarded as the cartel's 'quartermaster', Brady had gone under the radar for many years despite his standing within the cartel, as one source explained: 'He was one of the most senior members and was well known to Thompson. He had experience from the Crumlin and Drimnagh feud and was bringing in weapons for the use of cartel gang members. His arrest and subsequent conviction were a serious blow to the cartel.'

The Thompson brothers and Browne were sentenced for their part in the plot to kill Patsy Hutch, the Monk's older brother on 10 March 2018. The Thompsons were each jailed for twelve and a half years, while Browne received an eleven-and-a-half-year sentence for possessing firearms with intent to endanger life.

As gardaí continue to investigate Dublin's gangland, some of Thompson's closet associates remain in custody on serious charges connected to the feud and will appear before the Special Criminal Court over the coming months and years.

Acknowledgements

I would like to offer my sincere thanks to those who can't be named for sharing their in-depth knowledge of Freddie Thompson's background and criminal career over the last twenty years. First, I would like to thank the many members of An Garda Síochána – and four in particular – who took time to provide me with advice on the contents of this book. The first of the four gardaí is a man who encouraged me to write the book whilst having a coffee shortly after Thompson's arrest in November 2016. This book would not have been possible without him and I am grateful for his encouragement, wisdom and guidance. Special thanks also to a long-term friend whose knowledge of Thompson is second to none, and to another friend who took time to read over the material. A special note of thanks to 'The Jedi' for his continued friendship. Thanks to each of you for your support, which has been invaluable.

I am most grateful to the families of Trevor O'Neill and Noel Kirwan for sharing their stories of the devastation caused by the loss of their loved ones during the Kinahan and Hutch feud. They welcomed me into their homes during a period of immense grief for their families.

I also received valuable guidance and advice from a former colleague at the *Sunday Life* in Belfast, Damian McArdle. Credit must also go to Barry Cummins from RTÉ for his support, and to the author Mick McCaffrey from Virgin Media for allowing me to use his book *Cocaine Wars* as a reference point. I would like to thank the members of the legal profession who helped me with the project.

Praise is due to my editor at Penguin, Patricia Deevy, for all her hard work, advice and countless emails on this project. I would also like to thank my other editor, Aoife Barrett, for reshaping and improving my initial raw efforts. Thanks also to Michael McLoughlin, MD of Penguin Ireland, for his continued support and enthusiastic response to the project, and to the libel expert Kieran Kelly for his direction.

Thanks also to the ongoing support of the *Irish Sun*'s editor, Kieran McDaid, Neil Cotter, head of news, Mark May, associate head of content, Chris Doyle, picture editor, Declan Ferry, digital editor, and his team, and to all my colleagues at the paper. Thanks also to my colleague, and co-author of *The Cartel*, Owen Conlon, for his help on this project.

Thanks to the team on the *Irish Sun*'s picture desk for their assistance in compiling the images for the picture section. Huge thanks to Jon Lee, who worked tirelessly to source the images and to supply the captions. Special thanks to the photographers Padraig O'Reilly and Crispin Rodwell for taking many of the photographs. Thanks also to Collins Photo Agency and to Maxwell Photography for allowing us to use their images. Copyright as follows: 6 – Courtpix/Maxwells; 5, 18, 34 – the photojournalist Padraig O'Reilly; 11, 12, 19, 21 and 48 – Crispin Rodwell (for the *Irish Sun*); 4, 35, 36, 41, 44 and 45 – Collins. All other pictures supplied by the author.

ACKNOWLEDGEMENTS

And on a personal note . . .

I would like to thank my wife, Chrissie, and our sons, Tom and Finn, for all their love and for giving me the time to work on the project. Special thanks to Chrissie's parents, Go-Go and Grandpa, for looking after my family when they were sick during the writing process and also for allowing me to use their home. Thanks also to my mum, Lorraine, her husband, Brendan, my brother, Paul, and his wife, Toni, for their support.

FROM THE SAME AUTHOR...

THE CARTEL

BY STEPHEN BREEN AND OWEN CONLON

The definitive account of the rise of the Kinahan gang and the deadly feud that shocked the nation

February 2016. A daring gun attack in the Regency Hotel brings Dubliner Christy Kinahan and his international criminal cartel to a horrified public's attention.

Kinahan's son Daniel, the target of the attack, escapes. A trusted henchman dies at the scene. And the deadly rivalry between the Kinahans and the family and associates of the veteran Dublin gangster Gerry Hutch is now all-out war.

The Cartel offers a unique behind-the-scenes account of how Kinahan got so big, and why a local feud could bring about the unravelling of his global crime empire. Its authors – experienced crime journalists Stephen Breen and Owen Conlon – have written a meticulous, eye-opening and gripping story of double-crossing, vengeance and murder.

'Incisive, intriguing, fascinating' Ryan Tubridy, *RTÉ*

'Full of insights . . . thoroughly researched . . . impressive access' *Irish Examiner*